nirvana: the last nightmare

T0094523

OSHO

Extemporaneous talks given by Osho
at the OSHO International Meditation Resort, Pune, India

nirvana: the last nightmare

Learning to Trust in Life

ZEN PARABLES AS A MEDIUM TO TEACH RELAXATION

OSHO

Copyright © 1975, 2012 OSHO International Foundation, Switzerland
www.osho.com/copyrights

Osho image Copyright © OSHO International Foundation

All rights reserved. No part of this book may be reproduced or transmitted in
any form or by any means, electronic or mechanical, including photocopying,
recording, or by any information storage and retrieval system, without prior
written permission from the publisher.

OSHO is a registered trademark of OSHO International Foundation
www.osho.com/trademarks

This book is a series of original talks by Osho, given to a live audience. All of
Osho's talks have been published in full as books, and are also available as
original audio recordings. Audio recordings and the complete text archive can
be found via the online OSHO Library at www.osho.com/library

Osho comments in this work on excerpts from:
Material on p.121 is from *Zen Buddhism: An Introduction to Zen,* copyright ©
1959 Peter Pauper Press, Inc. Reprinted by permission.
Zen: Poems, Prayers, Sermons, Anecdotes, Interviews, 2nd edition, Selected and
translated by Lucien Stryk and Takashi Ikemoto. Reprinted with the permission
of Swallow Press/Ohio University Press, Athens, Ohio.

OSHO MEDIA INTERNATIONAL
New York • Zurich • Mumbai
an imprint of
OSHO INTERNATIONAL
www.osho.com/oshointernational

Distributed by Publishers Group Worldwide
www.pgw.com

Library of Congress Catalog-In-Publication Data is available

Printed in India by Manipal Technologies Limited, Karnataka

ISBN: 978-0-9836400-1-1
Also available as eBook ISBN: 978-0-88050-210-8

contents

preface

Nirvana is a state of unconditional acceptance. Wherever you are, if you can accept your life with totality, with joy, with gratitude, if you can see your life as a gift, then nirvana is never a problem. The problem arises only because you don't accept your life, you reject life. And the moment you reject life you start looking for some other life; you become worried about whether it is going to be better than this life or not. It may be worse. That's what hell is: the fear of a worse life than this. And that is nirvana: the greed for a better life than this. But there in no other life; there is no hell, no heaven. Only fools are interested in such things.

These heaven–hell concepts have nothing to do with geography or space, and they don't have anything to do with time either. So it is not a question of tomorrows, not a question of something after death. It is a question of understanding, it is a question of meditation. It is a question of becoming utterly silent, herenow. There is no other space than the here, and no other time than the now. These two words contain the whole existence: now, here.

My suggestion to you is, forget about nirvana. Nirvana means something that will happen after this life – don't be concerned about it. Be concerned about this moment because this is the only true moment there is, and enter into it. That very entrance is the entrance into nirvana. And once you have found it, nobody can take it away from you.

Osho
Tao: The Golden Gate, Vol.1

CHAPTER 1

mastered by zen

Date-Jitoku, a fine waka poet, wanted to master Zen. With this in mind he made an appointment to see Ekkei, abbot of Shokokuji in Kyoto. Jitoku went to the master full of hopes, but as soon as he entered the room he received a blow.

He was astonished and mortified: no one had ever dared to strike him before, but as it is a strict Zen rule never to say or do anything unless asked by the master, he withdrew, silently. He went at once to Dokuon, who was to succeed Ekkei as abbot, and told him that he planned to challenge Ekkei to a duel.

"Can't you see that the master was being kind to you?" said Dokuon. "Exert yourself in zazen and you will see for yourself what his treatment of you means."

For three days and nights Jitoku engaged in desperate contemplation, then, suddenly, he experienced an ecstatic awakening. This satori was approved by Ekkei.

Jitoku called on Dokuon and thanked him for his advice, saying: "If it hadn't been for your wisdom I would not have had such a transfiguring experience.

And as for the master, his blow was far from hard enough."

There are a thousand and one poisons, but nothing like idealism – it is the most poisonous of all poisons. Of course, the most subtle: it kills you, but kills you in such a way that you never become aware of it. It kills you with a style. The ways of idealism are very cunning. Rarely does a person become aware that he has been committing suicide through it. Once you become aware, you become religious.

Religion is not an ideology. Religion does not believe in any ideals. Religion is to become aware of the impossibility of idealism – of all idealism. Religion is to live here and now, and idealism goes on conditioning your mind to live somewhere else. And only the now exists. There is no other way to live.

The only way is to be here. You cannot be there. The tomorrow is nonexistent, it never comes, and idealism believes in the tomorrow. It sacrifices the today at the altar of the tomorrow. It goes on saying to you, "Do something, improve yourself. Do something, change yourself. Do something, become perfect." It appeals to the ego.

Idealism belongs to the world of the ego. It appeals to the ego that you can be more perfect than you are; in fact you should be more perfect than you are. But each moment is perfect and it cannot be more perfect than it is. To understand this is the beginning of a new life, is the beginning of life. To miss this is to commit suicide.

Then you go on destroying this moment for the moment which never comes. Then you go on destroying this life for some life which exists nowhere. You go on destroying this world for some other world – some paradise, some *moksha*, some nirvana. To sacrifice the present for the future is to be trapped in death.

To live the moment, to live it totally and freely, is to delight in existence, is to celebrate it. And that is the only way of being; there is no other way. Idealism has put you on the wrong track.

The first thing to be understood: you are perfect. If somebody says to you that you have to become perfect, he is the enemy. Beware of him! Escape from him as soon as possible. Don't let him poison your being. Don't let him destroy you. He may have been destroyed by others; now he is doing the same to you. He himself may be a victim. Have compassion on him, but don't allow him to destroy you. He has not lived his life. He has only hoped; he has not lived. He has only dreamt; he has not lived. He has only prepared, planned; he has not lived.

The idealist mind goes on preparing for something that never happens. It is a nightmare. It goes on preparing and preparing – infinite preparations for a journey that never starts. It goes on planning in a thousand and one ways: subtle, cunning, clever. But the whole thing is pointless, because each moment it is denying life.

Life is knocking at your door each moment and you are denying it, because you say you are preparing for it. You say, "How can I receive the guest right now? I am not ready." By and by you become so accustomed to preparing that preparation becomes your life.

You have missed. This type of mind is constantly missing, and the more it misses, the more it plans desperately – to go somewhere, to reach somewhere, to attain something, to be somebody. And the misery of all miseries is that it is not going to happen.

Life is already available. You need not prepare for it. You are already entitled to enjoy it. By just being alive, you are already ready. Because you breathe, you are already capable. Because you can be conscious, you are already ready. Nothing is lacking.

Once you take the first wrong step, the whole journey goes wrong. The first step defines and decides your whole life. Never try to be perfect, otherwise you will be caught in a dead routine – preparing and preparing. You can watch yourself, you can watch others. People who have become addicted to idealism live a life of ritual, of empty gestures. They are always waiting: some great thing is going to happen. It never happens of course, because it cannot happen that way.

It is happening right now, here, and their eyes are fixed somewhere there, far away. It is happening at close quarters. It is already happening near your heart. Where your heart is beating, it is already happening – and they are looking at the sky.

So they make a life of routine, dead routine. They move like dead corpses – waiting and waiting and waiting. And every day they know death is coming near; they become more and more desperate. Their whole life will turn into a mechanical routine.

If you want to really live, you have to be spontaneous. Life is spontaneous. Be available to this moment. Allow this moment to lead you. Don't plan for it otherwise you will live in empty gestures, obsessed with dead routine, just thinking as if, if you plan your life completely, some day or other the great happening is going to result.

Do you think life is a result? Life is not a result; it is already there. It is a grace. Nothing is to be done to attain to it. What have you done to be born? What have you done so that you can breathe? What have you done so that you can be conscious? What have you done so that you can fall in love? It has happened. It is a sheer grace, a gift. Yes, let me tell you – life is a gift. Don't think that it is going to be a result. Once you think it is going to be a result, it is never going to be there at all.

Then there are a few people who will go on waiting and waiting, and they will die. Almost ninety-nine percent of people die this way. Their whole life has been a sheer waste. One percent of people – sometimes by chance, accident – become aware that they are wasting their life. Then their whole training and conditioning takes a subtle revenge.

The day that they become aware they have been waiting for something which is not waiting for them, which is not going to happen, they start saying that life is meaningless. First they were waiting for some meaning; now, because that meaning is not happening, they say life is meaningless. First they were waiting for some purpose; now, because it is not happening, they say life is purposeless.

Ask Jean-Paul Sartre. He says, "Man is a useless passion." It does not say anything about man. It does not say anything about life. It does not say anything about existence. It simply says that Sartre has missed. It simply says that he was waiting for some utilitarian end to be fulfilled in life and now he has become aware that it is not going to be fulfilled. He was waiting for some meaning. Now, seeing it, realizing it – that that meaning is not going to be – he says life is meaningless.

Life is neither. It is neither meaningful nor is it meaningless. If there is really no meaning, how can life be meaningless? If there is no purpose, how can life be purposeless? For life to be purposeless there must be a purpose. For life to be meaningless, for even the word *meaningless* to be meaningful, there must be a meaning.

Life is neither. It simply is there in sheer beauty with no purpose. Look at the trees. Look at the sunlight. Just – it is. What is the purpose of the sun rising every day in the morning? What is the purpose of trees blossoming? What is the purpose of birds singing? No purpose. I don't say purposelessness; I simply say no purpose. It is.

Drop your search for meaning, because that search either will destroy your whole life and you will live in misery, or, one day if you become aware, then another anguish will surround you – the anguish of meaninglessness.

Sartre says, "Life is nauseating." He must have been expecting too much. Now the fulfillment is receding further away and he feels a rumbling in the stomach, nausea, an illness, a sea-sickness. He was expecting too much. Now all expectations are turning into frustrations and life has become nauseating.

It is not. Life has nothing to do with nausea, because it has nothing to do with your expectations. Once you get out of this trap of idealism, you are available to life and life is available to you.

Somewhere Friedrich Nietzsche has said, "Where can I feel at home? Where?" He must be seeking a womb, a home, a mother. He must have been a little childish. He must have been stuck somewhere in his growth. Why are you seeking a home?

Life is not a home, but it is not homelessness either. It is. Simply, it is. Enjoy it. Celebrate it. It is not going to become a home for you, but it is homelessness – no it is not that either. The very search for a home makes life look like homelessness. Drop the search. The very search throws you away from life. You go on missing the present moment.

So either you can wait – a futile waiting; or you can become angry – a futile anger. If you go on waiting, your life will be obsessed with routine. You will try to become an automaton.

Let me tell you an anecdote:

Mr. Smith had killed his wife, and his entire defense was based on temporary insanity. He was a witness on his own behalf and was asked by his lawyer to describe the crime in his own words.

"Your Honor," he began, "I am a quiet, peaceful man of systematic habits, who virtually never bothers anybody. I get up at seven every morning, have breakfast at half-past seven, punch in at work at nine, leave work at five, come home at six, find supper on the table, eat it, read, watch TV, bed. Until the day in question." Here he paused to breathe passionately.

His lawyer said gently, "Go on. What happened on the day in question?"

"On the day in question," said Smith, "I woke at seven, had breakfast at seven-thirty, began work at nine, left at five and came home at six. There was no supper on the table and no sign of my wife.

I searched through the house and found her in the bedroom in bed with a strange man. So I killed her."

"What were your emotions at the time you killed her?" asked the lawyer, anxious to get the point on the record.

"I was in a white-hot fury," said the defendant, "mad with rage, simply out of my mind, and unable to control myself." He turned to the jury and, pounding the arm of the witness chair, cried out, "Gentlemen, when I come home at six o'clock, supper has to be on the table!"

That was his reason for killing his wife – not that she was in bed with a strange man. "Supper has to be on the table exactly at six o'clock!"

Are you aware that you are also more or less obsessed with a dead routine? Why are people so obsessed with a dead routine? They are so obsessed with a dead routine because if the chain of their routine is broken, suddenly, underneath they see a futile life, a useless life, a meaningless life. Somehow they are trying to give it a feeling of meaning, an aroma of meaning. Somehow they are trying to forget that they are living uselessly, that they are not living at all.

They make a dead routine; they follow it. Just by following it like a mechanism, they have a feeling that everything is going perfectly well. They get up exactly at the right time, they go to the office, they come home, they read the newspaper, they watch TV, they take their food, they go to sleep – everything is going as it should go. A dead routine gives the feeling that everything is perfectly right. Underneath, everything is in chaos. They are missing life.

Idealism, to me, means living for some ideal to be fulfilled in the future. The future is not part of time; it is only part of desire. Ordinarily you think that past, present and future are divisions of time. You are wrong. They are not divisions of time. Time is only present, always present, never otherwise. The past is just in the memory, in the mind. It is not part of time; it is part of the mind. And the future is also part of the mind – the desire. The past, memory; the future, desire. And between the two is the very small moment, the atomic moment of time which is present, which is always present.

Time comes always as now. If you are missing the now, you are committing suicide. Maybe it is slow, that's why you are not aware. You are postponing life for some ideal. Then your life will become a dead routine, futile. You are simply wasting a great opportunity – but wasting for beautiful words. Somebody is trying to become perfect.

Somebody is trying to become a sage. Somebody is trying to become a mahatma. Somebody is trying to become something else. Be – and forget becoming. Becoming is the nightmare. Relax. You are perfect. Life as it is, is perfect, each moment of it. It is very difficult to accept it, because you have been conditioned for centuries. You have been given ideals and you go on comparing with ideals. You say, "How can I be perfect? – I still have anger in me. How can I be perfect? – I still have sex in me. How can I be perfect? – I still have violence in me. How can I be perfect?" You are comparing. Comparison is the disease, the very illness. You are you!

If anger is there, what can you do? You have to accept it. If you try first to be beyond anger and then live, you will never live. Listen to me. Accept the anger and live. And I tell you – by living, the anger will disappear. Transformation happens through living, not through preparations. The more you prepare, the more you become hung-up in the head. Relax. Enjoy. But the ego goes on like a hard taskmaster. It goes on saying, "Why are you wasting your time in small things, trivia? Become a great man! Become a Buddha, become a Mahavira, become a Christ!"

Christ was never trying to become a Christ, that's why he was a Christ. He simply accepted himself, through that acceptance he flowered. Mahavira was not trying to become somebody else. He had no ideals. He simply lived his life, he simply did his thing, and life happened to him. It always happens. It is always happening.

It is not that life is not happening; it is that you are missing it. It is a simple fact. I am not talking philosophy. It is a simple statement of a fact. Right now, look! What are you missing? Nobody is missing anything.

I was reading one of Emerson's essays. He says, "Man is timid and apologetic. He is no longer upright. He dares not say 'I am.' He is ashamed before the blade of grass or the blowing rose. These roses under my window make no reference to former roses or to better ones. They are what they are. They exist with God today."

Let this be the very foundation of your life, "They exist with God today." They don't refer to the former roses. They don't compare with better roses. They are simply themselves and "they exist with God today." There is no time to them. There is simply the rose. It is perfect in every moment of its existence.

Perfection is not a goal; it is already there. You are born perfect;

only perfection happens in this existence, nothing else. How can imperfection happen out of existence? Only perfection is possible. The idea that you have to be perfect makes you imperfect in the present, because the comparison arises. You go on comparing yourself with others: somebody is more beautiful, somebody is more intelligent, somebody is more moral, somebody is more sincere, somebody is healthier, somebody is stronger. You are crippled in these comparisons; such a dead weight falls on your head that you cannot move. But you have forgotten one thing: you are you, and you cannot be anybody else.

Once you accept the fact that you are you and whatsoever you do you are not going to be anybody else, you are going to remain yourself; once you accept it a transfiguration happens. You start living. Then you don't bother about the future. Then you are not in the rat race of being somebody else. Then you are no longer comparative, no longer competitive. Then you also become a rose under the window, you exist with God today. If you are not existing with it today, you will be in a nightmare.

Buddha realized this. He was the first man to realize it in its absoluteness. He dropped all ideals. People would come to him and ask, "Is there God?" and he would remain silent. Not that there is no God, but once he says there is, a desire arises in you to achieve, to know, to be – and then you are on the wrong track again. Buddha remained silent. He would not say anything about God. People would ask, "Okay, if God is not there, it is nothing to be worried about. Is there a soul inside?" Buddha would keep silent, because once he says, "Yes, there is a soul," then you are after it.

You have become such addicted chasers of shadows that any word, any hint will do, and you are on the track, running. Chasing has become your life. Chase something, money, *moksha* – it makes no difference, but chase. Power, prestige, meditation – it makes no difference, but chase.

I can understand how difficult it was for this man Buddha to keep quiet when he knew well that God is, when he knew well the soul is. How difficult it was to keep quiet. He resisted the temptation because he knew you. Never has anybody known humanity so deeply – and the madness of humanity, the obsession with ideals.

People would ask, "When we attain, when we become realized and enlightened, where will we be then? Will there be a *moksha*, a state of total freedom?" Buddha remained quiet. He dropped the old eastern term *moksha*, the state of total freedom. He invented a new term – *nirvana*.

The term is beautiful. The word is very significant. *Nirvana* simply means cessation. You will not be. Nothing will be. He used a negative term, just so that you cannot make an ideal of it. How can you make an ideal of a negative state? Anything positive becomes an ideal and you start chasing it. He used the most negative term, the absolute negativity – nirvana. Nothing will be there. Only nothingness will be there. You will cease to be.

Look at the human mind; the human mind has made a goal of it. Buddha tried to give you a totally negative term so that you cannot make an ideal of it. But since then people have made an ideal out of it, millions of people are chasing nirvana. They have completely forgotten that nirvana simply means nothing. It means absolute void. It means emptiness.

How can you chase emptiness? The chaser has to cease, only then is the emptiness there – so how can you chase it? How can you seek it? The seeker has to drop. You have to disappear completely, utterly.

People have even made a goal of that. The mind seems to be so addicted, that whatsoever is said, it will make a goal out of it. For example, I go on saying be here and now, and I know well you will try to be here and now. You miss the point – because in the very trying you have missed. You cannot try to be here and now, because by the time you are trying, the here and now is passing. You can simply relax. You can be, but you cannot try. If you understand me – finished! Then there is nothing to be done.

But you go on coming to me. You ask me, "What is to be done?" I go on telling you, "Do this, do that." That is just a way to tire you, to exhaust you. So that one day, out of sheer tiredness you say, "No more!" and you relax. Otherwise nothing is lacking. When I see you, you are buddhas – chasing empty shadows. Then each and everything becomes a nightmare.

An old man was sitting on a park bench, enjoying the late spring sunshine, when another old man sat down at the other end of the bench. They viewed each other cautiously and finally one of them heaved a tremendous, heartfelt sigh.

The other rose at once and said, "If you're going to talk politics, I'm leaving."

If you feel that somebody is going to give you an ideal and goal, leave him immediately, because the disease is very infectious and once you are caught in it, it becomes chronic. Nothing has to be done. The doing has to be dropped – not by effort, but by understanding.

If you understand that goals have not helped you, if you understand that becoming has not helped you, then in that understanding, something within you stops. In that understanding, something falls, drops of its own accord. Not that you drop it; otherwise you will come to me and ask, "How to drop it? How to drop this constant chasing? How to drop ideals?"

No, you cannot drop it. If you are trying to drop it – again here you go. You cannot drop it; it will drop of its own accord. Simply understand, understanding is enough; understanding is the only transformation.

When you are following an idea, an ideology, an ideal, a goal, you are bound to imitate others – bound to. You are bound to follow others, because from where will you get the cues? Then you are bound to follow Christ, Buddha, Mahavira. And never has there been a man like you or a woman like you. You are simply unique.

You cannot follow a Buddha, you cannot follow me. You can watch me, but you cannot follow me. You can love me, but you cannot follow me. You can understand me, but you cannot follow me. Once you follow me, you will become more blind. You are already blind. All beliefs lead to blindness. All following leads you away from you.

If you try to become a Buddha, one thing is certain: you will not be able to become yourself. Only one thing is certain: that you will not be yourself. And then follows the next thing: you can never be a Buddha, because you are you and a Buddha is Buddha. If you try to become a Buddha, you cannot be a Buddha; at the most you can be an imitation – a plastic flower, not a real rose.

You can imitate, you can become an actor, you can follow. You can completely follow Buddha and you can make a character exactly like him, but remember: a man like Buddha has no character. He lives spontaneously. He has awareness; he has no character. Each moment he responds to life. He does not follow any character. He does not follow the past. He does not follow any routine that he decided in the past, yesterday. He is herenow responding.

A man of character is always a dead man. A man of character means that he has created an armor around himself. He has taken a vow that he will never speak a lie; that's why he never speaks a lie. He wants to speak lies but he cannot because of his character, the ego involved in it. He suppresses. He can never be authentic and true, and he can never be flowing and open. He is always closed. A man of character carries his tomb around himself. He is not alive. The dead layer of character never allows him to meet life – to meet life herenow.

Buddha has no character, but if you follow him you will have to follow his character as you understand it. You cannot see his consciousness, you can only see how he behaves, and through that behavior you can find some cues. You will miss.

The only way to become a Buddha is to be yourself. It is going to be a totally different and unique phenomenon. It is not going to be a repetition. Existence never repeats. It is infinitely original. It never repeats; there is no need. It goes on innovating new persons, new beings. Never again will you be here; never before have you been here. You come totally new, fresh. Why try to become stale?

It happened in a very famous hotel that a new person was being recruited. The experienced veteran bellhop was explaining the ropes to the young trainee. "This thing," he said, "isn't all carrying bags. In a big hotel, you're forever encountering delicate situations and you have to think fast. For instance, I had to deliver some ice to a particular hotel room and walked into the one across the hall by mistake. The door shouldn't have been open, but it was. Inside the room, the bathroom door was open – which it shouldn't have been – and inside the bathroom was a fat lady taking a bath. In a minute, I knew the fat lady was going to scream her head off." Fat ladies are dangerous.

"Thinking fast, I said, 'Excuse me, sir,' and left. The 'excuse me' was politeness, but the 'sir' was tact, and it saved the day. She figured I hadn't been there long enough to see anything and she calmed down. Get it?"

The trainee got it – and there starts the trouble. The next day he was in the infirmary with a black eye and assorted bruises. The veteran said, "And what happened to you?"

The trainee said, "I was following your advice. I was delivering ice and got into the wrong room and there was a man and a woman on the couch with almost all their clothes off. So I said quickly, 'Pardon me, gentlemen,' and the guy got off that couch and nearly killed me.'

If you have got cues from anybody else other than your own awareness, you are moving into a very dangerous situation. You will miss yourself and you will not gain anything else. The cost is very high, and out of it no fulfillment ever comes.

If you follow a Buddha you will be in trouble – millions of people are in trouble. If you follow a Jesus you will be in trouble. Look at Christians, look at Jainas, look at people who are followers. They are bound to be in trouble, because life goes on changing every moment and you have dead principles.

Remember, there is only one golden rule: that there are no golden rules. Each rule is arbitrary. Every rule is arbitrary; no rule can be ultimate – it is useful in a certain situation, but it is not ultimate. It is not useful in any other situation.

The only thing to attain is consciousness. And consciousness simply comes if you live the moment. If you live here and now, responding, you become conscious. The consciousness has not come to you up to now because you have never lived in the present. It is a consequence of living in the present, call it meditation if you like. The only meditation there is, is to live in the present, to live herenow.

Eating, eat. Walking, walk. Sitting, just sit. Be alert! Enjoy it! It is a tremendous gift. Breathing, breathe. Enjoy it! Delight in it! Looking, look. Sleeping, sleep. Be ordinary if you want to become a buddha. Be simply ordinary and yourself, and do your thing and don't be worried about others, and don't try to follow anybody else.

If you are here with me, it is very simple to follow me – because in a follower the need for awareness is thrown away; you are no longer responsible. When I say "responsible," I mean you are no longer responding to life. You have a dead idea. You consult that dead idea and then you follow it. You don't look at life. The situations are constantly changing; it is a constantly flowing Ganges. It will never fit with your idea. That idea was a byproduct of a certain situation. That situation is not there.

Never follow a dead idea. If you are here with me, don't follow me. Try to understand me. If you love me, you will understand me. If you trust me, you will try to understand me, not try to follow. If you understand me, the only thing that has to be understood is that life is infinitely valuable. Don't waste it.

No ideals are valuable, more valuable than life. Life is the only reality and all else is just the mind. Avoid the mind. Follow reality. And wherever it leads, go courageously with it and you will never miss. You will become yourself. By being yourself, you will become yourself. I am not saying to try to become yourself. By being yourself, every moment you will become yourself. By and by the potentiality will be revealed, realized.

All the religions of the world have created a certain schizophrenic state in the human mind. They have created a division. Half of you is against the other half. You are never one. Angry, you are never totally angry. Somebody is standing by the side and condemning, saying, "This is wrong! Have you forgotten the great masters? What are you doing? This is wrong! Don't do it!" Making love, a part is standing against it and goes on saying, "Celibacy is purity."

Whatsoever you do – it is not a question of anger or love. If you try to become celibate, one part of you goes on saying, "You are missing life." Whatsoever the situation, you are divided.

If you are angry, you are divided. If you are not angry, you are divided. If you don't go into anger, one part of you goes on saying, "This is not good." The other will take advantage of it, he will think you are a weakling. And life is a struggle, and if people come to know that you are a weakling you will be oppressed. Stand on your feet and give a good fight! Don't be an escapist.

If you become angry, the mind goes on saying, "This is wrong. Anger is unawareness. It is irreligious. A religious person like you – and angry?" This doesn't fit with your ideals. This doesn't fit with your image. You have a very beautiful image of yourself: serene, calm, collected like a Buddha; of course a stone Buddha, unperturbed, centered.

Religions have created schizophrenia; you don't know how to do a thing totally. And this is the basic madness of humanity: everybody is divided. Divided, how can you enjoy? Divided, how can you celebrate? One part of you goes on against you continuously – as if one of your legs goes to the right and the other leg goes to the left. You are standing on two boats, which are moving in different directions, diametrically opposite. This is your anxiety.

So many people come to me and they ask, "How to get rid of

anxiety?" They don't know what this word *anxiety* implies. They think that something like transcendental meditation – just chanting a mantra and their anxiety will go. They are simply stupid. Things like transcendental meditation have appeal because of the stupidity of people, because they are in search of shortcuts, something easily done. Like instant coffee: you do it, finished!

Anxiety is a deep problem. The problem is schizophrenia. You are divided, constantly fighting with yourself. You are two, not one, and this tension creates anxiety. Now, repeating a mantra is not going to be of any help. It may give you a little deeper sleep, it may help you to be a little more together, but it is not going to help far enough. Your division remains, and sooner or later again you realize that now the trick is not working.

The schizophrenia has to be dropped in a deep understanding. Don't fight with yourself. And always remember that the top dog is wrong. Always remember that the natural is truer. Whenever there is a conflict, follow the natural. If there is a conflict between love and celibacy, follow love – and go totally in it. I know one day celibacy arises, but that comes out of a deep experience of love. *Brahmacharya* arises, but this is the flowering of profound love – love felt so deeply it becomes *brahmacharya*, it becomes innocence, it becomes virginity.

Virginity has nothing to do with the body; it has to do with profound love. You call a woman virgin because she has not made love yet. I don't call her a virgin. I call a woman virgin who has transcended love, who has loved so deeply that the very depth has become a transcendence.

I call a man virgin who has loved deeply and through love has become so one that now there is no need – no need to depend on the other. He feels grateful toward the other because the other has helped him to become so independent. Virginity is not in the beginning; it is in the end. Children are not virgin. They are just waiting to be violated.

I have heard...

Three children were sitting on the steps of a home, and one child was playing with toy motorcars, another was playing with a spaceship, and the third was reading a glossy *Playboy*-type magazine. A man passed. He looked at the three children. He asked the first, "What would you like to become in your life?"

The first said, "Of course, I would like to compete in car races. I want to become the greatest driver in the world."

The second said, "I want to become an astronaut."

And he asked the third, "What do you want to become?"

He looked at the man and said, "Grown-up, sir. Grown-up."

Children are not virgin. They are just waiting to become grown-up. In fact they are worried why it is taking so long, why it is being delayed.

I was reading the autobiography of a poet who came under the influence of a Christian missionary when he was a child. He must have been about eleven. He became very impressed by the Christian doctrine, that soon the world is going to end and Jesus will come, the "Second Coming." But he became very much afraid. He started praying "God, wait a little. Let my virginity be broken, violated. Wait a little! Just two or three years more. Don't finish the world so soon!"

Children are not virgin. In fact, children are not innocent – they just look it. They are getting ready to be corrupted. They are getting ready to move in the world.

Real innocence comes only in the end. It is a flowering; it is not a seed. It is not the beginning; it is the end.

If love is fulfilled, *brahmacharya* arises. If you have lived totally in anger, compassion comes. If you have moved in life, suddenly you have a transcending experience. But the old religions, all of them have created a divided mind, a guilty mind, a crazy, split mind.

Once it happened, a governor came to visit a madhouse. He was inspecting the new state-supported psychiatric hospital. On being taken through the isolation wards he was struck by the fact that in one cell there was a man sitting, of distinguished appearance, who was reading a copy of the *Wall Street Journal* and who was wearing nothing but a glossy silk top-hat.

The inmate looked up, and saw the governor and his surrounding cluster of doctors and other functionaries. The inmate thereupon rose, bowed politely, and said in cultured tones, "Sir, I perceive you are a man of importance and it strikes me that you must be curious as to why I sit here in the nude."

"Well, yes," said the governor cautiously. "The thought had indeed struck me."

"It is not at all mysterious," said the inmate. "The cell is air-conditioned, as you will note, and is maintained at a most comfortable temperature, and I am, moreover, quite private. Since clothing is not necessary either for warmth, modesty, or adornment, why bother with it at all?"

"True," muttered the governor, rather taken aback at the other's obvious rationality. "But tell me," he said, "in that case, why the top-hat?"

The inmate shrugged. "Oh well, someone might come."

This is the split mind. This is the basic schizophrenia of humanity – never total, this way or that.

My whole teaching is to be total whatsoever you do. I don't say don't be angry. I say that if you choose to be angry, if it happens to be, be total. I don't say don't be greedy. If it happens to you that you are greedy, then be total – because I have come to know that only through totality you transcend.

A split personality can never become non-greedy. It can try, but it can never become. A split personality can never go beyond anger. It can try, but it can never go beyond. A split personality can never go beyond sex. It can fight. So many monks in the monasteries are doing it. They don't go beyond sex; at the most their sexuality becomes perverted, their love becomes poisoned.

Whatsoever the case, I am not telling you to choose something against it. Whatsoever the case, be total in it. Let totality be the only concern, because that is the only way to be alive. And if you are alive, you are perfect. Then you are with existence today, not tomorrow. Because you will not find godliness tomorrow; it is always today. Godliness is today.

Tomorrow is hell. Today is nirvana. But the mind goes on making out that even nirvana belongs to tomorrow. Then nirvana itself becomes a nightmare. Now, the Zen story.

Date-Jitoku, a fine waka poet, wanted to master Zen.

The misery starts ...*wanted to master Zen.* If you want to master anything, you are on an ego trip. And particularly you cannot master Zen. Zen is something which can be found only when there is no ego.

Zen means *dhyan*, Zen means meditation. The very word comes from *dhyan*. It originated in India; Buddha called it *dhyan*. Then Bodhidharma took it to China; in China it became *ch'an*. Then from China it went to Japan; there it became *Zen*. *Zen* means *dhyan*. *Dhyan* means meditation.

You cannot master meditation, because you are the barrier. You drop and the meditation is there. Please don't come in, and there is meditation. If you come in, you are the disturbance.

Remember, as I was saying to you, you come in only when you are split. The ego is only when you are divided. You need an ego to make a connection between the divided parts of your being. You need a link, otherwise you will fall apart.

The ego is the link between your two diametrically opposite parts. It keeps them somehow together in a bundle. It is the rope around them, the link between them, the chain that keeps you together somehow. Otherwise you will fall apart. You will be like Humpty-Dumpty, and all the king's men will not be able to put you together again.

The ego is needed. It is the rope that helps you remain together somehow. Once you are together, the rope is not needed. Once you are one, the ego is not needed. You are, but there is no "I" in it. You are; perfectly you are, but there is no "I" in it. "I" is a tension.

Have you seen it? In certain moments even this miracle happens to you. You are in love with someone and love gives you an opportunity to be together. Suddenly there is no "I"; suddenly you are, without the "I" – an infinite vastness, an uncorrupted being, undivided totality.

Or suddenly someday looking at the sunset, the beauty is so tremendous, you become one. Or one day, listening to music or singing or dancing, suddenly you move so fast in dance that the very idea that you *are* cannot be retained. You move so fast that you become total.

Run fast, and see; dance fast, and see; whirl fast, and see: suddenly the action becomes so total it takes possession of you. The ego drops.

Date-Jitoku, a fine waka poet, wanted to master Zen. Now the wrong journey starts. You cannot master Zen. You can be mastered by Zen, but you cannot master it. It is not a skill to be mastered, it is not a technique to be mastered. It is your very being: to be possessed by it. It is your totality.

With this in mind he made an appointment to see Ekkei, abbot of Shokokuji in Kyoto.

With this in mind... If you come to a master with anything in the mind, you never come. If you have come to me with anything in the mind, you have not come at all. You have traveled, but you have not come. You are still traveling; you have not arrived. If you have come with nothing in the mind, you have come. Then you are close to me.

With nothing in the mind, mind disappears – because the mind can only be there if something is in the mind. The mind cannot exist without the content. The mind is nothing but the total of the contents. If the contents disappear, the mind disappears.

If you have come to me with something in the mind – that you have to achieve something, that you have to be something, that you are chasing some ideal, that you have to fulfill some image – then you will miss me. You will miss me utterly. To be with me, there is only one way: come to me without anything in the mind so that you are open, so that you are open for all things. If you have something in the mind, you are not open for all things. Then you are closed. *With this in mind he made an appointment to see Ekkei...*

Ekkei was one of the rare masters. You will see why I call him rare.

Jitoku went to the master full of hopes...

You should come to a master only when all your hopes have failed. To be full of hopes is to be in the world. A man who is living still with hopes is still living in the future, in the tomorrow. A man who has come to understand that all hopes have been futile, have not led anywhere, can come to a master.

Not that he becomes hopeless, because if you feel hopeless it simply means you are still hoping. Hopelessness is an indication of a mind which is still hoping.

When hopes have really been dropped, when you are suddenly without hope – not hopeless, simply without hope, without hopelessness – you are simply here. With the disappearance of hope, future disappears. Future is nothing but the extension of hope. Future is a hope-project.

Jitoku went to the master full of hopes, but as soon as he entered the room he received a blow.

The master did well. He had not even uttered a single word, he had not asked anything, and he had been hit hard. When you come with hopes, that is the only way to bring you to the moment. If I hit you hard on the head, at least for a single split moment you may come here. Otherwise you are in the future. Zen masters have been hitting their disciples out of their compassion.

Once you start understanding me, I am going to hit. Right now I know you will not understand; you will simply escape – so I go on persuading you to be near me. Once you are ready, a good hit on the head is simply a tremendous gift; one should receive it in deep gratitude. It brings you to the earth, it brings you to the herenow. You have gone so far away that only a hit on the head can bring you here.

...but as soon as he entered the room he received a blow.
He was astonished and mortified: No one had ever dared to strike
him before, but as it is a strict Zen rule never to say or do anything
unless asked by the master, he withdrew silently.

But he missed. He followed the rule, but he could not respond to the situation. When you follow a rule, you miss the situation. He knew that it is a rule that unless the master says something you are not expected even to utter a single word – and he had not said anything. He had to withdraw, but deep down he was hurt.

The master had hit his head to bring him herenow, but he felt hurt, his ego was hurt. He missed the point. He must have been really too obsessed with the future. And a person who is obsessed with the future is almost always obsessed with the past also. That is the way the pendulum of the mind goes on moving – from past to future, future to past. It never stays in the middle where time really exists.

Immediately he said, *No one had ever dared to strike him before...* He moved to the past. Inside he said, "No one has ever dared to hit me before." The master hit him to come herenow; he moved to the past. From the future he jumped to the past. He missed the middle point. As it was a rule, he followed it.

Rules are not helpful with a master. You have to respond not according to rules. You have to watch the situation. You are not to interpret according to your mind. You have to look without the mind to see the fact, what the master has done. The master had done a great act of compassion, but it had been missed. The ego came as a barrier.

He went at once to Dokuon, who was to succeed Ekkei as abbot, and told him that he planned to challenge Ekkei to a duel.
"Can't you see that the master was being kind to you?" said Dokuon. "Exert yourself in zazen and you will see for yourself what his treatment of you means."

It is a great act of compassion. A master is beyond anger, beyond ego, beyond hurting anybody, but out of his compassion he can even hit. The hit is surgical. The knife is not against you. The knife is not in the hands of the enemy. It is in the hands of a doctor, a surgeon. He's going to cut you deeply. He has to take out the growth, the cancerous growth inside you of the ego. It is the greatest surgery ever. And he has to be hard, because he loves you.

Dokuon said, "Don't be puzzled, don't be confused by it, and don't make any decision right now. For a few days sit in *zazen.*"

Zazen means to simply sit, do nothing. *Zazen* is a beautiful meditation. One simply sits looking at the wall, not doing anything. One goes on sitting, sitting, sitting.

If you simply sit and don't do anything, by and by the mind settles, because there is nothing to be done – the mind is not needed. In the beginning it rebels, in the beginning it thinks more – thoughts whirl in a mad whirlpool inside. But if you go on sitting and sitting, there is no point for them. By and by the dust settles; thoughts disappear, gaps appear. In those gaps, understanding is possible. When thoughts are not there, thinking is possible. When you have no thought in the mind, the whole energy that is invested in thinking, in thoughts, is released; it becomes your awareness.

"Exert yourself in zazen and you will see for yourself what his treatment of you means."
For three days and nights Jitoku engaged in desperate contemplation, then, suddenly, he experienced an ecstatic awakening. This satori was approved by Ekkei.

What happens when you simply sit? The whole energy that has been moving in the body, outside the body, in actions, is no longer moving. You become a pool of energy. The energy goes on gathering; you become a reservoir. In *zazen* you are not even allowed to sway or move your body, not even a slight movement, so no energy is invested in action. All energy becomes available. It goes on falling inside. It fills you, it starts overflowing. When the moment of overflowing comes, there is satori. Satori is a moment of energy overflowing.

Thinking stops by and by. It takes time – it takes almost three days. If you exert day and night, continuously, somewhere in three days the moment comes when the energy is so much it simply explodes. Everything calms down, a sudden lightning inside. Everything becomes clear, a clarity of perception is achieved. This is what is called satori in Japan.

Satori is a glimpse of *samadhi* – the first glimpse. Of course, in the first glimpse you cannot recognize what it is. It is so unknown; you have never known it before, you have never come across it before. It has to be approved by the master. The next time when it comes you will be able to recognize it, but for the first time you don't know what it is, how to understand it, how to interpret it.

It is so vast, and all your experiences are irrelevant to it. Your whole past is irrelevant to it. All your hopes for the future are irrelevant to it. It is something you had never hoped for. It is something you had not even imagined of. It is something you had not even dreamt. How can you recognize it? That's why the first satori has to be approved by the master. Up to the first satori one has to remain with the master. Then one can move on one's own, but not before that.

This satori was approved by Ekkei.

Jitoku called on Dokuon and thanked him for his advice, saying: "If it hadn't been for your wisdom I would not have had such a transfiguring experience. And as for the master, his blow was far from hard enough."

Now he understands. Had it been a little harder... That time he was offended. Now he says *"...his blow was far from hard enough."* Now he understands the compassion.

You are on the same journey. You are here with me to know what life is: to learn how to know that which is already available; to learn how to look into that which is in front of you, already standing; to learn how to feel that which is already surrounding you from all sides. Many times I have to hit you. It may not be a physical whack on your head, because to tolerate that is not very difficult. Just the other night a sannyasin came and he said, "Last time I came to you, you called me a coward!" He was very offended. Just because I called him a coward he was so offended. He missed an opportunity. The ego started thinking, the ego came in between. It was a hit on his head. He missed. Now I will have to take another opportunity.

And there are certain moments – only then can I hit you. Even then there is no certainty that you will not miss them. Only in rare moments can you be hit, and then too you can miss. Be alert. And don't philosophize, because that can again be a trick. When I hit you, respond. Be alert. It is not to offend you; it is to awaken you. And I know, the day you understand you are also going to feel ...*his blow was far from hard enough.*

To seek life, to search for truth, is to be ready to die – to die to that life that you have been thinking is life. It is not. I have to destroy you in many ways, in fact, dismantle you. Only then can the new arise. You need a crucifixion, and only then can there be a resurrection. Let me be a cross to you. Only then, and only then is there a possibility that you will be enthroned.

The path is hard, arduous, but once you realize the truth of your being, you will come to know that nothing was hard, nothing was hard enough. Then you will know that whatsoever you have attained is not because of your efforts. Your efforts were nothing compared to that which you have attained. That which you have attained is a sheer gift. And the paradox is, it is already in your hands; I have just to make you aware. It is already in you, I have just to point it to you.

Many times you will be offended in many ways. Many people come to me and leave. They become offended. If I have to think about them and not offend them, I am useless; then I cannot help. I have to go on offending. A hundred persons come: ninety are bound to leave by and by. Out of ten who will remain with me, even if one attains, it is enough – not because it is difficult to attain. The difficulty is not a part of truth, the difficulty is part of your conditioning, the schizophrenic conditioning.

The religions have completely poisoned your being, have made you fragmentary. To put all those fragments together again – not only putting them together, but melting them so that you can become a crystallized being – is difficult because of you.

If you are ready, it is not difficult; it is very simple. It is so easy, it can happen right this moment. If you have to wait, it is because of you – always remember.

It is a question of understanding. It is not a question of doing anything. That *waka* poet, just sitting for three days, day and night, doing nothing, came to realize – a sudden awakening, and it is always sudden.

Whenever you are full of energy and the energy starts overflowing, you attain to an inner orgasm. That orgasm is satori. When that orgasm becomes your constant state of being, that orgasm is called *samadhi*.

Enough for today.

enlightenment: a present possibility

The first question:

Osho,
You tell us to be herenow, without goals and without purpose, but then you allure us also by talking about ecstasy, enlightenment, freedom, and the possible fulfillment. It looks contradictory. Please explain.

t is not contradictory at all, it is a simple fact. But the mind tends to create problems where they don't exist. Mind is a problem-creating mechanism.

When I say that ecstasy is beautiful, when I say that enlightenment is blissful, I'm not talking about the future, I'm not alluring you. I'm simply stating a fact. When I say be herenow without any purpose and goal, I'm showing you the way, how enlightenment can happen right now.

Enlightenment is not a distant goal, it is a present possibility. You can miss it. That doesn't mean that it is far away from you, that simply means that you are fast asleep. You can miss it. That doesn't mean that you have to work hard to attain it, it simply means that you are not aware of something that is already surrounding you.

I will go on talking about enlightenment because without it you are not alive at all; without it you only seem to exist but you don't exist, without it you go on missing. But remember, I am not creating a goal for your desires. Enlightenment can never be a goal. This has to be understood. Nirvana cannot be desired.

Let me explain it to you. Whenever you desire something, you become tense. The desire creates disturbance. Whenever you desire something, of course you desire in the future. In the present, how can you desire? There is not enough space for a desire to exist in the present. It can only exist in the future. Desiring can only be concerned with something in the future, with something which is not here. That which is here cannot be desired.

You can delight in it, but you cannot desire it. You can live it, you can dance it, but you cannot desire it. Hence all the Buddhas say: "Become desireless." But the human problem is that we understand it as if they are saying: "Make desirelessness your goal."

We turn everything into a goal. Put anything into the mind, it immediately reduces it into a goal and the problem arises – immediately. And then the mind asks "How?" How to achieve this? How to get it? How to become it? Again you are on the track, again you have missed.

When Buddhas say: "Become desireless," they are not trying to create a goal for you. They are simply saying, "See, look into your desiring. Understand your desire and the futility of it. Look deeply into it, penetrate deeply into it, and that very penetration will help: desire disappears."

When you can see the total futility of desire, will you ask how to drop it? If you see the total futility of it, it drops by itself. You go on asking how, because you still want to cling. You still want to postpone it. You still think there must be something in it, "Maybe I am missing, maybe I am not making the right efforts, maybe I am not moving in the right direction – but there is something." You are still hoping.

When you look into the nature of desire, you will understand that it is like a horizon. It appears far away – there. Go, move – it moves with you. When you reach the point where you were thinking that the earth meets the sky, it is not meeting there. Again, at the same farther distance, the horizon exists. Again move, the horizon moves with you. The distance between you and the horizon remains constantly the same. If you look into desire, it is so simple to see. If you meditate on desire, this is a fact; this is not a theory about desire.

You have ten thousand rupees. The mind asks for twenty thousand rupees. The mind says, "How can you live happily unless you have twenty thousand rupees? It is impossible." You can get twenty thousand rupees. You will waste a long time for it; one day you will get it. By the time you have got twenty thousand rupees, the desire has gone further away. Now it asks for forty thousand rupees.

By the time you attain to twenty thousand rupees, you have become more addicted to comforts; now more comforts are needed. Now the old house looks small, the old car looks an insult; it has to be dropped. A new car is needed. By the time you reach the forty thousand line, the horizon has gone further away – it demands eighty thousand. It goes on doubling. The distance remains the same.

Between the desire and the fulfillment, the distance remains the same. It never changes, not even for a single inch. The beggar and the emperor are always in the same plight. If you look at the distance between their desire and fulfillment, you will see they are sailing in the same boat.

Once understood, desire drops by itself, of its own accord. Not that you drop it – so the question of "how" never arises. And when desire drops, there is desirelessness. Not that you have to make efforts for it to be there, not that you have to work hard to gain desirelessness: it is not a goal. When desires disappear – the absence of desire is desirelessness.

Let me say it in another way. Ordinarily whenever the word *desirelessness* is used, you think it is against desire. It is not. Desirelessness is not the opposite of desire. Desirelessness is simply the absence of desire, not the opposite. If it is the opposite then it can become the goal. It is not the opposite. You cannot make a goal out of it.

Love is not opposite to hate. If love is opposite to hate, in that love, hate will go on continuing, an undercurrent of hatred will go on flowing. The authentic love is not opposite to hate. The love of a buddha is not opposite to hate. It is simply absence of hate.

Compassion is not against anger. When anger disappears, compassion is. Compassion is not to be fought for; it is not against passion. When passion disappears, compassion is. Compassion is your nature.

Desirelessness is you. When all desires have gone and you are left alone, in that beautiful aloneness – pure aloneness, crystal-clear aloneness – there is desirelessness. Not even a trace of desire; no goal, nowhere to go. Then for the first time you live what life is, for the first time your song bursts, spreads all over the existence. For the first time you become capable of celebrating.

This is called enlightenment, nirvana. Nirvana can never be a goal. When you don't have any goal, nirvana comes to you. You never go toward nirvana. When you are not going anywhere, it comes to you. Or, if you want to use the language of *bhaktas* and devotees, you can use the word *godliness*.

You are not to go toward godliness. One can never go toward it. Where will you go? Either it is nowhere or it is everywhere. Where will you go? You cannot make an object of godliness. You cannot make an arrow of your desire moving toward the target of the divine. Either it is everywhere – so you cannot make a target; or it is nowhere – then too you cannot make a target.

Nobody has ever reached to it. When you stop all reaching, when you drop the whole nonsense of achievement, suddenly godliness comes to you. And when it comes, it comes from everywhere, from all directions. It simply enters in you from every pore of your being. You never reach to it; it always comes to you.

When people come to me, and they say that they are in search of the divine, I say, "Please, don't make that effort. You are on a futile journey. Simply rest, relax, wait, and allow it to come to you. Your very search will create a barrier."

A searching mind is a tense mind. A seeking mind is not at rest. A desiring mind is not at home – always wandering, wandering, going somewhere. If I come to you, do you think I will find you there? You may be somewhere else. You are always somewhere else. Wherever you seem to be, you are not there. If you are sitting in the temple, only your appearance is in the temple. You may be in the market. You may be in the shop or in the factory or in the office. When you are sitting in your office or in your shop, only your appearance is there – you appear to be there. Your mind may be anywhere, the world is vast.

You are never where you are. Just be there. Wherever you are, be there. This is the door to the divine and the divine enters in you.

Nirvana becomes a nightmare if you seek it. And then nirvana is the greatest nightmare there is. Wealth can be found if you seek it. Power, prestige, can be found if you seek it. Of course, it takes a long time, much effort and it is almost useless, because when you have found it you find nothing there. But you can find it.

If you are mad enough you can find anything in the world. You just have to be mad enough – almost insane, crazy. Then, you will win, because nobody will be able to compete with you – unless somebody crazier than you comes to compete with you. You can find anything in the world that you crave for. There will be a nightmare, but there is an end to it.

Nirvana is the last and the ultimate nightmare. Once you start seeking it, it is never going to happen, because the very nature of nirvana is such that the very nature prevents you from reaching it. So when I say be herenow, I am saying please help nirvana to come to you. Be at home, just wait, sooner or later you will see – it has knocked.

Jesus says: "Knock, and the door shall be opened unto you." I say to you: "Just wait. Existence will knock. Just remain alert and open the door when it knocks." Existence has been continuously, constantly knocking, but you are not there to hear, to listen. You are not there to open the door. The guest is always standing at the door, but the host is missing.

Be a host; that's what I mean when I say "be herenow." This simply means be a host to life, be a host to existence. Remain available, and everything is going to happen to you. Nothing is going to be debarred. There is nobody hindering the path except your own desire, except your own continuous running here and there. Rest a little while. And when I say rest, I mean rest herenow. Don't postpone it – because who can rest tomorrow?

I will go on singing the beauties of ecstasy, but don't misunderstand me. I'm not trying to convince you that nirvana has to be achieved. It is not a goal. It cannot be made a goal. It cannot be made an object of desire. It is available. Just look, have an alert look. Life is tremendously beautiful. It is showering on you from everywhere.

This, I call meditation. This is what Zen calls *zazen*. Just sit, in an infinite waiting. Watching, alert, aware, not going anywhere and the miracle of miracles happens – that which you were seeking and could not find, suddenly happens.

There is no contradiction in it, but your mind will make a contradiction, because unless your mind makes a contradiction out of it, the mind has no function to fulfill. First it creates a problem, then it tries to find a solution. Don't allow the mind to create a problem where none exists.

I have heard about a physician...

A man came to him; he was suffering from a common cold. The physician said, "Do one thing. The night is very cold. At midnight, go to the lake naked and jump in."

The man said, "Have you gone mad? I am suffering from a cold, and at midnight the lake is going to be just ice! I will get double pneumonia."

The physician said, "Don't be worried. I have a perfect medicine for pneumonia – but for the common cold I have none. I will cure it certainly. Just follow the instructions."

The mind goes on creating problems and then it goes on supplying solutions. Have you not watched this nonsense?

Cut the mind from the very root. Don't allow it to create a problem – that is the solution.

Otherwise, the mind will give you a solution. In the first place, the problem was false. How can the solution be right? If you solve a false problem, the solution is going to be false. Then you are caught in an infinite regress. Then in the solution the mind will again find problems. Then again, solutions have to be supplied. And then you go on and on.

If your own mind cannot give you a solution, you go to greater minds; they can supply solutions. You go to philosophers – people who have theories, doctrines, scriptures in their heads. If you cannot supply your own solution then you look to the experts; and then they supply you with a solution. But experts have not helped anybody yet. Fifty centuries of philosophy has not even given a single solution to any problem. On the contrary, it has created more and more problems. Cut the very root!

Whenever the mind is trying to create a problem, first try to find out whether the mind is playing the old trick again. Because as I see, life is absolutely simple. It has no problems. I don't mean that life is not a mystery. I mean that life is not a riddle. You cannot solve it.

Life is a tremendous mystery, but very simple. You cannot solve it. You can live it, you can enjoy it, you can merge into it, and doors upon doors open and it is an endless journey of revelations. Greater and greater revelations are waiting for you, but it is not a riddle that can be solved. The more you enter into it, the more unknowable it becomes. The more you know, the more you know that you don't know.

A moment comes when all knowledge seems futile. That is the

moment where consciousness goes through a conversion – from philosophy to religion; from futile, stale theories to a fresh and eternally
alive source of life.

Life is a mystery, it cannot be solved. It has no solution, it has no
answer. Don't try to solve it. That is what the mind is constantly
doing: to solve. Cut the root! Whenever the mind tries to bring a
problem, first try to see – is there a problem really?

It is such a simple thing that I have said: be herenow – and
enlightenment happens to you. It has already happened, you only
have to recognize it. It has happened even before you were born. It
has happened simultaneously with your life. Your very existence is
enlightened. Just a turning-in, a conversion, and the recognition.

The recognition is possible only if you turn herenow. If you go on
moving, chasing the shadows, then you will not have time and space
to move within. All future is without, and the present is within.

The present is not part of time. The present is eternity. It is now,
eternal. It is within you.

Once you turn in, you will start laughing.

It is said that when Bodhidharma attained, he started laughing, a
deep belly laughter. He started rolling on the ground and the disciples
gathered and they said, "What has happened? Have you gone mad?"
He looked really crazy. And he was sitting for nine years and nobody
had ever seen even a smile on his face. He was a very severe and
serious person.

For nine years continuously he was looking at the wall – continuously sitting near the wall and looking at the wall. He had not even
turned to talk to any man for nine years – a very serious man. And
he had decided that he would not get up unless he came to know
what truth is. Tradition has it that his legs withered away. Nine years
is a long time, maybe it really happened. But that is not the point.
One thing is certain. The legs are representative of activity, movement, desire, going, a goal. The legs are a representative of all that.
Certainly in those nine years, goals disappeared. There was nowhere
to go. All motivation, all desire to achieve disappeared. Certainly the
legs withered away.

Then one day suddenly this man is rolling and laughing – must
have gone mad. People must have been thinking that sitting for nine
years watching the wall is bound to create madness. But why was he

laughing? He was laughing at the whole absurdity, the very ridicu-
lousness of it – that all that he was seeking he had already within him
and he was not aware.

Your treasure is with you. Your treasure is already within you. I
can see it but you cannot see it. Being with me is just an opportunity
so that you can also see that which I can already see in you.

When you come to me, you are precisely valuable to me. When
you come to me, I see a buddha coming.

You are not aware. I would like to bow down and touch your feet,
but that can be dangerous for you, so I resist the temptation. You are
already mad – you will go even more mad. But that's what I would
like to do.

You are already there where you would like and wish to be. You
are fulfilled. I can see your flower has bloomed, it has always been
blooming there, but your eyes are wandering somewhere else.

So when I talk about enlightenment, I am simply stating a fact
about your being. I am not giving you a goal to be desired. Then
immediately I have to tell you to be herenow, because that is the way
you will be able to see the blossoming of your being.

There is no contradiction. If it appears to you, look again. Your
mind has deceived you. Cut the mind from the very root.

The second question is from a new seeker:

Osho,
I understand that none of your disciples have achieved. How can I
consider the idealism of preparing myself for losing my ego better
than the idealism of which you spoke today?

Who has told you that none of my disciples have yet achieved? I
cannot see a single person who has not achieved. They are all buddhas, enlightened people deceiving themselves, playing tricks with
themselves, in a hide-and-seek with themselves.

But it is difficult for you to see. Unless you have seen your own
enlightenment, you cannot see. Once you have seen your own enlightenment, the whole world is enlightened. The whole world, I say,
is enlightened the moment you are enlightened.

Then you know that that is their choice. If they want to deceive themselves it is perfectly okay – that is their freedom. If they want to play the game a little more, it's perfectly okay. Why shouldn't they? A few lives more. It is for you to decide.

Not only are my disciples enlightened, life is enlightened. These trees may be fast asleep, snoring, but they are also enlightened. Since the day I became enlightened I have not seen anything that is not enlightened. I cannot see otherwise.

So forget about others. It is a question only about you. Are you ready to stop the deception, the game that you are playing with yourself? Only that much should be your concern. Don't be worried about others.

"I understand that none of your disciples have yet achieved." The questioner must have a very deep-rooted desire for achievement, a very deep-rooted achieving mind. So he looks around through that achieving mind – and of course, an achieving mind cannot believe that anybody else has achieved. Even to concede that I have achieved, he must have struggled hard. In fact, he cannot believe that too. Just to be polite he has said, "I will grant it to this man – but no one else."

It is natural when it has not happened to you. How can it happen to anyone else before it has happened to you? That will look unjust. If it has to happen, it must happen to you first. That's the way of the ego. The ego goes on denying.

But please be a little alert, because if you go on denying that it has happened to others, by and by you will become convinced that it cannot happen, it is impossible, and then you are closing doors for your own enlightenment also. Once you accept that it has happened to somebody, the possibility also opens for you – that it can happen to you.

Just look again, a second look. Watch people. Come out of your achieving mind and have a look. Can you hear the birds singing? They are enlightened buddhas chatting. It has to be so. Godliness is not separate from life. Godliness is a synonym for life. Divinity is not something separate that happens or does not happen. It is hidden in everything that is. In a rock, in a tree, in a bird.

But for the first time you have to realize it within yourself, because that is the closest reality to you. Once you see it there, you see it everywhere.

And the second thing: "How can I consider the idealism of

preparing myself for losing my ego better than the idealism of which you spoke today?" I am not saying to you to prepare. I am not teaching any preparation. I am simply saying: look – this is the ego, and this is the block that is hindering the path. Drop it right now! Who is saying to you to prepare?

If you prepare, then you will prepare forever and ever. Have you not lived long enough already? Have you not been here so many millions of times? You have been repeating like a circle, a wheel – moving again and again, the same wheel. Birth, youth, old age, death, birth again. It goes on moving.

When I am talking about dropping the ego, I am not saying prepare for it. If you are not yet prepared, then when will you be prepared? Enough is enough. Drop it right now. Either you drop it right now or you don't drop it. Don't befool anybody that you are preparing. Preparation is a trick of deceiving others, and more basically, yourself: "I am preparing. One day I am going to drop the ego." But why "preparing" and why "one day"? Why not today? If you have seen the fact, then what is the need?

When you come across a snake on the path, do you prepare to jump? You simply jump out of the way. You don't say, "How can I jump right now? I see the snake, I see the danger, I see death standing in front of me, but how can I just immediately jump? It needs preparation. It needs rehearsal. First I will prepare and then I will jump."

No, your mind simply stops when you see a snake on the path. The mind has no space to think, no time to waste. You jump first and later on you think. Then you can think as much as you want – but first you jump. What I am showing you is that the snake is not as dangerous as your ego. It is your ego which is the real snake.

In the Christian parable of Adam and Eve and the snake, the snake is nobody else but the ego. The snake is symbolic because a snake is very cunning – ego is very cunning. A snake is very slippery and ego is very slippery. A snake moves without legs and the ego also moves without legs. It is a miracle. In fact the snake should not move. It is a miracle – without legs it goes on moving. The ego is not there and goes on moving.

In the Christian parable, the snake convinced Eve that the tree of knowledge is worth tasting. God has prohibited it because he does not want you to become knowledgeable; he does not want you to become wise, as he is. He is jealous. If you also become wise like him then who will worship him? He wants you to remain ignorant so you remain dependent. This is what the ego is doing. The ego convinced Eve. Eve convinced Adam. Why through Eve? That has to be understood.

The feminine mind is more prone to be egoistic. The reason is that the feminine mind lacks ego. The male mind is egoistic already, but the feminine mind lacks ego – it is a passive mind, not active, not aggressive. The male mind is already aggressive; the male mind is already egoistic. It is already outgoing. The male mind was not lacking it.

Whenever something appeals to you, it appeals only when you lack it. You see somebody beautiful – if you are ugly, it appeals. You see somebody strong – and if you are weak, it appeals. The appeal is always of the opposite, of that which you are not. A poor man is attracted toward riches. The really rich are those who renounce riches. A poor man cannot renounce riches.

The feminine mind is not egoistic. It is more surrendering, more receptive, hence the appeal. The trick worked on it. And once the feminine part is convinced, it is very difficult for the male part not to follow. The man has always been a follower of woman. Whatsoever the outward appearance he tries to show that he is the master – that too is because he lacks that. He may be the master in the world, but the moment he comes home he is no longer the master. In the home the woman remains the master. Even a Napoleon or an Alexander is nobody before the wife. Even a Napoleon becomes a coward.

The male mind follows the feminine mind. Once the ego convinced the feminine mind, sooner or later Adam followed. The snake is the old symbol for ego. I'm showing you the real snake on your path.

This snake has convinced you to eat the fruit of knowledge, and all religion is nothing but going back, unlearning. Religion is nothing but vomiting knowledge. What did Adam do? He ate the fruit of knowledge. Christ vomited the same fruit. Adam went far away from the divine source, from the Garden of Eden, from God's garden. Jesus entered it again.

When I am saying that ego is poisonous, I am just stating a fact. I'm not saying prepare to drop it. I am saying if you understand me, it will be dropped right now. Not even a single moment has to be wasted. Once you see the point, in the very seeing the ego has dropped. If it has not dropped in the seeing then you have not seen the point. Then you are playing a trick. Then you think you have understood but you have not understood.

The funniest joke I have ever heard on radio consisted of nothing but silence. On one of his radio shows, Jack Benny, notoriously the cheapest man in the world – at least in the image he had built up for himself – was stopped by a thief who said, "Your money or your life!"

There followed a lengthening silence, and in due course the audience, catching on, began to laugh louder and louder and louder. Finally, just in case there were a few people who didn't get the point, the thief said, once the laughter had died down, "Come on! Your money or your life!"

To which Mr. Benny replied, "I'm thinking. I'm thinking."

Money or life? If life is gone, what are you going to do with the money?

If you have understood me, in that very understanding is the dropping of the ego.

Not that you drop it. How can you drop it? You are to be dropped. How can you drop it? It is dropped. Suddenly you are not there. A totally different quality of energy arises in you, which was blocked by the ego. Yes, you are there and yet you are not there. A very strange experience – the most strange, the strangest – you are you, and yet, you are not you.

How can you drop it? If you drop it, the dropper will remain inside. The ego has deceived you. It drops. Once understood, it drops. There is no question of preparation. I am not saying prepare to drop it. If you prepare to drop it, you may become humble, more humble, more humble, but then the ego will hide behind your humbleness. And you will start thinking, "I am the most humble man in the world. I am the most humble man in the world." That "I am" still remains the same.

The ego can become pious, it can become religious. The ego can become saintly, but that doesn't make any difference. If poison becomes pious it makes no difference. A purified poison may become more poisonous and a purified ego is certainly more poisonous than an ordinary ego.

Look at the religious people: they have a very subtle ego, very polished, cultured, refined. It is difficult to catch it, more slippery than ordinary egos; more subtle in its ways, more cunning in its deceptions, better protected, better secured. Even your talk of godliness may be just a hiding place for it.

No, you cannot drop it. Understood, it drops on its own. Suddenly you see it is slipping out of your hands. There is no need to drop it. Only once you don't cling to it, it drops. In non-clinging it drops. And if you understand that you are holding a poisonous snake, is there any need to prepare?

No, I am not talking about preparation. If you have understood it, let it drop. If you have not understood it, please don't prepare. Then it is better as it is. Don't decorate it. It will make it more ornamental, more flowery – and it will be more difficult then to drop it. It will become more precious.

A man of character has more difficulties in dropping his ego than a man who is characterless. A man who is moral has more difficulties in dropping his ego than an immoral man. The immoral man's ego is already wounded, ill. The moral man's ego is decorated with medals. The moral man's ego is still giving a good pay-off. The moral man's ego is more like a flower and less like a thorn. It is more difficult to drop it.

It has happened – it looks paradoxical, but it has happened so many times – that sinners have achieved to godliness more easily than so-called saints. Of course, it is not recorded much, because all the records have been made by saints. Sinners have not bothered to make records and history and this and that.

A rabbi died – a very religious, very moral, moralistic man – and the same day a sinner also died. The rabbi could not believe it – he was being taken to hell! He started making much fuss. He said, "What is happening? I, a saint, and being taken to hell! And this sinner I have known my whole life, he lived just in front of the synagogue, and he is being taken to heaven! There must have been some mistake."

He made such a fuss that they both were presented before God. The rabbi said, "You know well – my whole life I have been praying and praying, and repeating your name. This man has never done any prayer, he has never been to the temple, and he has done all that is wrong. He has been the most immoral man in the town, and he is being given heaven and I am being taken to hell! This is injustice! Explain it!'

God said, "Yes, I know it – but he never bugged me. You were constantly bugging me. Even in the night it was difficult to sleep because of your remembrance."

Innocence is needed, and innocence is where ego has disappeared.

Simplicity is needed, and simplicity is not a cultivated thing.

When all cultivations disappear, complexities disappear, one becomes simple. One may go to the temple, may not go – it doesn't matter. One may pray, one may not pray – it is irrelevant.

But innocence, simplicity, a deep surrender... That one is no longer a doer, that one no longer thinks of himself as "I" – one has surrendered that "I." One is no longer like an island, one has become part of the mainland, the continent, one has said, "Let the whole live, I disappear in it." Then do whatsoever happens to you, and it is right. Let the whole live through you, and it is moral.

Morality is not something that you have to do and practice. It is something when you disappear and the whole is allowed to exist through you, when you flow with the river, when you don't go up current. Remember this. If you have understood, watch your ego slipping. Don't cling to it, that's all. Allow it to be dropped and shattered.

Once I knew a man. He was a professor, a very learned man. He came to see me. He was very sad, so I asked him, "You look pretty down in the mouth. What is the matter?"

He said, "My psychiatrist says I am in love with my umbrella, and that that is the source of my troubles."

"In love with your umbrella!" I was a little surprised.

"Yes," he said. "Isn't that ridiculous! I like and respect my umbrella and enjoy its company, but love?"

You may not think that you love your ego, but you love it. You can say, "I like and respect my umbrella and enjoy its company, but love?" But just changing words does not make much difference. You love it. Whatsoever miseries it brings, still you love it. Whatsoever troubles it creates, still you love it. In spite of all the hells that the ego creates, you go on loving it.

When you come to me and you ask how to drop it, I am simply surprised, I cannot believe it. If the ego itself has not convinced you by creating so many hells, so many miseries for you, that it is not worth carrying, then nobody can convince you. The ego has done everything that can be done to harm you, to hurt you. It is like a cancer. You are dying of it, but you go on clinging to it. There must be some deep-rooted reason in it.

The deep-rooted reason is that you feel afraid of nonbeing. If ego is gone, then you are gone. If ego is gone, it looks like death – ultimate death, utter death. The fear of nonbeing forces you to cling to the ego. At least – maybe it creates miseries, but you are, at least you are. You would like to suffer rather than not be. This is the problem. You would like to be in hell rather than not be. At least one is. If these are the two alternatives for you – one that you disappear, and the other that you live eternally in hell – just think, and you will choose hell. "At least I will be there. But this utter disappearance? This complete nonbeing?"

That's what Buddha means when he says nirvana. He says consciously choose nonbeing, only then will you be able to drop the ego.

That's what I mean when I go on praising the beauties of ecstasy, the blissfulness, the benediction of enlightenment. I am trying to create a situation in which nonbeing can be chosen.

Not to be is the most beautiful moment. Buddha called it *anatta*, nonbeing. He dropped the old word, *atma*, the self. He used the contrary word *no-self*. He says when you come to your self, you will come to no-self. There you will not find any self.

Many escaped him because they said, "We have come here to know our selves, to be our selves. We have come here to become crystallized beings, and you are teaching nonbeing." Many escaped him. And this country, a very religious country – at least apparently – completely forgot about Buddha. Buddha was born here, but he could not get roots here. Just one word, *anatta*, no-self, created the whole trouble. Had he used self, *atma*, there would have been no trouble; many would have followed him, because behind the word *atma*, self, the ego goes on hiding itself.

Buddha tried to cut the very roots of the problem. He said: "Become conscious; this thinking that you are, is your whole problem and your whole misery. Drop this very effort to be. Accept nonbeing, and all benediction is yours."

This problem is going to face you. The ego is not the problem. The real problem is to be or not to be. And my whole teaching is not to be, because that is the only way of being, that is the only way of authentic being. Paradoxical, but it is so. The more you think you are, the less you are.

Let me try to explain to you. Have you watched? When you have a headache, only then you have a head. With the headache comes head. When the headache disappears, the head also disappears.

If you go on feeling your head, that means you must be carrying some sort of headache, more or less, but the headache must be there; only then the head is felt. When the head is perfectly healthy it is not felt at all. It becomes nonbeing. When you are ill, you feel the body. When you are healthy, you don't feel the body at all. That is the criterion of a healthy body: that the body is not felt at all. One becomes completely bodiless, then one is healthy.

When health is there, nothing is there, not even the consciousness of health because that too belongs to an ill person. You must know many people, hypochondriacs, who go on talking about health, medicine, this and that. Not that they are healthy – their very talk shows that they are not healthy. A healthy person is not worried about it.

I was reading the life of Martin Luther, the founder of Protestant Christianity. He was continuously worried his whole life about his constipation. I don't think that he was praying when he was praying; he was thinking of constipation – continuously thinking about it – the stomach, the constipation, the motion. And it is said that his first satori happened on the toilet seat. It must have been so, it is bound to be so.

He must not have been a healthy person at all. Not only was he not healthy, I cannot think that he was even spiritual. You can remain ill, but there is no need to think about it continuously. There is no need to make much fuss about it, and contemplate about it. He was too body-oriented.

He must have had an achiever's mind, because all people who are too much in the future have constipation in the present. Constipation is a very spiritual disease. People who are too much ambitious are always constipated. You cannot find a politician who is not constipated. Because the mind is so tense, it cannot relax the intestinal system; everything is held back. If you are really healthy, you forget the body. If you are really there, you forget the ego.

When one perfectly is there is no I, the I does not arise out of it. There is amness but there is no I. Amness is infinite; it has no boundaries. The I is very atomic – a shrunken thing, a constipated thing, an ill, diseased thing.

Prepare yourself, not to drop the ego – but prepare yourself right now, not in the future. Don't make plans to understand. What preparation is needed to understand? Will you have to do many *yogasanas*, yoga postures, to understand? Will you have to stand on your head for many years to understand?

To understand, only one thing is needed: right listening, nothing else. Please listen to what is being told to you. What I am saying to you, just listen to it. If you can listen to it, in the very listening, seeing will happen; you will have a different vision. In that vision is transformation.

The third question:

Osho,
Wu-wei and the way of the heart – how are they interrelated?

They are not interrelated; they are one and the same thing – just two ways of saying the same thing.

Wu-wei means action without action. It means doing without doing. It means allowing that which wants to happen. Don't do it, allow it to happen. And that is the way of the heart.

The way of the heart means the way of love. Can you do love? It is impossible to do love. You can be in love but you cannot do it. But we go on using expressions, like "making love," which are foolish. How can you make love? When love is there, you are not there. When love is there, the manipulator, the maker, is not there. Love does not allow any maneuver on your part. It happens. It happens suddenly out of the blue. It is a gift. Just as life is a gift, love is a gift.

The way of the heart or the way of love or the way of *wu-wei*. They are all the same. They insist that the doer has to be dropped, forgotten, and you have to live your life not as a manipulator. You have to live your life as a flow of the unknown. Don't move up current and don't try to push the river. Flow with the river.

The river is already going to the sea. Just be one with the river and it will take you to the sea. There is no need even to swim. Relax, and let the river take you. Relax, and let existence possess you. Relax, and let the whole take the part.

Doing means the part is trying to do something against the whole, the part is trying to have its own will against the whole.

Wu-wei means the part has understood that it is only the part and has dropped all struggle. Now the whole is doing and the part is happy. The whole is dancing and the part is dancing with it. To be in tune with the whole, to be in step with the whole, to be in a deep orgasmic relationship with the whole, is the meaning of *wu-wei*. And that is the meaning of love.

That's why Jesus says, "God is love." He is creating a parallel, because in man's experience there is nothing else other than love that comes close to godliness.

Listen, you were born but then you were not aware at all. It was a happening, but it has already happened; nothing can be done now. You will die, someday it will happen in the future. This moment you are alive. The birth has happened, the death has to happen. Between the two there is only one possibility – love.

These are the three basic things: birth, love and death. They all happen. But birth has already happened – now you cannot become aware of it. And death has not happened – how can you become aware of it right now? Only love is the possibility between the two, which is happening right now. Become aware of it and see how it happens.

It is nothing on your part. You don't do anything. One day suddenly you feel a glow; one day suddenly you feel an energy arising. In the hands of the unknown, the god of love has knocked at the door. Suddenly you are no longer the same: the dullness has disappeared, the drabness has disappeared, that staleness has disappeared. Suddenly you are singing and bubbling with joy, suddenly you are no longer the same. At the peak the valleys are forgotten, the dark valleys. Sunlight and the peak – have you done anything for it?

People go on teaching love. How can you love? Because of this teaching, love has become impossible. The mother goes on saying to the child, "Love me, I am your mother." How is the child supposed to love? In fact, what is he supposed to do? The child cannot believe what to do, how to do it. And the mother goes on insisting. And the father goes on insisting, "When I come home love is expected!" By and by the child becomes a politician, he starts the politics of love – which is not love at all. He starts playing tricks. He becomes deceptive. He smiles when the mother comes close, and the mother feels "He loves me."

He has to do these things because he depends on them, his survival depends on them. He is helpless. He becomes a diplomat. He does not feel any love but he has to pretend. By and by the pretension becomes so deep-rooted he goes on pretending his whole life. Then he loves a woman because she is his wife; then she loves a man because he is her husband. One has to love. Love becomes a duty. Can you think of any more absurd possibility? Love becomes a duty, one has to do it. It is a commandment, one has to fulfill it. It is a responsibility.

Now real love will never happen to such a person, such a conditioned mind, because love is always a happening. You are always taken unawares. Suddenly from nowhere, it comes to you. The arrow comes, hits the heart; you feel the pain, the sweet pain of it, but you don't know from where and how it happens. Love still remains in the hands of existence. It is a happening.

Just the other day I was reading an anecdote...

Friederich Wilhelm I, who ruled Prussia in the early eighteenth century, was a fat eccentric who stood on no ceremony at all. He walked the streets of Berlin unattended and when anyone displeased him – and he was easily displeased – he did not hesitate to use his stout walking stick as a cudgel. The king, and behaving that way!

Small wonder then that when the Berliners saw him at a distance, they quietly left the vicinity. The roads were empty. Whenever they would see that he was coming, they would escape here and there.

One time as Friederich Wilhelm was pounding down one of the streets, a citizen espied him, but too late, and his attempt to slide quietly into a doorway proved a failure. "You!" called out Friederich Wilhelm. "Where are you going?"

"Into the house, your majesty," said the citizen, trembling violently.

"Is it your house?"

"No, your majesty."

"A friend's house?"

"No, your majesty."

"Why are you entering it then?"

The poor citizen, fearing he might be accused of burglary, and at his wits' end, finally decided to tell the truth and said, "In order to avoid you, your majesty."

Friederich Wilhelm frowned. "To avoid me? Why?"

"Because I fear you, your majesty."

Friederich Wilhelm promptly turned purple and lifting his cudgel pounded the other's shoulders crying, "You are not supposed to fear me! You are supposed to love me! Love me, scum! Love me!"

How is one supposed to love? Love cannot be a duty. Nobody can be supposed to love. Nobody can be commanded to love. Nobody can be told to love. If it happens, it happens. If it doesn't happen, it doesn't happen. The very concept that you can do something about it has created such a situation that love is not happening to many people. Rarely does it happen to somebody. It is as rare as godliness because godliness is love, because love is godliness.

If you are available for love, you will be available for godliness also. They are the same. Love is the beginning and godliness is the end. Love is the doorsteps of the temple of the divine.

The path of love or the path of heart simply means nothing is in your hands. Don't waste your time. The whole will take care of itself. Please relax; allow the whole to take you over.

The last question:

Osho,
I don't know how it happened, but I am here with you. What pushed me toward you – a search for something? But I don't know that either. Is that idealistic? Any expectation hidden under that?

Don't be worried. There is no need for a cause to be there. There is no need for a motivation to be there. It can just happen for no cause at all. And when it just happens it is tremendously beautiful. Then it has a grace of its own.

If you have come to me in search of something then you will be using me. Then I will be a means to some other end. There, you will miss me. If you have come with a motivation, that very motivation will become a barrier between me and you. Why be worried? You are here. I am here. That's enough.

Let us meet and merge. Let us be in such a togetherness that you can taste of something which is present in front of you; so that you can eat a little of me, drink a little of me.

There is no need to find any cause why you are here. This very search, of finding causes, is mind-oriented. Drop it. Why waste time with it? You are here – that's enough. Now don't waste this time. Otherwise, later on when you are not here you will think, "I was there and I missed. Why couldn't I enjoy that moment? Why couldn't I celebrate that moment?"

A man once came to me and he said, "I am very much attracted to Buddha, and I always think that had I been there in Buddha's time, I would have gone to his feet and surrendered."

He was just sitting near me, almost fast asleep. I shook his head and I told him, "What are you talking about? I know you were there. I have seen you there. But then you were talking about some other buddhas and you were saying, 'Had I been in the time of some past Buddha...'"

Then too he could not understand. I had to shake him again and I said, "Look at me. I am here. Then don't say later on after two thousand years that had you been with me you would have surrendered."

He said, "I will think about it."

Are you also going to think about it?

It can be done. It can be allowed to happen right now. All thinking is a postponement. Don't be worried why you are here. You are here. Be grateful. Don't miss this opportunity in worrying. Celebrate this moment.

If you can celebrate this moment, you will also become the same as I am. If you can celebrate this moment, through that celebration you will attain to that which is already attained. You will achieve that which is already achieved. You will come to know your own hidden treasure.

Enough for today.

CHAPTER 3

mere players of a game

Muso, the national teacher, and one of the most illustrious masters of his day, left the capital in the company of a disciple for a distant province. On reaching the Tenryu river they had to wait for an hour before boarding the ferry; just as it was about to leave the shore, a drunken samurai ran up and leapt into the packed boat, nearly swamping it. He tottered wildly as the small craft made its way across the river and, fearing for the safety of the passengers, the ferryman begged him to stand quietly.

"We're like sardines in here!" the samurai said gruffly. Then, pointing to Muso, "Why not toss out the bonze?"

"Please be patient," Muso said, "we'll reach the other side soon."

"What!" bawled the samurai, "Me be patient? Listen here, if you don't jump off this thing and start swimming, I swear I'll drown you!"

The master's continued calm so infuriated the samurai that he struck Muso's head with his iron fan, drawing blood. Muso's disciple had had enough by this time and, as he was a powerful man, wanted to challenge the samurai on the spot. "I can't permit him to go on living after this," he said to the master.

"Why get so worked up over a trifle?" Muso said with a smile. "It's

exactly in matters of this kind that the bonze's training proves itself.
Patience, you must remember, is more than just a word." He then
recited an extempore waka:
"The beater and the beaten:
mere players of a game
ephemeral as a dream."
When the boat reached shore and Muso and his disciple got off, the
samurai ran up and prostrated himself at the master's feet. Then
and there he became a disciple of the master.

Seeking for something, desiring for something, is the basic disease of the mind. Not seeking, not desiring, is the basic health
of your being.

It is very easy to go on changing the objects of desire, but that is
not the way of transformation. You can desire money, you can desire
power, you can change the objects of desire, you can start desiring godliness; but you remain the same because you go on desiring. The basic
change is to be brought not in the objects of desire, but in your subjectivity. If desiring stops – and remember, I am not saying that it has to be
stopped – if desiring stops then for the first time you are at home;
peaceful, patient, blissful. And for the first time life is available to you
and you are available to life. In fact, the very division between you and
life disappears, and this state of non-division is the state of existence.

People come to me from all over the world, they travel thousands
of miles. When they come to me and I ask, "Why have you come?"
Somebody says, "I am a seeker of the divine," somebody says, "I am
a seeker of truth." They are not aware what they are asking. They are
asking the impossible. The divine is not a thing. The divine is not an
object. You cannot seek it. Divinity is this whole. How can you seek
the whole? You can dissolve in it, you can merge in it, but you cannot
seek it. The seeking simply shows that you go on believing yourself
separate from the whole – you the seeker, and the whole the sought.

Sometimes you seek a woman, sometimes you seek a man.
Sometimes, frustrated from the world, you start seeking the other
world – but you are not yet frustrated with seeking itself.

A seeker is in trouble. A seeker is confused. He has not understood the basic problem itself. It is not that you have to seek the
divine and then everything will be solved. Just the opposite – if
everything is solved, suddenly there is divinity.

It happened once...

A bookseller from south India wrote to a house in New Delhi asking that a dozen copies of the book *Seekers after God* be shipped to him at once. Within two days he received this reply by telegraph: "No seekers after God in Delhi or Mumbai. Try Pune."

Of course they are all here. The seeking is a disease. Don't make it an ego trip. When somebody comes and says that he is a seeker of God, I can see the light of the ego that shows in his eyes – the condemnation of the world, that he is not a worldly man, he is a religious man. The way he says it shows his pride; that he is not an ordinary man, not part of the ordinary run of humanity. He is special, extraordinary. He is not seeking money, he is seeking meditation. He is not seeking anything material, he is seeking something spiritual.

But to me and to all those who have ever known, seeking is the world. There is no otherworldly seeking. Desiring is worldly. There is no otherworldly desire. In the very desiring the world exists. What you desire is irrelevant, that you desire is enough to make you worldly, because all desires are from a basic fallacy; the basic fallacy that you are missing something, that something is needed. In the first place you are not missing anything. Nothing is needed.

The world is a nightmare because of desiring, and then nirvana becomes the last nightmare. Of course the last, because if you wake up seeking God and nirvana – if you wake up, then all nightmares disappear.

You have dropped the world. Now you seek God. Please also drop God. This will look a little irreligious; it is not.

I was reading a statement of Albert Einstein. I loved it. Some-where he says, "I am a deeply religious nonbeliever." In fact a religious person cannot be a believer. A religious person can trust, but cannot believe. Trust comes out of existential experience; belief is just a mind-trip. Belief is just of ideology, concepts, scriptures, philosophy. Trust is of life.

The moment you say "God," you have used a belief. God is a belief. But life is not a belief, it is an experience. Let life be your only god. No other god is needed, because all other gods are human inventions. Einstein is true when he says, "I am a deeply religious person, but nonbelieving, not a believer." What does he mean?

The quality of being religious has nothing to do with the quality of a believer. A believer believes because he desires. A believer believes because he wants to seek something. A believer believes because he cannot live life without the mind. He always brings the mind in between life and himself. As if your hand is hiding behind a glove, you touch your beloved but not directly; your hand is hidden behind the glove. The glove touches the beloved, you touch your glove only.

A belief is like a glove, it surrounds you. You are never available to life directly, immediately. A religious person is naked in this sense – he has no clothes of beliefs. He is simply direct, in touch with life; in that touch the melting, in that touch the merging, in that touch somewhere you are no longer you. Somewhere you have become the whole and the whole has come to you. The ocean drops into the drop and the drop becomes the ocean.

Beliefs are dangerous. We go on changing beliefs: a Hindu can become a Mohammedan, a Christian can become a Hindu, or a religious person, a so-called religious person, can become a Communist; a theist can become an atheist. It makes no difference. You go on changing the glove, but the glove remains.

Can't you see life directly? Can't you love life directly? Is there really any need to believe in anything? Can't you trust life?

Let me say it in this way: people who cannot trust, believe. Belief is a substitute – a false coin, a deception. People who can trust need no beliefs. Life is enough. They don't superimpose any god, any nirvana, any *moksha* on top of it. There is no need. Life is more than enough. They live life.

Of course if you have a belief, you can create a future around it. If you don't have any belief then you don't have any future, because life is herenow. There is no need to wait. But we go on postponing – to the very moment death comes and takes the gift back.

I was reading…

Three men were engaged in one of those profitless conversations, which involve all of us at one time or another. They were considering the problem of what each would do if the doctor told him he had only six months to live.

Robinson said, "If my doctor said I had only six months to live, the first thing I would do would be to liquidate my business, withdraw my savings, and have the biggest fling on the French Riviera you ever saw.

I would play roulette, I would eat like a king, and most of all I would have girls, girls, and more girls."

This man must have been postponing, postponing for death. When a doctor says you have only six months to live, then... But that too seems to be just a wish; he may not be able – because when death knocks at the door, one is so shocked and shattered – when death has come near you, how can you enjoy? You could not enjoy when life was close. When life is receding farther away each moment, how can you enjoy? This is again just a way of believing that if it happens, then immediately I will start living. Who is preventing you from living right now?

The second man said, "If my doctor said I had only six months to live, the first thing I would do would be to visit a travel agency and plot out a world tour. There are thousands of places on earth I have not seen and I would like to see them before I die: the Grand Canyon, the Taj Mahal, Angkor Wat – all of them."

Who is preventing you? Why are you waiting for death to come, then you will go and see the Taj Mahal? Will you be able to see the Taj Mahal then? Your eyes will be so filled with darkness that the Taj Mahal won't look like a Taj Mahal. It will be impossible to see when death has come into the mind. It will make you blind. An inner trembling will overpower you. You will not be able to hear, you will not be able to see, you will not be able even to breathe. But why do people go on postponing?

The third man said, "If my doctor said I had only six months to live, the first thing I would do would be to consult another doctor."

This seems to be the most representative of all men. This is what you are also going to do. You are not going to live even then. You will try another doctor who can again give you hope, who can again give you future, who can again tell you, "No need to be worried – you can still postpone. No need to be in a hurry – death is far away." You will find, you will seek someone who can still give you hope.

Hope is a way of postponing life. All desiring is a way of postponing life, and all beliefs are tricks of how to avoid that which is and how to go on thinking about that which is not. God is not; life is. Please don't be seekers of God. Nirvana is not; life is. Please don't be seekers of nirvana.

And if you stop seeking nirvana, you will find nirvana hidden in life itself. If you stop seeking God, you will find godliness everywhere – in each particle, in each moment of life. God is another name for life. Nirvana is another name for life lived. You have just heard the word *life*; it is not a lived experience.

Drop all beliefs, they are hindrances. Don't be a Christian, don't be a Hindu, don't be a Mohammedan. Just be alive. Let that be your only religion.

Life, the only religion. Life, the only temple. Life, the only prayerfulness.

I have heard...

A disciple came to a Zen master, bowed down, touched his feet and said, "How long do I have to wait for my enlightenment?"

The master looked at him for a long, long time. The disciple started getting restless. He again said, "Why are you looking at me for so long? Why don't you answer me?"

And the master answered a really Zen answer. He said, "Kill me."

The disciple could not believe that this is the answer for his enlightenment. He went to ask the chief disciple. The chief disciple laughed and he said, "He did the same to me also. And he is right. He is saying, 'Why do you go on asking me? Drop this master. Drop this asking. Kill me. Drop all ideology. Who am I? I am not preventing you. Life is available. Why don't you start living? Why do you go on preparing, when and how?'"

This seems to be the most difficult thing for the human mind: just to live naked; just to live without any arrangements; just to live the raw and the wild life; just to live the moment. And this is the whole teaching of all the great teachers, but you go on making philosophies out of them. Then you create a doctrine, and then you start believing in the doctrine.

There are many Zen people who believe in Zen – and Zen teaches trust, not belief. There are many people around me who believe in me – and I teach you trust, not belief. If you trust your life, you have trusted me. No intellectual belief is needed.

Let this truth go as deep in you as possible: that life is already here, arrived. You are standing on the goal. Don't ask about the path. In Franz Kafka there is a parable; it looks like Zen, almost Zen. Kafka says:

I was staying in a strange town. I was a new arrival there, and I had to catch the train early in the morning. But when I got up and looked at my watch, I was already late so I started running. When I came to the tower and looked at the tower-clock I became even more afraid that I would miss the train, because my watch itself was late. So I started running, not knowing the path, not knowing the way. And the streets were clean and deserted early in the morning – a cold winter morning and I couldn't see anybody.

Then suddenly I saw a policeman. Hope came into me. I went to the policeman and I asked about the way, and the policeman said, "The way? Why are you asking me?"

And I said to him, "I am a stranger in this town and I don't know the way, that's why. Please show me the way, and don't waste time – I am already late and I will miss the train, and it is important to catch the train."

The policeman laughed and he said, "Who can show the way to anybody else?"

The policeman said this, and he waved a hand and moved away smiling.

Here ends the parable. It looks exactly Zen. In the West they think this is surrealistic, absurd. It is not. Of course from a policeman it looks more absurd than from a Zen master, but sometimes policemen can be Zen masters.

Who can show you the way? – because basically the way does not exist. You are always on the goal. Wherever you are is the goal. The way does not exist. If you go on asking about the way, you are trying to create future again and again – and future is the nightmare.

Look. This very moment life is pouring from everywhere. A single moment of witnessing and you will laugh at the very absurdity of asking for a path, or a way, or a method. Nothing is to be done.

A woman came up to a policeman and said, "Oh officer, there is a man following me and I think he must be crazy."

The officer took a good look at her. "Yes," he answered, "he must be."

Whenever you come to me asking for a way, I say within myself, "Here comes a crazy man again." If I don't show you the path, I look hard, unkind. If I show you the path, I mislead you. The only thing that can be done is that you should be thrown to yourself. So I have to devise ways that are not ways, which only appear to be ways. They don't lead anywhere because there is nowhere to go. Everybody is already there. There is nowhere to go. I devise paths and methods just to tire you, exhaust you. So one day, in deep exhaustion, you simply drop all seeking. Exhausted, you fall down on the ground tired, tired of all ways and all methods; tired of the very seeking and the search. And suddenly a peace descends on you – the peace that is beyond understanding. You will laugh because it was always possible. It was because of you that it was not descending. You were running away.

All paths lead where? Truth is here. All paths lead somewhere, and truth is always here. No paths can bring you to yourself.

That's why I say try hard, so that you can be tired soon. Don't go slow. Lukewarm, you can go for lives and lives, hoping and hoping. Try hard. Try absolutely, totally, so that you can be tired – so much so that the sheer tiredness drops the whole effort, and suddenly lying on the ground you become aware of the reality that is here.

God is not a thing. It is the whole performance. You cannot catch hold of it. Nirvana is not somewhere. It is the whole performance of life.

I was reading a little story:

It was springtime and a teacher said to his little pupils, "I saw something the other day, and I wonder if any of you have seen it. If you know it, don't say what it is. I went out and saw it coming up from the ground about ten inches high, and on top of it was a little round ball of fluff, and if you went *woof*, a whole galaxy of stars flew out. Now what was it like before the little ball of stars appeared?"

One said, "It was a little yellow flower, like a sunflower, only very small."

"And what was it like before that?"

A little girl said, "It was like a tiny green umbrella, half closed, with a yellow lining showing."

"Yes, but what was it like before that?"

One of them said, "It was a little rosette of green leaves coming out of the ground."

"Now, do you all know what it is?"

They roared back, "Dandelion!"

"And did you ever pick dandelions?" Most of them said yes, but the teacher said, "No, you cannot pick a dandelion. That is impossible. A dandelion is all these things you mentioned, and more, so whatever you picked, you got only a fragment of something or other. You can't pick a dandelion because a dandelion is not a thing. It is a process and a performance. And, you know, everything is a process and a performance – even you."

You cannot pick even a dandelion, even a small flower, in its totality because the totality is tremendous. How can you pick life? You cannot pick a small flower. Life is this whole performance. All that is today is life; all that has ever been is life; all that is ever going to be is life. Life is not a thing, it is a process. And so infinite and so vast – how can you seek it? It is impossible.

You can live, you can drop into this infinite ocean of godliness. And that door opens right now. There is no need to wait.

The whole Zen attitude is to bring to your notice the fact that there is no effort to be made. The Zen attitude is that of effortlessness. That is where it differs from Yoga. Yoga is effort; Zen is effortlessness.

And of course effort can lead somewhere, but it cannot lead to the ultimate. Effort can give you a better ego, more polished, more crystallized. But it cannot give you nirvana, it cannot give you godliness. That is beyond effort. When all efforts cease, in that silence, in this beautiful emptiness, in that void, whatsoever is found is godliness.

Then what is to be done? The question naturally arises – then what to do? Understanding, more awareness, more witnessing. Watch yourself moving, living, being. Try to understand each moment that passes by you. Become a witness.

Remember, witnessing does not mean judgment. You are not to judge that this is good and this is bad. The moment you judge, you lose the witness. If you say this is bad, you are already identified. If you say this is good, you have already slipped out of witnessing – you have become a judge.

A witness is a simple witness. Just watch as you watch the

traffic on the road, or someday you lie down on the ground and you watch the clouds in the sky. You don't say this is good, that is bad; you simply don't make any judgments. You watch. You are unconcerned with what is good, what is bad. You are not trying to be moral. You are not trying any concepts – a pure witnessing. Out of that, more and more understanding arises and by and by you start feeling that the ordinary life is the only life; there is no other life.

To be ordinary is the only way to be religious. All other extraordinary things are ego trips.

Just to be ordinary is the most extraordinary thing in the world, because everybody wants to be extraordinary. Nobody wants to be ordinary. To be ordinary is the only extraordinary thing. Very rarely does somebody relax and becomes ordinary. If you ask Zen masters, "What do you do?" they will say, "We fetch wood from the forest, we carry water from the well. We eat when we feel hungry, we drink when we feel thirsty, we go to sleep when we feel tired. This is all."

It does not look very appealing – fetching wood, carrying water, sleeping, sitting, eating. You will say, "These are ordinary things. Everybody is doing them." These are not ordinary things, and nobody is doing them. When you are fetching wood, you are condemning it – you would like to be the president of some country. You don't want to be a woodcutter. You go on condemning the present for some imaginary future.

Carrying water from the well, you feel you are wasting your life. You are angry. You were not made for such ordinary things. You had come with a great destiny – to lead the whole world toward a paradise, some utopia. These are all ego trips. These are all ill states of consciousness.

Just to be ordinary – and then suddenly what you call trivia is no longer trivia, what you call profane is no longer profane. Everything becomes sacred. Carrying wood becomes sacred. Fetching water from the well becomes sacred.

When every act becomes sacred, when every act becomes meditative and prayerful, only then are you moving deeper into life – and then life opens all the mysteries to you. Then you are becoming capable. Then you are becoming receptive. The more receptive you become, the more life becomes available.

This is my whole teaching: to be ordinary, to be so ordinary that the very desire to be extraordinary disappears. Only then can you be in the present; otherwise you cannot be in the present.

Montaigne has written: "We seek other conditions because we know not how to enjoy our own, and go outside of ourselves for want of knowing what it is like inside of us. So it is no use raising ourselves on stilts, for even on stilts we have to walk on our own legs, and sitting on the loftiest throne in the world we are still sitting on our behind." Wherever you are – fetching wood or sitting on the throne as a king or as a president or a prime minister – makes no difference. Wherever you are, you are yourself.

If you are miserable in carrying wood, you will be miserable in being a president, because outside things can change nothing. If you are happy being a beggar, only then can you be happy being an emperor. There is no other way.

Your happiness has something to do with your quality of consciousness. It has nothing to do with outside things. Unless you become awake, everything is going to make you more and more miserable. Once you are awake, everything brings tremendous happiness, tremendous benediction. It does not depend on anything else; it simply depends on the depth of your being, on your receptivity.

Carry wood, and when carrying wood just carry wood – and enjoy the beauty of it. Don't go on thinking of something else. Don't compare it. This moment is tremendously beautiful. This moment can become a satori. This moment can become the moment of *samadhi.*

Fetching water, be so totally in it that nothing is left outside. Fetching water, you are not there; only the process of fetching water is there. This is what nirvana is, enlightenment is.

I am talking to you; I am not there – just enjoying a chitchat with you, gossiping with you.

Listening to me, if you are also not there, then everything is perfectly fulfilled. If you are there listening to me, watching by the corner, standing there; if something valuable is being said so that you can hold it for future use; if something meaningful is said so that you can make it part of your knowledge – "It will be helpful to seek something, to be something" – then you will miss me.

I am not saying anything meaningful. I am not saying anything for any purpose in view. I am not giving you some knowledge. I am not here to make you more knowledgeable.

If you can listen to me the way I am talking to you – this moment is total, you are not moving outside it, the future has disappeared – then you will have a glimpse of satori. Remember that we are engaging here in a certain activity. This activity has to be so prayerful, so meditative, that in this activity, the past is no longer a burden and the future does not corrupt it, and this moment remains pure – this moment simply remains this moment.

Then, I am not here and you are not there. Then, this crowd disappears. Then, we become waves of one ocean – that ocean is life, that ocean is existence, that ocean is nirvana. Nirvana is such a deep relaxation of your being that you disappear in that relaxation. Tense, you are; relaxed, you are not. Your ego can only exist if you are tense. If you are relaxed, existence is, you are not.

Now the story, a very simple story. All Zen stories are very simple. If you understand them, they show something. If you don't understand them then they say nothing.

All the great masters of the world have used the parable as a medium for their message, because the parable creates a picture. It is less conceptual; it brings things more to the heart. It reveals more, says less. There is no need for the mind to intellectualize about it. The parable is there, completely clear.

Muso, the national teacher, and one of the most illustrious masters of his day, left the capital in the company of a disciple for a distant province. On reaching the Tenryu river they had to wait for an hour before boarding the ferry; just as it was about to leave the shore, a drunken samurai ran up and leapt into the packed boat, nearly swamping it.

A drunken samurai... He may not be ordinarily drunk, but a samurai is always drunk. A samurai is a man who is after power. A samurai is a warrior. A samurai is drunk with the ego. He may not be drunk ordinarily – that is not the point. He may have been drunk, but all people who are after power are drunk.

The more you are after power, the more you are unconscious, because only unconsciousness can seek power. Consciousness lives life. Consciousness does not bother about power, because what is the use of power?

The use of power is that someday you can live through it. First you collect power – maybe it is hidden in money, or in the sword – first you prepare, power is a preparation, and then someday you will live.

*...a drunken samurai ran up and leapt into the packed boat, nearly
swamping it. He tottered wildly as the small craft made its way
across the river and, fearing for the safety of the passengers, the
ferryman begged him to stand quietly.*
*"We're like sardines in here!" said the samurai gruffly. Then,
pointing to Muso, "Why not toss out the bonze?"*

Bonze means a Zen priest, a Zen monk.

The story is beautiful. If politicians were allowed, then they would
not like religious people on the earth at all. They would kill them,
they would toss them out of the boat – because the only danger for
the politician is religious consciousness. The more people become
religious, the more politics loses luster.

The politician is after power and the religious man is not after
anything. The religious man wants to live herenow, and the politician
is always preparing for some future, future which never comes. The
politician is always after some utopia; chasing it, after some dream.
It never comes.

All political revolutions have failed, failed utterly – because
you go on sacrificing for the future, sacrificing the present for the
future. And if the present is destroyed, from where is the future to
come? It is going to be born out of the present. You go on murdering the present in the hope that someday a beautiful future will
be born out of it. A beautiful future can be born only if the present
is lived beautifully.

Politicians are always against religious people. If they are not,
that simply means religious people are not religious people. Then
religious people are also playing politics in the name of religion.
Christianity, Islam, Hinduism – all politics in the name of religion.

A really religious person wants to live herenow. He is not worried
about the future and he is not trying to bring any revolution into the
world, because he knows there is only one life and there is only one
revolution and there is only one radical transformation – and that is
one's own being.

He wants to love, he wants to live, he wants to pray, he wants to
meditate. He wants to be left alone, nobody should disturb. He does
not want to interfere in anybody's life and he does not want that anybody should be allowed to interfere in his life. And the whole politics
is nothing but this – interfering in others' lives. Maybe you pretend

that you are interfering for their own sake – but you are interfering in people's lives.

The story is beautiful. Out of all persons the samurai said, "Why not throw this bonze out of the boat? It is much too crowded."

"We're like sardines in here!" the samurai said gruffly. Then, pointing to Muso, "Why not toss out the bonze?"
"Please be patient," Muso said, "we'll reach the other side soon."

Ordinarily we should expect him to become angry, but he simply says, "Please be patient. The other shore is not very far away."

It is a very symbolic sentence. A religious person remains patient because he sees, continuously understands, that this life is not worth being impatient about – the other shore is continuously coming close. Nothing is worth being impatient about. Patience is better paying, gives you more of life. Becoming impatient means you will miss this moment, you will become restless.

He said, "Don't be worried. It is a question of a few moments. No need to throw me or anybody else; no need to create any conflict. The other shore is coming close by. We will reach the other side soon."

This is the whole attitude of a religious person. He is not worried about trivia. Somebody has stolen his money. He is not worried about it, it doesn't matter. Somebody has insulted him – it does not matter.

It matters only to people who are not living life. Then ordinary, useless things, meaningless things, become very meaningful. A person who is living his life totally is so happy with it he is not disturbed. Whatsoever happens on the periphery makes no difference to the center. He remains the center of the cyclone.

"What!" bawled the samurai, "Me be patient? Listen here, if you don't jump off this thing and start swimming, I swear I'll drown you!"

A politician, a power-oriented person, cannot be patient. The more impatient he is, the more possibility of succeeding in the world of power and politics. He cannot be patient because time is running fast. Only a religious person can be patient because he has come to know the quality of eternity. Paradoxically, the religious person knows that this life is going to end, but underneath this life there is a life which never ends. Paradoxically he knows this time is going to end in death but hidden beneath this time is eternity.

If you enter life you enter eternity. If you remain on the surface you remain in time. Time is impatience.

Look: in the West people are more time-conscious and of course more impatient. In the East people are not so time-conscious, naturally they are not so impatient. Time brings impatience.

Christians are more impatient than Hindus because Hindus have an idea of rebirth and Christians don't have any idea of rebirth. Only this life, such a small life, seventy years – almost one-third is lost in sleep. By the time one becomes a little aware, half of the life is gone, and then in small things: earning the bread, making a house, working for the children, the wife – the life is gone. One becomes impatient.

How to live more in such a small time? The only way the West has found is to go on increasing speed – the only way. If it used to take one day to travel, travel in five minutes so that you can save time. This too great a hankering for speed is part of impatience. You can save time but then you don't know what to do with that time. You use it in saving more time, and this goes on and on.

Impatience is a feverish way of living. One should relax. Once you relax time disappears and eternity reveals to you its own nature.

"What!" bawled the samurai, Me be patient? Listen here, if you don't jump off this thing and start swimming, I swear I'll drown you." A politician can't be patient. You cannot think of Lenin or Hitler meditating. It would be a sheer waste of time.

When you come to me from the West and you start meditating it is really a miracle. It is against all the conditioning that you have gone through. When you go back nobody will be able to understand what has happened to you – just wasting time – because time has to be used. It is already too short. "Life is short and so many desires to be fulfilled – why waste it in sitting with closed eyes and watching the navel? Do something before life is gone." If you live on the surface, you will remain impatient. If you enter deeper into the stream, you will come to feel that this life is not all and the periphery is not the total; and the waves belong to the ocean, but the ocean itself is not only the waves – hidden just underneath the waves of time is the ocean of eternity.

A religious person can be patient, can be infinitely patient because he knows nothing begins and nothing ends.

*The master's continued calm so infuriated the samurai that he
struck Muso's head with his iron fan, drawing blood.*

And it happens. If the master had been angry, the samurai could
have understood the language, his own language, but because the
master remained silent – not only silent, absolutely patient – this infuriated him very much.

If somebody insults you and you remain silent, as if nothing has
happened, the person will get more angry; he will get angrier. If you
had been angry he could have understood it, but he cannot understand the silence. In fact, in your silence he feels very much insulted.
In your silence you become a tower, a height. In your silence he
becomes like a worm, a very small thing. That hurts.

Jesus has said, "If somebody slaps your right cheek, give him
the left also." Nietzsche commented on this, saying, "Never do this,
because this will insult the other person more. Rather, hit him hard.
He will respect that more. At least you accept him as your equal."

Nietzsche is also right. He has a very penetrating eye. The very
presence of a religious person infuriates the politician. And when he
is insulted and he takes it easily, as if nothing has happened, that
drives the other person almost mad.

That's how they crucified Jesus. The priests, the politicians, the
power-addicted people, could not tolerate this humble and simple
man. He was not doing any harm to them. In fact, he was teaching
people harmless things. He was teaching them to become innocent
like children. He was teaching them "Blessed are the meek." But
they became infuriated. They had to kill him, because his very presence became very humiliating to them. Such a tower, such a peak,
a pinnacle of love, compassion, humbleness – they could not tolerate him.

*Muso's disciple had had enough by this time and, as he was a
powerful man, wanted to challenge the samurai on the spot. "I
can't permit him to go on living after this," he said to the master.*

A disciple is a disciple. He has not yet understood. He is still in the
same ego. Maybe he has become religious, but the ego continues.

If somebody says something against me, you will feel angry. Now
your ego is attached to me. If somebody says, "This man is nothing,"

you become angry. Not because you are too much concerned with this man, but because if this man is nothing and you are following this man, you are even worse than nothing. It hits the ego. If you follow me I must be the greatest master in the world. You are following me – how can you follow me if I am not the greatest master in the world?

Remember, that is again a game of the ego. You will try to prove that "My master is the greatest master in the world." It is not a question of the master. How can you be a follower of a lesser master? Impossible. You – and a follower of a lesser master? That's not possible.

> *"I can't permit him to go on living after this." He said to the master.*
> *"Why get so worked up over a trifle?" Muso said with a smile. "It's exactly in matters of this kind that the bonze's training proves itself. Patience, you must remember, is more than just a word."*

It is a great experience. Now this is the moment to be patient and to enjoy it. This fellow has given a beautiful opportunity to be patient. Be thankful to him. He has given a challenge. But don't let that challenge become a challenge for your ego. Let that be a challenge for your patience. The same situation – but you can use it or you can be used by it.

If you are used by it you are an unconscious man. Then you react. All reaction is unconscious. If you are conscious you never react. You act. Action is conscious, reaction is unconscious.

Reaction means that that man became the master of the situation: he pushed the button and you became angry. You became a puppet in his hands. But if you remain patient, if you smile, suddenly you are out of the vicious circle of unconsciousness.

Use situations and then you will come to see that even enemies are friends and even the darkest nights will bring beautiful dawns. When there was anger thrown at you, you will see compassion arising in you. These are the rarest moments. And you will feel thankful and grateful to the person who created the situation.

> *"Why get so worked up over a trifle?" Muso said with a smile. "It's exactly in matters of this kind that the bonze's training proves itself. Patience, you must remember, is more than just a word."*

Patience is a great experience, a great existential experience.

He then recited an extempore waka:
"The beater and the beaten:
mere players of a game
ephemeral as a dream."

This is what witnessing is all about. If you can become a witness in a situation, suddenly you are out of it, no longer part of it. If you lose your witnessing, even in a dream you become part of it. You go to the movie, you watch the movie; you are just a watcher there. But sooner or later you forget all about your being a watcher – you become part of the story. You smile, you cry, you weep, you become angry, you become agitated – and there is nothing on the screen, just shadows passing, but you have lost the witnessing. You are almost identified now. You are part of the story now. Then even shadows passing on the screen become realities.

Just the opposite happens if you stand by the side of the road and simply watch people passing. Suddenly you will see real persons have become ephemeral, shadows on the screen.

The whole thing depends on you. If you are identified, an unreal thing becomes real. If you are unidentified, even a real thing becomes unreal. A man who comes to know what witnessing is, for him this whole life is nothing but a big dream, a big drama.

"The beater and the beaten: mere players of a game ephemeral as a dream." This is one of the greatest insights the East has achieved – that life, life that you know as life, is ephemeral, illusory, *maya*. It is not real.

There is another life. If you become aware, then you enter the temple of reality. Unawareness allows you only to live in a dream.

When the boat reached shore and Muso and his disciple got off, the samurai ran up and prostrated himself at the master's feet. Then and there he became a disciple of the master.

First, if you remain silent when the situation was ordinarily demanding anger, if you remain patient when the other was expecting impatience and trouble, he will be infuriated, he will be hurt, humiliated. He would like to take revenge – you are playing God to him.

But if you continue, if you are not tempted and you remain in your silence, in your tranquility – you remain centered and rooted in your being – sooner or later the other is going to relax, because silence is such a power, silence is such a transforming force, silence is so alchemical. It is the only magic in the world; the other is bound to be transformed.

Just wait a little. Don't be in a hurry. The other will take a little time. Give him an opportunity.

The samurai ran, fell at the feet of the master.

Then and there he became a disciple... Whenever you come against something like this – a real patience, a real substantial silence – deep down something is touched in your heart also. Deep down you are no longer the same. Something real has penetrated like a ray of light into your darkness.

The world is transformed by people who live in this world as if this world is just a dream. People are changed, transfigured, by those who live in this world unconcerned, indifferent to trivia; who live a life of inner centering, who live in the world but don't allow the world to enter them, who live in the world but the world does not live in them, who remain untouched; who carry their silence everywhere. In the marketplace they remain in their inner temple – nothing distracts them from their being.

These people become catalytic agents. These people bring a totally new quality to human consciousness. A Buddha, a Jesus, a Krishna, a Mohammed, bring another world into this world.

That is the meaning of the Hindu word *avatar.* It means they bring godliness into the world; godliness descends through them. A vision, they become windows. Through them you can have a vision, a glimpse of something that is beyond.

One of the most influential writers, authors and thinkers of the West was Aldous Huxley. He was very much in tune with the Eastern idea of inner centering. He was one of the Western minds who penetrated very deeply into the Eastern attitude toward life. It is said that when a Californian brushfire destroyed a lifetime's possessions, Aldous Huxley felt only an unexpected freedom. "I feel clean," he said.

He had a really beautiful collection of rare antiques, rare books, rare paintings – a whole life's possessions – and all his possessions were destroyed in a fire. Looking at the flames, he could not believe it himself that he simply felt unburdened, a sense of freedom: not at all disturbed, on the contrary, a sense of freedom – as if the fire had been a friend. And later on he said, "I feel clean." This is the Eastern attitude.

If you are centered, nothing can be destroyed. No fire can

destroy your centering. Not even death is capable of distracting you.

And this centering is possible only if you start living each moment meditatively, fully alert, aware. Don't move like an automaton. Don't react like a mechanism. Become conscious. Collect yourself more and more so that a crystallized consciousness continuously illuminates your inner being, a flame goes on burning there and it lights wherever you move. The path, the way, whatsoever you do, it lights it.

This inner flame, this inner light is there, potentially there, like a seed. Once you start using it, it sprouts. Soon you will see – the spring has come and it is blossoming and you are full of the fragrance of the unknown and the unknowable. The divine has descended in you.

Enough for today.

CHAPTER 4

creativity: a dynamic energy

The first question:

Osho,
I don't understand – what does the word *God* mean? I really don't
understand. God – what is that? You say life is everything. Life is
what is, what counts, here and now – no planning, no wishing, no
wanting, no hoping, no searching. Live now, spontaneously. Just
be. Yes, I understand that, but what is God? Is *God* another word
for life, what is? But why do we use the word *God* and not just *life*?
They say God is the one who created the world. Is that what it is?

The question is of course from somebody who is very new
here. Many things will have to be understood.
First: there is no need to understand what God is, because
whatsoever God is cannot be understood. Understanding is not the
right direction toward God. Understanding means you are trying intellectually – through logic, reason, concepts – and that's the sure way to
miss God.

It is as if somebody is trying to see through the ears. He will not
be able to see. Or somebody is trying to hear with the eyes. He will

not be able to hear. The ears are to hear and the eyes are to see.

The intellect is utilitarian. It helps while you are moving outside of your being. It is helpful as a guide in the world of the without. The moment you turn inward it becomes useless, it is no longer a guide. Then it misguides. There is a limit to the intellect, and God can only be felt, not understood.

When you are moving inward, you come closer to the source of your own being, and that is the source of all being. If I can come to my own self, I have come to the supreme self, because at the center I am no longer "I am"; I am the whole. But the movement has to be inward, the movement has to be somewhere deep in the depth.

Intellect is superficial – so if you are trying to understand God, you will go on missing. The first thing to be understood is that understanding is not the right direction. Feeling...

Once a Christian missionary asked a very primitive man, an aboriginal, "Who told you what you know of God?"

The primitive laughed and replied, "Told? Whoever is so stupid that they have got to be told about God? Never did any man know God by 'tolds.' You get God by 'feels.' All the 'told' there is to it, is his name. You call him God, I call him Gallah. I say Gallah's name in English so you can understand me, but whoever has got anything by 'tolds'?"

Whatsoever you know about God is through "tolds" – the parents, the society, the culture. It is your conditioning. And now you have got a concept about God and you are trying to understand that word. God is not a word. The word *God* is not God. The word is simply a word, in itself empty and meaningless.

If you really want to know what God is, you will have to drop the word and move into feeling. You will have to drop the mind and move into no-mind. Love will bring you closer to it than thinking.

When I say "Life is God," I am saying that if you want, you can experience God but you cannot understand. Life cannot be understood. You can live it – that is the only understanding there is. But you are worried, you say that you understand that – but what is God? If you understand that, if you understand what life is, you will never ask what God is. In that very understanding, the problem of God is solved.

A man who has lived life in its totality has understood all that is there to understand. He will be full of godliness. He has given enough of God to himself and there will be no problem of understanding.

You have not given anything of life to yourself. Empty you live; hiding in a cocoon you live; blind, deaf, you live; dead you live. You have not given any life at all to your being – and *there* is the flavor, *there* is the taste of what God is. You have to eat out of life. You have to drink out of life. You have to live, merge into it.

But the mind is cunning, it goes on thinking about God. Thinking is a very secure situation. You never go out of yourself. You go on playing with words. If you are too interested in the word, if you want to know what the word *God* means, it doesn't mean God. If you are only interested in the linguistic symbol *God* then you can ask the linguists, don't come to me. They say that *God* is derived from a word *ghu-to*. That *ghu-to* means "the called one," nothing else.

If you call life, it becomes God – the called one. If you provoke life, it becomes God. God is a certain situation in life when you provoke it, when you open to it, when you are in a deep dialogue with it. When you look at the sky and you say, "Father, who art in heaven..." you have called life. Now life is no longer just life – it has become the called one, the provoked one. The word *God* simply means that.

In deep love, someday one cries, one starts uttering words – a dialogue arises. Life is no longer "it"; it becomes a "thou." That is the meaning of the word *God*. If life becomes your beloved, if life becomes a thou and you are in deep relationship with it, suddenly life has become God.

God is a deep communion with life.

If you are just trying to understand the word... Yes, there is a need to use a different word – *God* – rather than just calling it "life" – life-provoked, called life in deep relationship.

An ordinary woman passes by. She is a woman, but if love calls in your heart she is no longer a woman, she is a beloved. We can say all beloveds are women. To become a beloved is a certain function in the being of a woman – when she is called, when she is no longer just a "she," she becomes "thou," becomes related.

Have you watched this transfiguration? The woman may have passed you many times; you may have seen her many times, yet she was just a woman, as there are millions of women. Then suddenly one day something changes. The woman is no longer an ordinary woman, she has become divine. She is a beloved. Now suddenly she has come close to you, your heart has called.

Or a man. You know him as one of so many men – just a statistic, just a number in millions of men. He has no particular face for you, is unrelated to you. If that man disappears and is replaced by another, you will not even notice the difference. He is only a number, is not yet a person to you. Unprovoked, uncalled, he remains anonymous, he has no name. Then suddenly one day love arises. He is no longer an ordinary man, he has become a god.

You have become provoked, called, related. A communion has happened. And not only the man has changed; you are also changed simultaneously. Something of the beyond has entered.

Yes, there is a function of the word *God*: life provoked, life become a thou, life become a person. You are no longer indifferent to it. You feel for it – a communion has happened. Then life becomes God. Then life is no longer with a lower case *l*; now it is with a capital *L* – Life.

But there is no way to understand God through intellect, because there is no way to understand love through intellect. God is love provoked. And in that light of love, everything is transformed. It is alchemical, magical.

Give a little of God to yourself – that's my whole effort. When I say "Life is God," I am meaning to say don't see God in the temples and the mosques and the churches. There you will find the God of the philosophers, theologians – which is a bogus God, a false coin, counterfeit. Look in the trees, in the flowers, in the stars, in humanity, in animals, in birds. Wherever there is life, look deep down there. Provoke God there. Be prayerful there. Be prayerful before a tree. Be prayerful before an animal. Be prayerful before the stars. Provoke God there. There is the real temple.

When I say "Life is God," I mean this: don't be confined in temples and don't be confined in churches and don't be confined by Bibles and Gitas and Korans. Don't be confined at all. Life is infinite. Meet life as it is. Meet the infinite. Don't be afraid of the infinite.

Where is the fear of the infinite? The fear is that with the infinite you will disappear. In a church you cannot disappear. You can manage. A church is your construction. It is arbitrary. It is artificial. It is a plastic flower. You can control it, manipulate it. Behind the curtain are your hands. The God in the church is your creation.

The real God is totally different. If you come to the real God – life – then you are God's creation. Then God is behind everything. In the church you are behind everything. The church is a deception.

So when I say "Life is God," I simply mean don't create substitute gods, don't create substitute temples. This vast space is the temple and this infinitely moving life is God. Give a little of God to yourself and then you will understand. And that understanding will not be of the intellect; that will be more of your total being. It will be more of the blood and the guts.

I was reading an anecdote:

A man was brooding over his beer at the bar, and said to his friend, "I tell you, Mulligan, I don't know what I am going to do about my wife."

"What is it now?"

"The same old thing – money. She is always asking for money. Only last Thursday she wanted ten dollars, yesterday she was around asking for twenty, and this morning, if you please, she demanded fifty dollars!"

"What does she do with all the money, for heaven's sake?" asked the friend.

"There is no way of finding out. I never give her any."

Give a little of God to yourself, then you will stop asking what God is. If you don't give yourself a little of God then you go on asking. Nobody else can give it to you, remember. You will have to come to terms with it on your own. I cannot give it to you. It is not a commodity, it is not a thing. It is such an experience that only you can have it.

You will have to move alone. You will have to go totally alone, naked of all thoughts, totally naked, naked of all philosophies, naked of all scriptures. And once you have tasted a little, you will understand.

Love life, and by and by a light will arise in your being. Through deep love of life one comes to understand what it is.

The last part of the question is: "They say God is the one who created the world." God *is* the world. The mind goes on creating dualisms. It says, "God is the one who created the world" – then "the world" is separate and "God" is separate. God is not separate, he cannot be separate from his world. If he is separate, the world cannot exist for a single moment without him. He is the very life of life.

So don't imagine God as a painter who paints on a canvas and then the canvas is separate and God is separate – the painter can die but the painting can continue.

Because of this duality, Nietzsche could say, "God is dead." What is the need of him? He created the world – finished! Why go on carrying the load? What is the need of God? Once he created the world then what is the need? The world is there, you are there. This God can only be a hindrance. He will come between you and your life; be finished with him!

Nietzsche was right in a way; that is the logical conclusion of duality. The world is perfectly right without him. Why bring him in? In fact, the more you bring him in, the more trouble arises. Look at the religions: how many wars, murders, violence? What has not happened in the name of religion? The world has suffered tremendously.

Be finished with God! He created the world; give him a last thank you and be finished. Now he is no longer needed. Already too old, almost a ruin. Nietzsche said, "God is dead, and man is free now." This is the logical conclusion of dualistic thinking.

In the East we have never thought of God as a painter, we have thought of God as a dancer. The dance cannot be separated from the dancer; the painting can be separated. That's why dance is alive and painting is dead. Howsoever beautiful a painting, it is dead. It is separate from the creator. The moment it is separate it is dead. It may have lived a life in the mind of the painter; it may have been alive when it was not painted. The moment it is painted it is finished; it is already a dead product. But a dance...

In India we call God *nataraj*, the god of dancers. You must have seen Shiva dancing. That is the Eastern concept about the divine – a non-dual concept. When the dancer stops, the dancing stops. You cannot separate the dancing from the dancer. And dancing comes to a culmination, to a crescendo, when the dancer is completely lost in it; when there is neither a dancer nor a dancing; both are one – one movement of sheer energy and delight.

That's why nothing can be compared with dancing: poetry, painting, sculpture, nothing comes close to it. Dancing remains the supreme art. And that is the first art that was born and that will remain the last art also, because dancing has some quality in it of life itself.

God is a dancer. He is not a creator in the sense of a painter; he is a creator in the sense of a dancer. Then let me say it in another way. God is not a creator but creativity; a dynamic energy. The moment you say creator, he is dead. The very word *creator* has a full-stop in it. Creativity with an open end; tremendously moving and moving and reaching to higher and higher peaks.

The animals are a dance of God, the trees are also a dance of God, humanity is also a dance of God, reaching higher and higher. God is moving faster and faster – more mad, more fast, getting dissolved into his dance.

A Buddha or a Jesus is the ultimate of his dance – where the dancer is so completely drunk and mad that he has become the dance. That's why I say that if you live life in its dynamism you will come closer to God, because he is still dancing. Don't say that he created the world; he is still creating. Otherwise how do the trees go on growing? How do the flowers go on blooming? Every moment the world is being renewed. Every morning fresh life is released.

No, the Christian God is false – the God who created the world in six days and then rested on the seventh. It doesn't seem true; a holiday for a God will be a death. Just think of it: a holiday for a God will be a death to his creation. The dancer cannot go for a holiday, otherwise the dance will disappear. And the very idea that God got tired is stupid. He is still creating – he is nothing but creativity.

Think in terms of energy; don't think in terms of things. Think in terms of energy. The wild ocean – God is a wild ocean of energy – goes on and on, waves upon waves, unending. There has never been a beginning. The very idea of a beginning is of the mind. How can the world begin?

Before Darwin, Christians used to believe that God created the world on a particular date. One foolish theologian even decided the date and the day – four thousand and four years before Jesus, exactly on a Monday he started. It must have been the first of January!

Then the question arises: what was he doing before that? Don't ask Christians; they will get angry. Even a man like Saint Augustine became very, very angry. One man asked – the question seems to be relevant and innocent – he asked, "I can understand that God created the world four thousand and four years before Jesus Christ was born, but what was he doing before that?"

Of course there is no answer to it in Christian theology. Saint

Augustine became very angry and he said, "He was brooding and thinking about punishments for people like you who ask such questions."

This is not very saintly. The question was very innocent, this anger is irrelevant. But the man raised a question which topples the whole of Christian theology. No, there has never been a beginning – there cannot be, because then the question will always arise: what was there before the beginning? And there is never going to be any end, because the question will arise: then what will be after the end? If you can conceive of anything before the beginning, then that was not the beginning. If you can conceive of anything after the end, then that is not the end.

The world is an ongoing process. God is creativity – creating and creating and creating. In fact, the moment I say "creating" I don't feel very happy. Language is not exactly capable of expressing it. The moment I say "creating," again it seems that he is separate.

No, God is the creator and the created. God is the same energy which becomes a rock, becomes a tree, becomes a man; the same energy which becomes a sinner and becomes a saint; the same energy which weeps and cries and laughs; the same energy which becomes the day and the night, life and death, summer and winter – non-dual.

Existence is God called through love, provoked through love. The moment you become capable of prayerfulness, existence becomes godly. The moment you become capable of deep love, life becomes godly. It is a transfiguration of the same energy.

So, God is not something which exists there like an object. If I have experienced him, I cannot show him to you. Unless you provoke him, unless you come to terms with him, unless you kneel down in prayer, unless you call him, you cannot know him.

The dilemma is that first you want to be perfectly certain whether he is, then you can be prayerful. And only through prayerfulness he is; only through trust he is. And you want first to be certain about the very hypothesis that God is, then you can trust. Now this is the dilemma: if you choose that first you need certainty, then you will never be able to know what God is.

It is only for gamblers to know God: who are not worried about certainty, who are ready to move in danger, who are ready to move in insecurity, who are ready to move into the unknown, who are ready to leave the comfortable past, the convenient past – who are like small children, always wondering and always wandering. God is only for those who are courageous. It is the greatest courage there is because it is the most difficult thing – almost impossible for the mind to do. First comes trust and then arises God. You create God through your trust. Here you open the eyes of trust and suddenly life takes a change, is transformed – it becomes godly, it becomes divine.

God is your subjectivity, your innermost rest, coming home. God has nothing to do with theology; it has something to do with the way you live your life – whether you live through the mind or you live through the heart.

If you live through the heart, forget all about God – he will take care himself! He will come, he will knock at your heart. Sooner or later you will hear the sound of his footsteps coming closer and closer. Your very heartbeats will become the footsteps, the sound of his footsteps. Your very breathing will be his coming in and his going out.

The second question:

Osho,
If one is in the situation of Muso's disciple – wishing to terminate a samurai for daring to assault the master – should one do it with concrete totality, and meditate afterward, or suppress the ego-based impulse, or is there a third alternative?

The first thing, and the most basic to be understood, is that whatsoever you do, it should not be a reaction. If it is an act then there is no problem.

If Muso's disciple had acted out of his spontaneity, Muso would have certainly blessed him. But he started saying that he would like to do this, he cannot allow this man to live any longer, he has insulted his master. If he had acted rather than brooding about it, rather than thinking about it, rather than bringing the mind in; if he had acted with no-mind, the master would have certainly blessed him.

Action is always good; reaction always bad. So try first to understand this term *reaction*. It means you are acting unconsciously. Somebody is manipulating you. Somebody says something, does something, and you react. The real master of the situation is somebody else. Somebody comes and insults you and you react, you become angry. Somebody comes and praises you and you smile and you become happy. Both are the same. You are a slave and the other knows how to push your buttons. You are behaving like a mechanism. You are an automaton, not yet a man. Act, don't react. Don't be a plaything in the hands of others.

You cannot predict a man who acts out of no-mind; only mind is predictable. If the disciple was a realized man, a man alert, nobody can say what turn the story would have taken – nobody can say. Nobody can say; a thousand and one alternatives open for consciousness.

The story would have been totally different, that much is certain. He may have thrown the samurai out of the boat, or he himself may have jumped out of the boat, or he may have even thrown Muso, his master, out of the boat. Nobody knows.

Consciousness is total freedom. But one thing is certain: whatsoever would have happened, the master would have blessed it – if it was out of no-mind, spontaneous, an act totally in the present, not controlled by anybody else, coming out of his own being.

We react according to our conditionings. If you have been born in a vegetarian family and nonvegetarian food is placed on your table, you will feel nausea, vomiting, sickness – not because of the nonvegetarian food, but because of your conditioning. Somebody else who has been conditioned for nonvegetarian food will relish the very sight of it, will feel appetite not nausea, will feel happy, will be thrilled. That too is a conditioning.

We react because we have been conditioned in a certain way. You can be conditioned to be very polite. You can be conditioned to always be in control. You can be conditioned to be silent. You can be conditioned to remain still in situations where people ordinarily become disturbed and distracted. But if it is a conditioning then it has nothing to do with religion; then it has something to do with psychology. And Buddha or Jesus are not masters there; B. F. Skinner and Pavlov, they are the masters there. It is a conditioned reflex.

I have heard a story:

In B. F. Skinner's lab, a new mouse was introduced.

They go on working with mice, because they don't give any more credit to man. They think that if they can understand the mind of a mouse, they have understood humanity.

The old mouse, who had been there with Skinner for a very long time, initiated the new. He said, "Look, this professor B. F. Skinner is a very good man, but you have to condition him first. Push this button and immediately breakfast comes in. I have conditioned him perfectly."

B. F. Skinner thinks he has conditioned his lab mice, and they think they have conditioned him!

Conditioning is a murder; the spontaneity is killed. The mind is fed with certain ideas and you are not allowed to respond; you are only allowed to react. In small things or great things, it is the same.

If you have been brought up in a religious family, the word *God* is so beautiful, so holy. But if you have been brought up in a Communist family in Soviet Russia, then the very word is ugly, nauseating. To utter the word, one feels as if it would leave a bad taste in the mouth.

Small or big is not the question. If you go on behaving the way you have been conditioned, you are functioning as a machine; the man has not been born yet.

It is said that when you tell an Englishman a joke, he will laugh three times. He will laugh the first time – when you tell it – to be polite. He will laugh a second time – when you explain it – again to be polite. That is the training of the Englishman, continuously being polite. Finally, he will laugh a third time in the middle of the night when he wakes from a sound sleep and suddenly gets it.

When you tell a German the same joke, he will laugh twice. He will laugh first – when you tell it – to be polite. He will laugh a second time – when you explain it – to be polite. He will never laugh a third time, because he will never get it.

When you tell an American the same joke, he will laugh once – when you tell it, for he will get it.

And when you tell a Jew the same joke, he won't laugh at all. Instead he will say, "It's an old joke, and besides, you are telling it all wrong."

It may be a joke, or it may be a great philosophy; it may be trivia or the divine itself – it makes no difference. People behave the way they are conditioned to behave, the way they are brought up to be, the way they are expected to behave. Nature is not allowed to function; only nurture is allowed to function. This is the man whom we call a slave.

When you become free, when you drop all conditioning and for the first time you look at life with fresh eyes, with no clouds of conditioning in between, then you become unpredictable. Then nobody knows, then nobody can imagine what is going to happen. Because then you are no longer there; life acts through you. Right now only society goes on acting through you.

Once you are simply alert, ready to respond, with no fixed idea, with no prejudice, with no plan, you become true and authentic whatsoever happens in the moment.

Remember two words – *authority* and *authenticity*. Ordinarily you behave according to the authority that has conditioned you: the priest, the politician, the parents. You behave according to the authority.

A religious man behaves not according to the authority; he behaves through his own authenticity. He responds. A situation arises there, a challenge is there – he responds with his total being. Even he himself cannot predict it.

When you ask a question, even I don't know what answer I am going to give to you. When I give it, only then I also know; only then I say, so, this was the answer. Your question is there, I am here – a response is bound to happen.

Response is responsibility. Response is authenticity. Response is living in the moment.

So I don't know, if the disciple was a little more aware, what would have happened. I don't know; nobody can say. You can always predict for unconscious people. I can say that if you were there instead of that disciple, the same would have happened – the same. Only two possibilities are there: either you would have been a coward or you would have been a brave man. If you were strong, you would have behaved in the same way the disciple behaved. If you were a weakling, you would have found some rationalizations to hide behind. These are the two alternatives.

But for a real man of understanding there are no alternatives – all possibilities are always open; no door is closed. And each moment decides. He does not carry a decision beforehand; he has no ready-made decisions. Fresh, virgin, he moves. That is the virginity of an enlightened man – uncorrupted by the past.

Listening to this story, you can do two things. One: you can try to be patient, as the master said to his disciple. If you try to be patient, that will be a suppression. It is not going to help. That patience is not going to be true; deep down there will be turmoil, a crowd, impatience, and on the surface you will pretend that you are patient.

The second possibility is that you understand that the reaction was just a reaction, a mechanical reaction, and you become more alert. Not that you suppress your impatience; you become more alert, you become more aware, and patience follows like a shadow.

Awareness is the key. If you become aware, everything follows. Don't try to become anything – patient, loving, nonviolent, peaceful. Don't try. If you try, you will force yourself and you will become a hypocrite. That's how the whole religion has turned into hypocrisy. Inside you are different; on the outside painted. You smile, and inside you would have liked to kill. Inside you carry on all rubbish and on the outside you go on sprinkling perfume. Inside you stink; on the outside you create an illusion as if you are a roseflower.

Never repress. Repression is the greatest calamity that has happened to man. And it has happened for very beautiful reasons. You look at a Buddha or a Muso – so silent, undisturbed. A greed arises: you would also like to be like them. What to do? You start trying to be a stone statue. Whenever there is a situation and you can be disturbed, you hold yourself. You control yourself.

Control is a dirty word. It has not four letters in it, but it is a four-letter word. Freedom, and when I say freedom I don't mean license. When I say freedom you may understand license, because that's how things go. A controlled mind, whenever it hears about freedom, immediately understands it as license. License is the opposite pole of control. Freedom is just in between, just exactly in the middle, where there is no control and no license.

Freedom has its own discipline, but it is not forced by any authority. It comes out of your awareness, out of authenticity. Freedom should never be misunderstood as license, otherwise you will again miss.

Awareness brings freedom. In freedom there is no need for control, because there is no possibility for license. It is because of license that you have been forced to control, and if you remain licentious the society will go on controlling you. It is because of your licentiousness that the policeman exists and the judge and the politician and the courts, and they go on forcing you to control yourself. And in controlling yourself you miss the whole point of being alive, because you miss celebration. How can you celebrate if you are too controlled?

It happens almost every day. When people come to see me who

are very much controlled and disciplined, it is almost impossible to penetrate their skulls; they are too thick, walls of stone around them. They have become stony, they have become ice cold. The warmth is lost because if you are warm, there is fear – you may do something. So, they have killed themselves, completely poisoned themselves. To remain in control, they have found only one solution and that is not to live at all.

So be a stone buddha, then you will be able to pretend that you are patient, silent, disciplined. But that is not what I am teaching here. Control has to be dropped as much as license. Now you will be puzzled. You can choose either control or license. You say, "If I drop control, I will become licentious. If I drop license then I have to become controlled." But I tell you, if you become aware, control and license both go down the same drain. They are two aspects of the same coin, and in awareness they are not needed.

It happened...

A boy, just eighteen years old, came down from his room. He had always been somewhat shy and retiring, but that evening he decided to change himself. All slicked up, he snapped at his father, "Look, I'm going out on the town – I'm going to find some beautiful girls. I'm going to get blind drunk and have a great time. I'm going to do all the things a fellow of my age should be doing in the prime of life and get a bit of adventure and excitement, so just don't try and stop me!"

His old man said, "Try and stop you? Hold on, my son, I'm coming with you."

All controlled people are in that state – bubbling inside to explode into licentiousness. Go and see your monks in the monasteries.

In India we have that type of neurosis very much. They are all neurotics. This is something to be understood – either you become erotic or you become neurotic. If you repress your *eros*, eroticism, you become neurotic. If you drop your neurosis, you become erotic.

Both are sorts of madness. One should be simply oneself – neither neurotic nor erotic, available to all situations, ready to face whatsoever life brings, ready to accept and live – but always alert, conscious, aware, mindful.

So the only thing to be constantly remembered is self-remembrance. You should not forget yourself. And always move from the innermost core of your being. Let actions flow from there, from your very center of being, and whatsoever you do will be virtuous. Virtue is a function of awareness.

If you do something from the periphery it may not look like a sin, but it is sin. The society may be happy with you, but you cannot be happy with yourself. The society may praise you, but deep down you will go on condemning yourself because you will know you have missed life – and missed for nothing.

What is it – the praise of the society? If people call you a saint, what is it? Nothing but gossip. How does it matter? You have missed existence for gossip. You have missed life for these foolish people who are all around, for their good opinion.

Live life from your very center. And this is all that meditation is about. By and by you will come to feel a discipline that is not forced, not cultivated, arises spontaneously – arises naturally like a flower blooms. Then you will have the whole life available, and you will have your whole being available. And when your whole being and the whole life meet, between the two arises that which is godly, between the two arises that which is nirvana.

The third question:

Osho,
This happened to my mother when she was a child.

A very beautiful question; listen carefully.

Her horse and buggy was in the street and she was sitting there. Further up the road was a horse and cart outside the saddler's shop. The farm-boy was going to change the horse's bridle in the street.
He took off the blinkers and for the first time the horse caught sight of the cart he had been pulling for years. Suddenly it became a fearsome object looming up behind him and he took off in fright, galloping down the street with the cart in tow.
My mother jumped out of her buggy just as the terrified horse and his cart leaped over it, knocking down the horse and buggy. He kept going, tied to the cart he was trying to escape.
I am the horse. What is the cart?

There you miss: you are the cart. Ask who is the horse.

You have not yet known who the horse is within you. All that you know about yourself is the cart. If you think, "I am the horse," from the very beginning you have taken a wrong step. Now there will be no freedom. This "I" is your bondage. This "I" is your slavery. This "I" consists of nothing but blinkers. This "I" is your blindness.

And you ask: "I am the horse. What is the cart?" Of course you cannot see the cart because you are misunderstanding the cart for yourself. You are misunderstanding. You are thinking you are the horse; that's why you cannot see where the cart is. You are the cart. Look for the horse. And if you start looking for the horse, suddenly you will see your whole "I" consists of imprisonments, bondages, chains.

But the mind is very cunning and goes on and on deceiving. The story is beautiful, the incident beautiful, it can almost become a situation for a satori. If your mother had been a little more aware, that moment would have become a moment of breakthrough. But you are also missing the point, and that's how mind deceives.

I was reading a story:

The fires of hell are occasionally banked for individual sinners for a longer or shorter period of time, depending on the egregiousness of their particular sins. At one time, three inmates of the hot place, their brief vacations happening to coincide, met and engaged in conversation.

One said, "I was Jewish when I was on earth, but my weakness, frankly, was ham sandwiches. So you see what happened."

"We could eat ham freely," said the second, "because I was a Catholic. Unfortunately I was too free with the ladies. Adultery was my chief sin and that is the reason I am here."

The third remained silent and the other two turned to him. "Well," they asked, "why are you in the hot place?"

And the third said firmly, "I am a Christian scientist. This place is not hot and I am not here."

Now, even in hell you can remain a Christian Scientist. You can deny. Because Christian scientists go on saying that it is a question of mind: if you say it is, it is; if you say it is not, it is not. Had it been so easy; it is not so easy.

One man met a Christian Scientist and the Christian Scientist asked him, "How is your uncle?"

The man said, "He is very weak and ill."

The Christian Scientist said, "He simply thinks so. He is not ill and he is not weak. This is just mind. He thinks it."

After seven days they met again and the Christian Scientist again asked, "How is your uncle?"

The man said, "Now he is in more trouble. Now, for two days he thinks that he is dead."

The mind can continue playing new games. First you try to escape. If you cannot escape then you create the idea that you are not here. Beware of it.

You are the cart. Don't say, "I am not the cart, I am the horse." This is the trick of the mind. Once you accept it, you will look in vain. You will never find where the cart is and you will never find who the horse is. Then everything becomes confused.

All that you know about yourself is not you. It is not your reality. All that you think about yourself is others' opinions that you have collected. Just look at what you think about yourself and you will find bits collected from here and there.

Somebody says you are beautiful; then go and stand before the mirror and you will find yourself a little more beautiful. Somebody says you have never been so beautiful. You must be, otherwise why should he bother? People say you are clever; you start thinking you are clever.

People go on saying things around you and you go on collecting opinions, cuttings from newspapers, and that is your whole being. Just have a look and you will find – this bit comes from your mother, this bit comes from your father, this bit comes from your brother, this bit from the teacher, this bit from the priest. Just go on looking how the whole cart has accumulated around you.

Once you see that it is borrowed from others then there is no difficulty in dropping it. In that very seeing, it drops and then awareness will arise. That awareness is the horse, and there you will not find any "I am." At the most it is *am-ness, is-ness*, but there is no "I" in it.

The ego is the most false thing in the world. But if you accept it, it goes on creating more and more illusions. It is very productive. It does not believe in birth control. It goes on producing more illusions, more illusions. The ego is the mother of all illusions.

The fourth question:

Osho,
How can you be a witness when totally in love with the moment? I
feel confused, because when involved with the beloved it seems
phony to be watching the situation.

Who has told you to watch? I am not saying to go on watching. I
am saying be alert – and they are totally different. When you watch,
you watch through the mind. When you are alert, you are simply
alert; there is no watching. When I say "alert," I simply mean don't
fall asleep.

Alertness has nothing to do with the mind. Watching has everything to do with the mind. Watching means you are trying from outside
the situation. Being alert means being in the situation but not asleep.

Of course, you will miss the whole thing, the whole beauty of
love, if you are watching. But people go on doing that; they have
become watchers. And that's why when I say "witness," inside, you
immediately think inside "watching."

People have turned into watchers. Particularly in the West, the
whole humanity have become watchers. Either watch the movie
or the TV or the football match or somebody dancing or somebody making love. You are just a watcher. In the film somebody else
is making love and you are sitting in your chair and watching. What
foolishness! Either make love or go home. Why go on watching? The
whole society seems to have turned into a voyeur. That's the only
thing – go on watching. What are you going to gain out of watching?

I have heard about people who cannot make love in darkness
because they would like to watch. They would like to watch themselves making love. Flooded with light they make love. Something
is missed. Love is a mystery and only happens in deep darkness.
The moment you start watching, there love disappears. You have
become a voyeur.

Women are more instinctively alert of the phenomenon. They
always close their eyes when they make love. And if they don't close
their eyes you can be certain they belong to the lib-movement. They
are trying to be like men, as foolish as men are. A woman always
closes the eyes because it is so tremendously beautiful to be inside
and alert. So much is happening inside; such a flow of energy, such a

deep resonance, such music, such silence, such a great dance of orgasmic feelings – who bothers to watch? One enjoys, one delights in it, one dances in it, one is bathed in it. Who bothers to watch?

I have heard about people who not only need light in their bedroom; they fix mirrors all over so that from every side they can watch themselves making love. Love is not important; the watching is important. Peeping Toms – looking into others' bathroom doors and keyholes. You would even like to look at yourself through your keyhole. But it is impossible – either you can be in the bathroom or you can be at the keyhole. So people have created many devices.

I have heard about people who have fixed automatic cameras in their bedrooms so they can make love at ease and the camera can go on taking photos. And later on they can review the whole thing. The thing in itself is not important – the reviewing is.

This is a disease. If you pull up a tree to see the roots, the tree will die. The roots have to be left in darkness. Existence works more in darkness than in light, because light is a little violating. A child is born in the deep womb of the mother; dark, no light enters. There he grows. A seed grows in the earth, in the dark womb of the earth – there it sprouts, comes up. All that is beautiful is born in the dark. Never be a watcher.

Witnessing is totally different. These words create trouble because witnessing also means watching. But try to understand me. Alertness simply means that you are making love and you are not asleep, that's all. Move into it as deeply as possible. Be merged into it. Let the orgasm take over. Be possessed by the godliness of love. Tremble like a small leaf in the strong wind. Let the godliness of love come to you from all over, from all directions. Let yourself be drowned, but don't fall asleep. Remain alert.

I'm not saying watch, because the moment you watch you have become the eyes and the whole being is lost. When you are alert, you are alert as a whole totality. Every cell of your body is alert. The whole body is alert. Alertness has a totally different quality.

But words create trouble. And we have become so knowledgeable; and we can always find ways in words. We can always go on playing games.

It happened:

In a museum, Muskovitch, having spent considerable time

tramping the corridors, paused for a refreshing cigar. He had not been smoking long when a museum guard appeared, approached him angrily and said, "Do you see that?" He was pointing to a sign on the wall which said in glaring red letters: No Smoking.

Muskovitch regarded it for a moment, then said to the guard, "It doesn't say positively."

You can always find ways, means, through words. I say "alert." I never said "watch." Watching is a tense activity. You become narrowed. Alertness is a very broad consciousness. You are not narrowed; you are widely open.

Watching is concentration. You concentrate – as if you want to hit a target with an arrow. Then you concentrate. Then you exclude everything from your vision; only the target, only the target remains in your eyes. You forget everything. Now everything has to be excluded and your whole consciousness has to become pinpointed. This is what watching is.

Alertness is meditation. You are wide open, all doors open; not narrow, absolutely vulnerable. Everything is allowed.

You can listen to me in two ways. You can concentrate. Then the singing of the birds will be a distraction because you have to exclude it. You can meditate with me. Listening to me meditatively, then birds become part of it; they are not to be excluded. They are saying the same thing in their way and they are not enemies and you are wide open. Everything is allowed: all windows open, all doors open, winds from every direction allowed. There is no distraction because you are not trying to concentrate.

People come to me and they say, "We feel very distracted. How to avoid distraction?" I tell them, "Avoid concentration. Don't avoid distraction. You are creating the problem of distraction because you are trying to concentrate."

Meditation is not a concentration. It doesn't exclude anything. It includes all. Just look at the difference. Not just a slit is open in you; you are completely open. Everything is allowed. Then the birds enrich. Then a dog barks somewhere – that too enriches. Nothing distracts if you are not concentrating. You create the problem by concentration.

Being alert means being open, alive, not sleepy, not unconscious. But it is not a question of watching; otherwise you will become tense. If you are trying to watch then you are divided. Then one part of you is making love; another is patrolling like a policeman. Then you will never be totally in it. There will be no love to be watched. Dissolve.

If you dissolve totally in love, you will find a certain quality of awareness in you; not like a torchlight – the torchlight is concentrated, pin-pointed, narrow – but like a lamp, the light falling in all directions. Let love be total and awareness will come out of it. Don't create problems for yourself.

I know you go on misunderstanding because you go on interpreting. Whatsoever I say, you interpret it according to your conditionings and thoughts and ideology, and then you destroy everything. Listen to me and don't try to interpret it. Leave it as pure as possible.

I am not saying difficult things to you. I am saying very simple truths. You make them difficult, you make them complex. You are addicted to complexity. Once the mind makes trouble then the mind becomes the master in solving it.

If you listen to me rightly, alert, aware, you can feel what I am trying to say. It is difficult to say, but if you are sympathetic, in love, in trust, you will have the feel of it.

That's why trust is so needed. That's why I go on insisting that you become part of my family. You can be here as an outsider, you can be here as a visitor, you can be here without being a sannyasin: you will miss much. I will be talking to you the same, but you will miss much, because the doubt, the mistrusting mind will be standing there and destroying and corrupting everything.

Once you relax, once you accept, once you surrender, once you trust, then whatsoever I am saying has a totally different quality to it. Only then does understanding arise.

The fifth question:

Osho,
I have been listening to you for the last year. Still I feel every morning is a new adventure. I wait for your arrival with a thrilled heart and with a strange excitement. Does this happen even after listening to you for one year? Please say something about it.

If you have really listened in love, then for years and years and lives I can go on talking and every morning you will be again excited. Love makes everything new, because love never accumulates the past. Love never becomes a burden; it never collects dust. The mirror remains clean.

If you are listening through the mind then it will be difficult. Then even one year is too much. Then you will have collected so much in the head, you will have become heavy, and you will start getting restless and the excitement will be lost – because the mind always becomes old. Mind is old because it accumulates past.

If you have heard me through the heart then there is no accumulation. Every morning you come as a morning – fresh like the morning dew, a newly-opened bud of a flower.

What I am doing here is not really saying something. Rather, I am playing on your innermost core of being. The words are just excuses. The words are just to keep you engaged somewhere so that I can go on penetrating deeper in you. The words simply create a climate in which I can penetrate deep in you and reach to your innermost core.

If you listen from the heart, then this can go on and on and you will always be excited. Love is always excited because love is always new. The heart is always excited – never bored, never burdened. Mind is always bored and burdened.

Feel happy and blessed. It is a benediction – rarely happens, to very few people. These birds have been singing here continuously, but when they sing again, it is again new, because that singing does not mean anything.

If I have some meaning to convey to you, then sooner or later the mind will feel, "Now, it is enough." I have nothing to convey. I have no message. On the contrary, I am the message.

I have nothing to convey to you except myself. I am not giving you a doctrine. I am not a teacher. Remember me as a singer, as a poet, as a dancer – that will be truer.

The last question:

Osho,
A love letter. You talk too much.

Since I became enlightened I have not uttered a single word. You must have been listening to somebody else, not to me. I am keeping silence. Try to listen again and you will not find a single word uttered.

Somewhere there has been a mistake. In your dream you may have heard me talking. I have not talked.

When you are unconscious you talk. When you become conscious you become silent.

An anecdote:

George Johnson, a hard-bitten man of early middle age, had evaded many a marital trap, but was now helplessly in love with a pretty young girl. Finally he said, "Will you marry me, Nancy?"

She smiled and said, "Oh yes, George." There followed a long silence until Nancy said, "Well, say something more George."

And Johnson said hollowly, "I think I have said too much as it is."

In your unconsciousness, even if you don't say much, you say much. And you are caught in whatsoever you say. If people who are unconscious remain silent, the world will be very much better.

When you become conscious, you can go on saying – it is never enough. And people who have attained, if they remain silent, the world will be very much poorer.

Enough for today.

CHAPTER 5

the flavor of an enlightened being

Sato-Kaiseki was very much disturbed by the implications of Copernicus' heliocentric theory, which, of course, was inconsistent with the old Buddhist cosmology in which Mount Sumeru occupies the center of the universe. He reasoned that if the Buddhist view of the cosmos were proved false, the triple world and the twenty-five forms of existence would be reduced to nonsense, resulting in the negation of Buddhism itself. Immediately he set about writing a book in defense of the Mount Sumeru position, sparing himself no effort as a champion of Buddhism.
When he had finished the work, he took it at once to Master Ekido and presented it to him triumphantly. After leafing through only the first few pages, however, the master thrust the book back and, shaking his head, said, "How stupid! Don't you realize that the basic aim of Buddhism is to shatter the triple world and the twenty-five forms of existence? Why stick to such utterly worthless things and treasure Mount Sumeru? Blockhead!"
Dumbfounded, Kaiseki shoved the book under his arm and quickly went home.

Metaphysics is nonsense, but even then it must be serving some object, otherwise it would not have existed so long. Man finds himself helpless in a strange, unfamiliar world – not only unknown, but unknowable also. This darkness, this cloud of unknowing, disturbs the human mind tremendously. Somehow he has to console himself. Somehow he has to create knowledge.

Even if that knowledge is not true knowledge, it will give an appearance that you are grounded. It will give an appearance that you are not absolutely helpless. You can pretend through it that you are not a stranger in this world – a chance, a coincidence – but a master. At least you can play with words and do whatsoever you like with words and can create a false illusion of your power.

This is what metaphysics has always been doing. It gives you a sense of power where in fact no power exists in you. It gives you an illusion of knowledge where no knowledge really exists.

The very word *God* becomes substantial. Just by using the word *God*, you feel as if you are doing something, as if you are relating to existence. As if you are not alone, a helpless child on the earth, but a father in heaven is taking care of you, continuously watching, worrying about you, about your welfare.

This is a very childish attitude – but man is helpless. And there are very few men who really become mature. Men remain childish. And remember the difference between childishness and the innocence of children. To be childish is to be stuck somewhere. To be like children is to be simply innocent, flowing, with no blocks in your being.

Man remains childish. The psychological age remains nearabout twelve; it never goes beyond that. You may become sixty, seventy, eighty – your physical body goes on moving in time – but your mind is stuck somewhere nearabout ten or twelve at the most.

One thing: metaphysics, words like *god, nirvana, enlightenment,* almost become things. You start believing in words. If somebody suddenly shouts "Fire!" a fear arises in you; you start running. You can create a nuisance in any theater at night. When the lights are put off suddenly shout, "Fire! Fire!" and people will start running.

The very word *fire* creates the illusion as if there is fire and life is in danger. The very word *lemon* – think about it, meditate on it, and saliva starts flowing in your mouth. The very word *lemon?* It has nothing in it. But man has become addicted to words.

There is a school of linguists called The General Semantics Group, founded by Alfred Korzybski. They have a little song; it is relevant. Their song is:

> Oh, the word is not the thing,
> the word is not the thing.
> Hi ho the derry-o,
> the word is not the thing.

That is their essential teaching.

Of course, you cannot be burned by the word *fire*, and you cannot get wet from the word *water*. But the word *God*, the word *religion*, the word *christ*, the word *buddha* – how many people have sacrificed their lives for these words?

Somebody insults Christianity – what is he doing? Christianity is a word – but Christians are offended; there is going to be bloodshed. Humanity has been fighting and fighting for words – *country, liberty, socialism, the flag* – and millions of people have died. Words have become more significant than life itself. This is a sort of madness.

So metaphysics is not only nonsense, it is also madness – of course, with a method. It is very methodological. Metaphysicians go on building skyscrapers of words – the Tower of Babel. They go on building it. And once you are caught in the words, the reality recedes farther away from you. You start living behind a wall of words. And a wall of words is stronger than any wall. Even a wall of stones, rocks, is not so strong.

The strength of words lies in their being transparent: you can go on looking through them and you will never become aware that you are looking through words. They are almost invisible, transparent – like pure glass. You can stand near a window. If the glass is really pure, you will not become aware of the glass. You will think that the window is open and you are seeing the sky and the trees and the sun rising, and you will never become aware that there is glass between you and the reality. Metaphysics is a glass. It goes on hiding reality from you, and it goes on distorting reality.

People cling to words because they don't know what reality is. So they start believing in words – it is a make-believe. At least it gives a sense that you know. When you use the word *God*, suddenly you feel as if you know godliness. You don't know anything about godliness, you only know the word *God*. That too you have only heard, but it has become your foundation rock.

One Dutch poet and thinker, Huub Oosterhuis, has written in his diary, "I heard someone crying "God" in a broken voice, and I saw someone else muttering.

I asked him, "What are you muttering about?"

He said, "I am praying to God" – but neither of them could tell me whether they had ever received any answer.

"Then why do you both keep calling upon him? When the answer has never come to you, why do you go on praying?" I asked.

They both answered, "Keeping quiet is even worse."

You go on praying, you go on believing, because to live without belief needs tremendous courage. You go on praying because just keeping quiet, you become more afraid.

Have you watched yourself? Sometimes when passing through a lonely street on a dark night, you start singing and whistling. What are you doing? That is metaphysics. You are creating a sense that you are not alone. Whistling, listening to your own voice, gives a feeling as if somebody else is also there. It warms you up.

Singing – and if you are a religious person, then praying – and you feel that God is there and everything is okay. For the moment you become occupied in your singing, in your praying, in your utterances, in your whistling. You become so occupied that you forget that the night is dark, and the street is lonely and there is danger everywhere.

Because of death, man goes on whistling. That whistling is metaphysics. One goes on avoiding the fact that death is. One goes on avoiding the fact that your life may just be a chance coincidence. There may be no creator. There may be nobody who is controlling. Once you understand that there is nobody who is controlling, you will be in a panic. Then anything can go wrong, any moment, and you will not even be able to complain. There is nobody to complain to.

Metaphysics creates a dream world around you, of beautiful words – *heaven, paradise*, for you; *hell* for others. *Hell* for the enemies, *heaven* for you. These are wish-fulfillments.

Psychologists have become aware of a certain state which every child has to pass. Have you watched small children? They become addicted to certain things – a rag doll, or a piece of blanket, or anything will do – the thing is immaterial. Whatsoever is handy, they will catch hold of it, and by and by that certain object becomes almost sacred, religious. You cannot take that object away without hurting the child. He will go to sleep with the rag doll. Every child is a Linus with his blanket. It gives security.

That object is not an ordinary object – it has a special quality to it. It has to be understood, because the whole metaphysics is the blanket of the child, the rag doll. If you take the rag doll the child cannot go to sleep, he is missing something. That is his TM, transcendental meditation. That is his prayer – that rag doll is his god.

To you, that rag doll seems outside. To the child, it is not outside his being; it is part of his innermost being. That rag doll exists somewhere on the boundary of inside and outside. The outside is the world of objects and the inside is the world of your being, and that rag doll exists just on the boundary, part of both. In a sense, part of the world; in a sense, part of your innermost being. It is the most strange thing in the world – but it gives security, it protects you. You never feel alone; you are always occupied.

It becomes a ritual. The first thing in the morning, the child will look for his rag doll. If it is there then everything is okay, things are in their place. He goes to sleep with it; first thing in the morning, he looks for it. If the rag doll is there then everything is still okay, nothing is disturbed. That rag doll is his world.

He has systematized the world. The world is vast and the child is impotent. He cannot boss over the world, but he can boss over the rag doll. With the rag-doll, he becomes a master. With the world, he is just a helpless child in the hands of others – too big, too incomprehensible.

With the rag doll, he is no longer a small child; he is somebody big, a boss. He can do whatsoever he wants with the rag doll: he can throw it, he can be angry at it, he can beat it. Then he can praise it and persuade it and love it and hug it and kiss it. Whatsoever he wants he can do, and the rag doll is absolutely impotent. He is the absolute master of the situation.

All metaphysics is of the same quality. Your gods or your rag dolls – your Linus is still holding a piece of blanket. If you really want to know what life is, all rag dolls have to be dropped, shattered. All illusions have to be shattered so that you can become capable of knowing what truly is. All make-believes have to be dropped.

People go on hiding behind their make-believes. They are your caves. No light enters, no fresh air comes – but you feel protected. Your beliefs almost become your death – but still you feel protected. That's why I always say that a religious man is the most courageous man in the world. And there is no other way to live life than to be ready to face the danger of it.

I have heard an anecdote:

During a Yiddish play, the curtain fell suddenly and the manager of the theater stepped out before the audience, in the last degree of agitation.

"Ladies and gentlemen," he said, "I'm distressed to have to tell you that the great and beloved actor, Mendel Kalb, has just had a fatal heart-attack in his dressing-room and we cannot continue."

Whereupon a formidable, middle-aged woman in the balcony rose and cried out, "Quick! Give him some chicken soup!"

The manager, surprised, said, "Madam, I said it was a fatal heart attack. The great Mendel Kalb is dead."

The woman repeated, "So quick! Give him some chicken soup."

The manager screeched in desperation, "Madam! The man is dead! What good will chicken soup do?"

And the woman shouted back, "What harm?"

All metaphysics – at the most, one thing can be said in its favor: it cannot do any harm. It is chicken soup to a dead man. Nothing good comes out of it. Nothing can come out of it – mere words, a mere play of words. Nothing good can come out of it. Of course, no harm also. It is a futile activity; not even harm comes out of it.

And remember, something can be harmful only if it can be beneficial also. If it cannot be harmful, it cannot be beneficial. If something can be beneficial then it can be harmful also; then it depends on how it is to be used. Poison is harmful: it can be beneficial, it can become medicinal. It depends on how you use it.

But with metaphysics, these are mere words. But the human mind tends to believe in words. By and by it completely forgets that the reality is not in the words; it is beyond the words. It has to be approached through silence. It has to be approached through meditation, not through mind. If your mind goes on creating more and more rows of words, you will continuously be in a futile activity – "much ado about nothing."

Why do people cling to their metaphysical attitudes? They cling, because if they drop those metaphysical attitudes they call their philosophies, religion, Christianity, Hinduism, Buddhism... If you drop them, suddenly you are naked. If you drop them, suddenly your trembling child is there without the rag doll. If you drop them, then you don't know who you are. If you drop them, suddenly you lose your identity; your name, your form. Everything starts disappearing, you start falling into an abyss; that is the fear.

People go on clinging to words. Words create more words. Words create more questions and more answers are needed, and then answers create more questions again, and so on and so forth.

There is a story of a workman who had been mortally wounded. A priest was sent for, and he began his ministrations by asking, "Do you believe in God the Father? Do you believe in God the Son? And do you believe in God the Holy Ghost?"

The man looked at those around him and murmured, "Here am I dying and he asks me riddles."

Life is continuously in the hands of death. Don't waste time in words and riddles.

Buddha used to say, "I see you in great danger and you go on wasting your time in solving riddles, which have nothing to do with reality." He used to say, "You are like a man who has been wounded by a poisonous arrow, and who is lying there. The physician comes and wants to take the arrow out of his body, but the man is a great philosopher and he says, "Wait. First I have to come to a conclusion whether the arrow is real or illusory, whether the world is real or illusory, *maya*. First I have to come to a decision whether the arrow has been thrown at me by accident, or whether somebody has done it purposely. Why did God create the world? Is there somebody who has created the world?" The fatally wounded philosopher asks, "Wait! First convince me whether life is worth saving."

Buddha used to tell this story again and again, and he used to say, "When I see you, I see the same man in you."

Your life is fleeting. The water of life is slipping through your fingers, any moment and death may strike – and you are trying to solve metaphysical puzzles? "Who created the world? Whether anybody created it or not? Who is God? What is his form?"

People go on constantly discussing, debating. It seems they are avoiding something through these discussions. They are avoiding existence. They are trying to remain occupied in something so that the reality of life and death is not encountered.

I have heard a story. It is tremendously beautiful; it happened in the Middle Ages in Rome.

Back in medieval times, the Roman Pope was persuaded by some of his more conservative advisors to no longer endure the presence of Jews in the very heart and core of world Christianity. The Jews of Rome were therefore ordered to be evicted from their home by a certain date.

To the Jews of Rome this was a great tragedy, for they knew no refuge where they might not expect worse treatment than in Rome. They appealed to the Pope for reconsideration and the Pope, a fair-minded man, suggested a sporting proposition. If the Jews would appoint one of their own members to engage in a debate with him in pantomime, and if the Jewish representative were to win the debate, the Jews might remain.

The Jewish leaders gathered in the synagogue that night and considered the proposition. It seemed the only way out, but none of their number wished to volunteer to debate. As the Chief Rabbi said, "It is impossible to win a debate in which the Pope will be both a participant and a judge. And how can I face the possibility that the eviction of the Jews will be a result of my specific failure?"

The synagogue janitor, who had been quietly sweeping the floor through all this, suddenly spoke up. "I will debate," he said.

They stared at him in astonishment. "You, a chief janitor," said the Chief Rabbi, "debate with the Pope?"

"Someone has to," said the janitor, "and none of you will."

So in default of anyone else, the janitor was made the representative of the Jewish community and was appointed to debate with the Pope.

Then came the great day of the debate. In the square before St. Peter's was the Pope, surrounded by the College of Cardinals in full panoply, with crowds of bishops and other church functionaries. Approaching was the Jewish janitor, surrounded by a few leaders of the Jewish community, in their somber black garb and their long gray beards. The Pope faced the janitor and the debate began.

Gravely, the Pope raised a finger and swept it across the heavens. Without hesitation, the janitor pointed firmly toward the ground, and the Pope looked surprised.

Even more gravely, the Pope raised one finger again, keeping it firmly before the janitor's face. With the trace of a sneer, the janitor raised three fingers, holding them before the Pope just as firmly, and a look of deep astonishment crossed the Pope's face again.

Then the Pope thrust his hand deep into his robes and produced an apple. The janitor thereupon opened a paper bag that was sticking out of his hip pocket and took out a flat piece of matzo. At this the Pope exclaimed in a loud voice, "The Jewish representative has won the debate. The Jews may remain in Rome."

The janitor backed off, the Jewish leaders surrounded him, and all walked hastily out of the square. They were no sooner gone than the church leaders clustered about the Pope. "What happened, Your Holiness?" they demanded. "We didn't follow the rapid give and take."

The Pope passed a shaking hand across his brow. "The man facing me," he said, "was a master at the art of debate. Consider. I began the debate by sweeping my hand across the sky to indicate that God ruled all the universe. Without pausing an instant, that old Jew pointed downward to indicate that nevertheless, the Devil has been assigned a dominion of his own below.

"I then raised one finger to indicate there was but one God, assuming I would catch him in the error of his own theology. Yet he instantly raised three fingers to indicate that one God had three manifestations – a clear acceptance of the doctrine of the trinity.

"Abandoning theology, I produced an apple to indicate that certain blind followers of so-called science were flying in the face of revealed truth by declaring that the earth was as round as an apple. Instantly he produced a flat piece of unleavened bread to indicate that the earth, in accord with revelation, was nevertheless flat. So I granted him victory."

By now the Jews and the janitor had reached the ghetto. All surrounded the janitor, demanding, "What happened?"

The janitor said indignantly, "The whole thing was nonsense. Listen. First the Pope waves his hand like he is saying the Jews must get out of Rome. So I point downward to say the Jews are going to stay right here. So he points his finger at me as if to say drop dead, but the Jews are leaving. So I point three fingers at him to say "Drop dead three times! The Jews are staying. So then I see he is taking out his lunch, so I take out mine."

The whole metaphysical debate goes on like this. Impotent gestures, meaningless gestures – you can give any meaning to them. Empty words – you can make them appear in any way you like. It is your game.

Reality does not bother about your words – what humanity is thinking, what the human mind decides is truth. The truth is not worried about it. It is not a question of your deciding what truth is. You are befooling nobody except yourself. Your truth is your truth; it is not the truth.

Whatsoever mind comes to conclude is mind's conclusion. It shows something about the mind; it shows nothing about the reality. Truth is not a conviction of the mind. Truth is a transformation of being.

Here I am not giving you any metaphysics. People come to me and they ask, "What is your doctrine?" There is no doctrine here. All doctrines are dangerous, because they become dogmas. All doctrines are dangerous because they become occupations – so much so that the whole human energy is wasted in them. Drop all doctrines, dogmas, beliefs, "isms." Be clean of them – young, fresh. Then you will be intelligent.

Intelligence is not intellect. Intellect is accumulated knowledge. Intelligence is your freshness of being, the virginity of your being, the innocence of your being.

An intelligent person is one who faces life without words: who comes to life naked of all beliefs; who comes to life without any scriptures; who looks at life, direct and immediate, with no clouds in his mind. He has nothing to prove. He has not decided anything beforehand. He has no fixed ideas. And then he is never frustrated. He simply is open, vulnerable, and the reality penetrates him from every nook and corner, from every cell of his being. He becomes like a sponge: he is soaked with reality.

Be a fresh sponge – totally empty – so that you can soak the whole of the reality that there is. This is what meditation is all about. Meditation means dropping the mind, dropping metaphysics, dropping doctrines about reality so that reality itself can penetrate you and enter you.

Once you become addicted to a doctrine, then it is intellect that functions, not intelligence. An intelligent person is always free; intellect is never free. Intellect always tries to be consistent with the past. Intelligence always tries to respond with the present. An intellectual will be consistent. An intelligent person will be very paradoxical. An intellectual will be logical, in fact too logical – hair-splitting, logic-chopping. An intelligent man is not logical; he is simply real – and reality is paradoxical. He has no fixed ideas to force on reality. He has no fixed modes to force on reality. He is flexible, fluid, like water. He is ready to move with reality. Whatsoever shape the reality gives to him, he is available. He never says no.

Remember this: an intellectual always remains with the no, an intelligent person lives with the yes. He says yes to reality, whatsoever it is. He has no fight. He has nothing to grind against reality. He is part of it.

To be intelligent is totally different from being intellectual. To be intellectual is just trying, pretending, that you are intelligent. It is a false substitute. And once you become intellectual, you will become egoistic. Once you become egoistic, you are closed.

If you are an intellectual and trying to solve reality, and carrying some doctrines within you according to which you hope that you will be able to find the key and open the lock of reality, that key will be the very barrier – because the lock has never been locked. The doors are open.

You must have heard about Houdini, the magician, who used to get out of all sorts of locks, chains, prison cells, within minutes – at the most, three minutes. But once, only once in his life, was he deceived.

In Italy he was exhibiting his talents, and he could not get out for one hour. People who had come to watch became worried – it had never been so. Within three minutes, sometimes even within seconds, he was out. What had happened? And when he came out after one hour, he was perspiring, completely tired. He looked weird.

They asked, "What happened?"

He said, "The people befooled me. They had not locked the door. The door was open, and I was trying to find the key. There was no lock, just a hole, and in that hole I was trying to open the lock, the nonexistent lock."

Of course, if there is no lock you cannot open it. He became more and more worried, and he could not imagine that they may have played a trick and the door was not locked. It was a simple hole; there was no lock in it, so no key would fit.

Jesus says, "Knock, and the door shall be opened unto you." The basic meaning is: "Knock, and you will find the doors are always open. They have always remained open."

Intellect tries to create keys. Because of your keys you go on missing. And once you have a key, of course, it looks like a key – it is not a key because it never fits, and it cannot fit because there is no lock; but it looks like a key. Once you have a key, you go on defending it. It becomes a blanket, a rag doll.

Hindus go on defending their religion. They are not so worried about using it; they go on defending it. Mohammedans go on defending their religion. Christians go on producing rubbish literature. I have never come across more rubbishy literature than Christian literature – just simple rot. But they go on producing it – in defense. They have to argue. They have never used what they are saying, the key has never been helpful to them, but they are defending it.

People find outlandish ways to defend their keys and their doctrines. Their whole energy becomes blocked in a futile effort. Have you watched? If you don't have any doctrine, you can enjoy it; it is very funny when people start rationalizing and defending their doctrines.

Many times it happens; they come to me:

A Christian missionary came a few years ago and he started talking about his theology. For half an hour I listened to him, and then I asked him, "Just one thing I want to ask – has it helped you? Because you look almost crazy." You must have come across Jehovah's witnesses and other crazy people... But he wouldn't listen; as if he was not there. He went on and on.

Again, after one hour had passed, I said, "Just wait a minute. What are you talking about? Has it helped you?"

He confessed that it had not helped him, but he hoped it would help. I told him, "Something has helped me – are you ready to listen to it?"

He said, "I will come some other time." He never came.

People cling desperately to their beliefs. They are not convincing others; in fact, in convincing others, they are convincing themselves. Alone, left to themselves, they become afraid. "Who knows whether

what I am believing is true or not?" When they convince others, and
somebody says, "Yes, it is right," they become confident. Now they
know that they must have something true; otherwise how can other
people be impressed?

Once it happened...

Two young disciples were disputing the comparative piety of
their respective rabbinical teachers.

"My rabbi," said the first, "is so holy that he receives the special
attention of the good lord. One time last spring when it was raining
all over the city, there was a little circle around my rabbi's head
where no rain fell and where, instead, beams of sunlight shone down
to illuminate him."

"Just the same," said the second, "my rabbi is much more pious."

"How can you say that?" said the first in shocked tones. "Your
rabbi lacks the very basic elements of piety. My rabbi is incomparable.
Why, on last Yom Kippur – the holiest day of the year, when fasting is
obligatory – I saw your rabbi eating a chicken sandwich."

"Exactly," said the second in triumph. "While all over the city it
was Yom Kippur, in a little circle around my rabbi's head, it was the
day after Yom Kippur."

People go to absurd lengths to defend themselves. They go on
believing in something, because if that belief is broken, they will be
falling into a bottomless abyss.

But that bottomless abyss is real. Once you accept it, all fear disappears. Once you accept that life is a mystery and cannot be solved,
once you accept that life basically is unknowable, all fear disappears
and all efforts to know, and all efforts to formulate doctrines, stop.

Suddenly you are again part of reality; the division is no longer
there. The seeker and the sought are one. The thinker and the thought
are one. The observer and the observed are one. The seer and the
seen are one. Suddenly the division is no longer there. The division is
created by your doctrines.

This Zen story is tremendously beautiful.

Sato-Kaiseki was very much disturbed...

Disturbed, because whatsoever belief he was clinging to was

being shattered by scientific discoveries. He was very much disturbed...

...by the implications of Copernicus' heliocentric theory...

All the religions of the world were disturbed by Copernicus. He created one of the greatest revolutions in human consciousness. Before him, all religions believed that the earth was the center of existence. Not that they knew – it was part of human ego to believe that the earth is the center of the whole universe. It was part of an ego trip.

If the earth is the center of the whole universe, then man is the center of all life. How can it be otherwise? When man lives on earth, how can the center be anywhere else? And when Copernicus said that the earth is not the center – in fact, the earth is a very, very distant, mediocre place, not at all important, very insignificant – that the universe is vast and the earth is not the center...

...which, of course, was inconsistent with the old Buddhist cosmology in which Mount Sumeru occupies the center of the universe.

Mount Sumeru is the center of the Buddhist cosmology, is the center of the whole universe. Of course, Buddhists were disturbed. Christians were very disturbed. They punished Copernicus, they punished Galileo. They tried hard to shut up these new discoveries completely, so that their old idea of the earth being the center could continue – man being the center of life could continue. But it is difficult. Whenever a truth is discovered, it is impossible to force it back into darkness.

He reasoned that if the Buddhist view of the cosmos were proved false, the triple world and the twenty-five forms of existence would be reduced to nonsense...

Religious people are always afraid. If even one doctrine is proved false then their whole structure is toppled. Because if one thing can be wrong then why not others?

If Jesus says that the earth is flat, and later on we find that it is not flat, it is round, circular, it is a globe, then Christians become afraid. If the son of God was so ignorant that he did not know that the earth is round, then what about other things? He may be wrong about the other things also. And the very claim that he is the son of God seems to be disproved. At least the son of God must know.

If one doctrine goes wrong, if one loophole is found, then the whole structure starts falling down. So religious people go on insisting, for trivia also. I came across a man, a Jaina monk, who is trying to prove that the Americans and the Russians have not reached the moon – because it is against Jaina cosmology.

In Jaina cosmology, the moon is the abode of *devas*, angels. If these people have reached there and have found that there is nobody, no *devas*, then the whole Jaina cosmology falls down. Then what to say about Mahavira and his knowledge, his absolute knowledge? His omniscience is shattered.

Jainas claim that Mahavira knows everything of the past, of the present, of the future. There is nothing hidden from him; his knowledge is omniscient, absolute. He is infallible. So what to do now? If people have reached the moon – as they have – then the whole Jaina philosophy is suddenly shattered.

So this Jaina monk is trying to prove that they have not reached. He is trying to prove that they have been deceiving the whole world; that on television, people are seeing nothing but studio performances; that nobody has reached there.

The same thing happened when Copernicus proved that the earth was no longer the center, the sun is the center. Sumeru is the Buddhist concept. Sumeru means there is a mountain, immovable, the highest in existence, which is at the center of the world. Now what will happen to Sumeru?

This Sato-Kaiseki was very much disturbed. If one concept is proved wrong then what will happen to other concepts?

...the twenty-five forms of existence would be reduced to nonsense, resulting in the negation of Buddhism itself. Immediately he set about writing a book in defense of the Mount Sumeru position, sparing himself no effort as a champion of Buddhism.
When he had finished the work, he took it at once to Master Ekido and presented it to him triumphantly.

Zen masters are rare people. If there had been even one pope like a Zen master, the whole conflict between science and religion would have been avoided. It still continues because Christian popes go on being stupid. They go on talking nonsense. Whatsoever new is revealed, they go on avoiding it. They lag behind humanity. The gap between them and humanity is almost of two thousand years. They still live in the time of Jesus. Had there been even one pope like Master Ekido, things would have been totally different.

This disciple was very happy that he had proved. Of course, he had proved only logically – hair-splitting. He could not prove in any other way. The proof could not be experimental; it could only be logical.

The master took the book in his hand.

After leafing through only the first few pages, however, the master thrust the book back and, shaking his head, said, "How stupid! Don't you realize that the basic aim of Buddhism is to shatter the triple world and the twenty-five forms of existence? Why stick to such utterly worthless things and treasure Mount Sumeru? Blockhead!"
Dumbfounded, Kaiseki shoved the book under his arm and quickly went home.

This is the taste of an enlightened being, the flavor.

One has to get rid of all doctrines, scriptures, theories, because basically one has to get rid of one's own ego. One has to get rid of all religions to be really religious. One has to get rid of all theories to come face to face with truth.

Zen monks are rare in the whole history of religion. They have burned their own scriptures. They have burned Buddha statues because the night was cold and there was no other wood available in the temple. Rare people. Worshipping Buddha, you cannot find more loving, trusting people. They worship Buddha, but if the time comes and it is winter and the night is very cold, they can burn Buddha just to keep themselves warm, with not the slightest bit of guilt. In the morning they will again be worshipping Buddha.

Very difficult to understand, but this is how enlightenment is. If you have become aware, then you don't cling to foolish things. If you have become aware, then awareness is the only worthy thing; then everything else is worthless.

The master said, "Who bothers about Sumeru? All nonsense!

Who bothers about the metaphysics, the cosmology, the philosophy? All nonsense! Good! Be happy that Copernicus has toppled it.
He has done a beautiful thing. Bless him."

Basically the whole effort is how to come out of the mind.
Whenever you cling to a dogma, you are clinging to your mind. Whenever you cling to a doctrine, you are clinging to words.

Right he is when he says:

*"How stupid! Don't you realize that the basic aim of Buddhism is
to shatter the triple world and the twenty-five forms of existence? Why
stick to such utterly worthless things and treasure Mount Sumeru?
Blockhead!"* When Buddha was dying, Ananda started crying and
weeping. He had lived forty years with him, like a shadow, and he
said, "I could not attain, and now you are leaving. You were with me
twenty-four hours a day for forty years and then too I missed. Now
there is no hope. When you are not here, for lives and lives I will be in
darkness, wandering here and there. Now there seems to be no possibility for me. All doors are closed. I have not yet attained."

Buddha smiled and said, "Maybe when I am gone you will be
capable of attaining it. As I see it, I have become a hindrance. You
cling too much to me. So remember one thing: when I am gone, let
me be gone completely. Don't cling. Drop me completely – and be a
light unto yourself."

And it is said that the next day Ananda became enlightened.
Buddha dead, now nothing to cling to – the last barrier dropped.

Zen masters say, "If you meet Buddha on the way, kill him immediately" – because he is so beautiful, so lovely, you may start being
attached to him. "Kill him immediately." Zen masters say, "If you by
chance utter the name of Buddha, clean, rinse your mouth well,
immediately!"

What do they mean? And they go on worshipping, and they go
on putting flowers at Buddha's feet, and they go on bowing down,
and they go on surrendering to him. They go on singing "*Buddham
sharanam gachchhami*" – "I seek refuge in your feet, my lord." They
go on saying it. It looks very paradoxical, but if you can see the
point, it is simple.

One respects an enlightened person because he has shown the
way. One feels grateful because he has shown the way in darkness,
he has become a light in darkness. But one never clings to him,

because if you cling, then the same person who was going to be a door has become a wall. You missed.

A disciple was leaving his master's house one dark night. He was afraid. The master said, "Wait, don't be afraid. I will give you a lamp."

He gave him a lamp. The disciple was very happy, more confident. When he was going down the steps of the master's house, the master called him back and blew out the lamp. The disciple said, "What? What have you done? The night is very dark."

The master said, "Buddhas can only show the way, but you have to travel alone – and with your own light. Be a light unto yourself."

Don't be worried about futile things – god, nirvana, *moksha*, absolute truth, who created the world, the heaven and the hell – all theories and theories and theories. All words. Beware of words. Put aside all words so you can be immediately in front of reality. Reality is herenow. You are missing it because of your metaphysical ideas.

In your being, there are two possibilities: one is intellect, another is intelligence. Intellect is male, intelligence is female. Intellect is aggressive, intelligence is passive. Intellect is violent, intelligence is nonviolent. Intellect tries to penetrate the reality forcibly – that's what science is doing. It is a rape on reality; it is ugly. Intelligence simply opens the door and waits for the light to come. It is receptive like a woman. It is like a womb – just receptive, passive.

Allow your intelligence to rule you. Don't allow your intellect to overpower you.

Have you watched, that whenever you fall in love, the woman starts unknowingly overpowering you? You may be a great man in the world, but with your beloved, your ego simply disappears. Even a very delicate and fragile woman will overpower the strongest man in the world.

Once it happened...

An eccentric king sent a henchman around the countryside. He was to interview the householders, and to every man who was boss in his house he was to give a horse. To every man who was henpecked he would give a chicken.

Everywhere the henchman went, he handed out chickens, with never an occasion to give anyone a horse. At last though, he arrived at the house of a burly farmer with a bristly, unshaven face, a deep bass voice, and muscles like an ox. In the background was his thin and wizened wife.

The henchman said, "Are you boss in your family, sir?"

The farmer leaned his head back and bellowed with laughter, "You bet, little man!" he said. "What I say around here, goes." And he opened and closed his fists, the size of hams.

The henchman was convinced. "You get a horse," he said. "Do you want a brown horse or a gray horse?"

The farmer leaned his head back and shouted, "Tilda, do we get a brown horse or a gray horse?"

And the henchman said, "You get a chicken."

It happens according to a certain eternal law. The feminine is more powerful, but very paradoxical. The feminine looks very powerless – therein is the power. In the very powerlessness is the power. The feminine looks fragile – therein precisely is the power and the strength.

Everybody has both inside them. A man has a woman inside him and a man, and a woman has a woman inside her and a man. Now it depends on you. This is how the focus has to be changed. Intellect is male; intelligence is female. Mind is male; meditation is female, receptive, passive.

If you go on clinging to the intellect you will miss, because reality opens its door only to those who are passive – passive, alert – but absolutely passive, not doing anything. Change the focus from intellect to intelligence. Change the focus from thoughts to feelings.

Truth can never be known; it can only be felt. You cannot go to truth; you can only be available for it to come to you. Nobody ever reaches truth; whenever you are ready, truth reaches you.

If you are trying to work it out through the intellect, you will become a metaphysician, a philosopher, a systematizer, a logician – but you will miss. You will miss absolutely. Drop all logic, all systematizing, all hair-splitting. Drop all aggressiveness. The active has to be dropped. Become passive.

Sit silently, be silent – and wait. And one day suddenly, when you are really settled in your passivity, when you are really centered in your receptivity, when you are just a door, an opening, truth comes to you, nirvana happens to you.

Enough for today.

CHAPTER 6

taking the risk

The first question:

Osho,
In the beginning you told me what I had to do. It was hard. Now
you tell me that I can decide for myself, that I can do what I feel.
This is hard, too. I am afraid of making a wrong decision. Please
explain.

These are the only two possibilities. Either you surrender and in
that surrender you stop thinking about decisions, conse-
quences; in your surrender you have surrendered the responsibility itself, and you are totally free – free to move without any worry,
without any burden on your mind. But that is difficult because of the
ego. You cannot surrender totally. You would like to control your life
on your own. It becomes hard for the ego.

The second possibility is that you take things in your own hands,
do whatsoever you like to do. Again the problem arises, because you
don't have any awareness. You don't know what to do and what not
to do. Then you are afraid of making a wrong decision. Then you are
afraid of moving in a wrong direction. The ego is there, and with the

ego, the shadow of the ego –ignorance is there. They both go together, or they remain together. If you drop the ego, ignorance disappears. If you drop ignorance, ego disappears – they cannot exist separately.

So these are the two paths. Either you surrender – the ego has to be dropped, then by and by you will feel the shadow has disappeared on its own accord. Or, you have to become more aware, more alert, so that more light is within your being and ignorance disappears.

When the ignorance disappears, the ego disappears automatically. Ego and ignorance are two aspects of the same coin. You can throw the coin in both ways, but one decision you have to take – either to drop the ego or to drop the ignorance. And if it is difficult to drop the ego, then it is going to be very difficult to drop the ignorance.

These are the two eternal paths – the path of will and the path of surrender. In surrender, the "I" is completely dropped. On the path of will, the "I" is purified, cleaned of all impurities, is made transparent. It becomes a light unto itself. But one decision you have to make – either to follow the path of will or to follow the path of surrender.

The path of surrender is easier, because it can become a total jump in a single step. The journey of a thousand and one miles is complete in a single step. The path of will is gradual – you move inch by inch. But if you choose that, if you like that, there is nothing wrong in it. It is up to you to decide.

Of course, both are hard. And whatsoever you choose will appear harder than the one that you have not chosen. But nothing can be done; one has to choose sooner or later. You have to commit your being to a certain path. The only wrong that you can do is to remain indecisive. The only sin that you can commit with yourself is to remain indecisive and postpone.

Don't be indecisive. Decide. Even if sometimes you commit mistakes, nothing is wrong in them. By committing mistakes you will learn much. Nobody learns without committing mistakes. Even if you go astray, don't be afraid. Go with courage. Go alert. Sooner or later you will realize that you have gone astray. You can come back.

Whenever you come back after wandering, committing many mistakes, you will see that your consciousness has been enriched. If you simply sit in your home and never move because of the fear that something may go wrong, you may do something wrong; if you remain tethered to the place where you are, of course you will not commit any mistakes, but your life will be a life of unfulfillment. You can avoid mistakes, but in avoiding mistakes you will be avoiding all those beautiful experiences that life can give to you. This is an escape. Be courageous. Have the courage to be.

There are many people, millions of people, who simply miss their lives because of the fear that something may go wrong. And this is the only wrong, this is the only mistake. They go on hiding, they go on escaping from situations. Wherever they find a possibility of a wrong movement, they stop all movement. They never grow. They remain immature.

There is nothing wrong in committing mistakes. Just remember one thing: don't commit the same mistake again and again; that's enough. Each mistake brings a lesson. Each going astray is coming to the right path in a deep way.

I have heard one anecdote:

Two Jews were up against the wall, hands tied behind their backs, waiting to be shot. The officer in charge of the firing squad came to them and asked curtly, "Do you want a final cigarette?"

The first Jew replied, "Keep your cigarette, you murdering bum!"

Whereupon the second Jew whispered anxiously, "Quiet, Jack, quiet. Don't make trouble."

When you are going to be shot, what difference does it make to create trouble or not to create trouble?

Death is approaching. Everybody is tied against the wall to be shot. Don't be afraid. Whether you are afraid or not makes no difference – death is approaching. Even if you don't do anything, death will come – it is already coming. The days are shortening every day. Your life is being cut every day. You are being uprooted from life every day.

For what are you waiting? Do something. Be decisive.

I know it is human to tremble when a decision is to be taken. I can understand the helplessness, but nothing can be done about it. It is so. Whenever you take a decision, a trembling comes – one may be wrong. But still the decision has to be taken. One may be wrong – still the decision has to be taken, because how is one going to know whether the decision was going to be wrong or not? You have to take it to know it.

People come to me and they say they are wavering whether to

take sannyas or not. I can understand wavering, I can understand an inner turmoil. I can understand that it is difficult to take a step in the dark, into the unknown.

But I tell them only one thing: you have lived up to now as a non-sannyasin – uncommitted you have moved, lived your life, and have never taken a decision which can become a radical transformation. Try it this time. If nothing happens, you can always go back. Who can hinder you from going back? But if something happens, just the possibility of something happening is worth the risk. Who knows?

There is no other way to know beforehand. That is the cowardly mind, who wants everything guaranteed. They ask me, "Will something certainly happen if I become a sannyasin?" Who can say? How can it be made certain? It is not a thing that I can give to you. It is something which is always in the unknown. It can happen, it may not happen. It depends on a thousand and one things. But the possibility is there. It is not impossible – this much can be said. It has happened to me. This much can be said – it is not impossible. But nobody can make it a certainty, nobody can give you a guarantee.

The Western mind particularly has become too afraid of commitment. You love a woman, but you are afraid to commit. You love a man, but you are afraid to commit. You remain in indecisiveness. You go on playing, but you never move in the deep waters of life because then you are afraid you may be caught: it may become a bondage, it may become a chain around your being. You may be imprisoned.

That risk has to be taken. Whenever you move in anything deep, the possibility is there: you may become more free or you may become more imprisoned. But one who takes the risk always learns something out of it, always is enriched.

So decide. Either you take everything in your hands, or you leave everything to me. It cannot be fifty-fifty. You would like to leave a part to me and to keep part in your own hands – that is not going to work. That is not going to work at all.

I have a friend. He is very satisfied with his marriage, with his wife. I asked, "How do you manage?"

He said, "The day we got married we made a contract, we made an agreement: fifty-fifty – half the decisions I have to take, and half the wife has to take."

So I asked him, "How did you divide?"

He said, "All the great decisions I take, and all the small decisions she takes."

I was still not clear, so I asked again, "Just enlighten me a little more."

He said, "Decisions like what should happen in Vietnam, or who should now become the prime minister of China – such great things I decide. And to what school the child is to go, and what type of car we have to purchase, and in what type of house we have to live, and what food we have to eat – things, small things like this – my wife decides. Fifty-fifty it goes – and everything is perfectly good."

So if you make this type of agreement with me then it is okay. If great things you decide and small things you leave to me, then it is perfectly okay. Then you can decide whether God exists as three or as one – I leave it to you. But how to meditate I will decide – small things.

The second question:

Osho,
You are the survivor of a shipwreck. You are able to find a small plank just capable of staying afloat with one person on it. Just then another survivor appears and attempts to join you on the plank. What would you do?

If I am myself, then I will jump off the plank and help the other person to survive. If I am you, then too I will jump off the plank and help the other person to survive. In both the cases I will do the same, but for different reasons.

If I am myself, then I know life is immortal, life is deathless. There is no problem for me. If I am you, then first let me tell an anecdote:

A British diplomat was visiting the mountain hideout where Adolf Hitler, in those terrifying days of the late nineteen-thirties, was deliberately attempting to break Western will by displaying how hopeless resistance was.

"What can the British do," he demanded, "against an army so devoted to me that they will go to their death at my nod? Do you see that soldier there? Soldier, jump out of the window!"

Without a moment's hesitation the soldier leaped out of the

window to his death, leaving the British diplomat frozen in horror. Hitler smiled grimly. "I will show you once more. Soldier, jump out of that window!" A second soldier jumped.

A third time Hitler ordered suicide, but this time the British diplomat could not sit there idly. He seized the third German soldier by the arm, even as he headed for the window, and cried, "How can you abandon life so lightly!"

The soldier replied, "You call this a life?" Then he broke away and jumped.

Whatsoever you call life is not life at all. If I am you, I will jump. What I call life is eternal. If I am myself, then too I will jump – because there is going to be no death.

But the reasons will be absolutely different. Sometimes actions can be similar and reasons can be absolutely different. So never pay too much attention to the action. Always pay much more attention to the reason behind it.

Buddha may behave just like you, the action may be exactly the same, but it cannot be similar, because a Buddha-consciousness is so different from you. The action will only be similar in appearance; deep down there must be a great difference – it has to be so.

Buddha also lives an ordinary life – eats, sleeps, feels thirsty. But the reasons are totally different. When Buddha drinks water, he is just quenching the thirst of the body. When you drink water, you are quenching your thirst.

When Buddha eats food, he is just helping the body to be alive so that it can be used. It is a means, a vehicle – all care has to be taken of it. When you eat food, it is a question of life and death. Food is life.

When Buddha sleeps and you sleep, both are in the same way sleeping. The posture may be the same, the eyes will be closed, but deep down there is a great difference. Even in deep sleep, Buddha is aware. He never sleeps, only the body sleeps. The inner light goes on burning. Never for a second is there any discontinuity in inner awareness. When you sleep, you are completely asleep. You become unconscious. You completely lose your being into unconsciousness, into darkness.

So never judge anything by the action. Always judge the thing by the innermost core of it.

The third question:

Osho,
You have mentioned many times the Christian trinity: the Father,
the Son, and the Holy Ghost. Could you tell us please, what
happened to the mother?

All the religions of the world were founded by men; not a single
religion has been founded by any woman. And of course the male
ego, the male chauvinism, has been the root cause of all the doctrines that have been created to explain existence.

It is very difficult for the male ego to think of woman as the creator. Even to give a small portion in the trinity to woman seems to be
difficult. Everything has been managed by man. Man has been the
manager in this world and, of course, he has created the concept of
the other world. There also he goes on managing.

"God is man, the Holy Ghost is man, the Son is man." Not that it
is so. If there is any God, he is bound to be both man and woman. He
cannot be just male – that is impossible, that will be incomplete.
He must be a complete circle – male–female, yin–yang.

In the East we have been more aware. In Sanskrit, the *brahman*,
the ultimate, is neither male nor female. That's truer – because it
is both. It does not belong to any gender. It is beyond gender. That
seems to be truer, a better concept, because life exists in polarities.
Life cannot exist with one pole. Electricity cannot exist only as
positive or only as negative. The negative and the positive – both
poles are needed. Between these poles exists the phenomenon of
electricity.

Humanity cannot exist just as man or as woman. Both are needed
to make it a complete whole; a graceful, elegant whole. Man alone is
incomplete. Woman alone is also incomplete. Look at life. All polarities are joined together there: life and death, love and hate, day and
night, summer and winter. All polarities are joined together, the earth
and the sky. Existence is the total, the whole. The whole cannot be
just male. This is a male attitude, if people say that the whole is just
male. It is a male chauvinist attitude.

Now women are reacting to it. Women who are in the lib movement have started calling God "she." They don't call God "he" anymore. That is a reaction. One can understand the reaction. But the

reaction is again the same – the same mistake is again committed. The ultimate is both he and she.

In Sanskrit we don't use *he* or *she*. We use *tat*. *Tat* means that. An indication, a simple indication without saying who God is – he or she. *Tat* – that. A simple indication without saying anything about God's gender. Sooner or later humanity will come to understand this, that man and woman are complementary. Opposites, yet complementary, creating one whole.

Because of this idea that "God is man," man has created such absurd theories that you cannot imagine. In India also, Jainas say that a woman cannot be liberated, cannot become liberated from the female body. First she will have to be born as a man; only man can become liberated. Stupid! – because the soul is neither man nor woman. Even Buddha, for many years, would not allow women to be initiated as sannyasins. Only very late in his life did he relax.

People come to me and they say, "What is happening in this ashram? So many women, so many men!" Because in the past, ashrams have existed always for men. If ashrams existed for women then they were purely for women.

Religions have been separating man and woman. There are Christian monasteries in the West where no woman has ever entered, where no woman is allowed to enter. There are Trappist monasteries where, once a man enters, he never comes out because of the fear of meeting some woman in the town, in the city somewhere.

Sex has been the forbidden thing. Love has been the condemned thing. And man has tried to become completely independent – as if that is possible. That is not possible. The energy needs the opposite. Hindus are more scientific in that way. If you go to a Hindu temple, there you will find Krishna with Radha, Shiva with Parvati, Ram with Sita. The feminine energy is there. It has to be there to make the ultimate complete.

In a Jaina temple, Mahavira stands alone. It looks a little awkward, a little incomplete. In a Buddhist temple, Buddha sits alone. In a Christian church, Jesus is crucified, is on the cross, but alone. Of course, if a church looks very sad, it is natural. The other energy, which can make it a celebration, is missing. When man and woman are together, life celebrates; there is rejoicing.

Have you watched twenty men sitting in a room? You will feel a certain sadness settling. Then a woman comes in, suddenly a flare-up of energy – *kundalini* arises. Everybody becomes alert, dust is shaken, something is happening. It is not a question of bodies, it is a question of energy. The opposite polarity has come in, sparks start happening. The opposite energy is there, the magnetism starts functioning.

A world only of men will be a very drab and dull world. The trinity must be bored by now. The Father, the Holy Ghost and the Son – what are they doing now? It must be very boring company. Just thinking of it, one should get scared!

No, it cannot make life complete. A mixing of energy is needed, only then does life go on reaching to higher levels. It is a dialectic: the thesis, the antithesis, and between the two arises the peak of synthesis. Then the synthesis again functions as a thesis, again antithesis – a higher synthesis arises. It is a continuous creation of a symphony of energies.

So this place is very strange. That's why you don't see many Indians here. They cannot believe that this is an ashram. They have known only sad people sitting in ashrams, almost dead. They cannot believe so much rejoicing, so much delight.

Just the other day an Indian wrote a letter and he said, "Everything is okay, but after the meditations, or even after your lecture, there are a few couples who start hugging each other, kissing each other. This looks irreligious." What can be more religious?

Love is religion, but for centuries love has been condemned. For centuries love has been a sin. For centuries man and woman have existed separately, meeting only in the dark of the night when nobody knows that they are meeting, and then separating again. And feeling guilty for the meeting, and feeling deeply troubled that the desire arises for the woman or the desire arises for the man. It is simply natural. It is not a question of you; it is a question of energies – positive and negative energies meeting. When they meet, new life arises.

The Christian doctrine is certainly wrong. Godliness should be given more freedom so that it can move between the polarities. In India we have a concept of Shiva as Ardhanarishwar – that seems to be one of the highest peaks of understanding.

Ardhanarishwar means: God is half-man, half-woman. You may have seen the statue or a photograph of the statue of Ardhanarishwar in which Shiva is half-man, half-woman. It is greatly symbolic; deeply indicative of understanding. This is how it should be.

It happened once:

A vicar was awarding prizes at the local dog-show. He was very much scandalized at the costumes worn by some members of the younger fair sex.

"Look at that youngster," he said, "the one with cropped hair, the cigarette and the breeches, and holding two pups. Is it a boy or a girl?"

"A girl," said his companion. "She is my daughter."

"My dear sir," the vicar was flustered, "do forgive me. I would never have been so outspoken had I known you were her father."

"I'm not," said the other. "I am her mother."

Someday this is going to be the case with God. And it will be a beautiful day when God will be in unisex costumes, and no one will be able to say who is coming – she or he. That will be a great day of liberation from male concepts. That will be a great day of human understanding about godliness – not man's understanding or woman's understanding.

The fourth question:

Osho,
Could you please talk about the difference between the patient non-reaction of the Zen master and the poisonous non-reaction of repressive self-control?

There is a great difference – as great as possible. When one is patient, one has nothing repressed in him. Otherwise patience is not possible. Because patience is not disturbed by somebody else insulting you; patience is disturbed by your own anger, hatred, jealousies, which are repressed within you. The other's insult functions only as an excuse; the real thing happens because of your repressions.

You go on repressing anger. It goes on piling up within you. Then just a spark of insult and there is going to be a great fire within you. It is absolutely out of proportion to the insult. And you also realize many times that it was not such a great thing: "But why did I become so mad?"

Sometimes the other has not even provoked it; the other was not even aware that he was insulting you and you became insulted. And you became mad. You must have been carrying anger for a long time; it was overflowing. It was just waiting to find some situation where you could rationalize and throw the responsibility on some-body else's shoulders. Patience is possible only if you are not repres-sive. Otherwise you will be impatient.

Look, ordinarily anger is not bad. Ordinarily, anger is part of nat-ural life; it comes and goes. But if you repress it, then it becomes a problem. Then you go on accumulating it. Then it is not a question of coming and going, it becomes your very being. Then it is not that you are sometimes angry; you remain angry, you remain in rage, and you just wait for somebody to provoke it. Or even a hint of provocation, and you catch fire and you do things for which, later on, you will say, "I did it in spite of me."

Analyze this expression "in spite of me." How can you do any-thing in spite of you? But the expression is exactly right.

Repressed anger becomes a temporary madness. Something hap-pens which is beyond your control. If you could have, you would have controlled it still – but suddenly it was overflowing. Suddenly it was beyond you. You couldn't do anything, you felt helpless and it came out. Such a person may not be angry, but he moves and lives in anger.

If you look at people – stand by the road and just watch – you will find two types of people. Just go on watching their faces. The whole humanity is divided into two types of people. One is the sad type, who will look very sad, dragging somehow. Another is the angry type – just bubbling with madness, ready to explode at any excuse.

Anger is active sadness; sadness is inactive anger. They are not two things. Watch your own behavior. When do you find yourself sad? You find yourself sad only in situations where you cannot be angry. The boss in the office says something and you cannot be angry; it is uneconomical. You cannot be angry and you have to go on smiling – then you become sad. The energy has become inactive. You go home, and with your wife you find some small thing, something irrel-evant, and you become angry.

People enjoy anger, they relish it, because at least they feel they are doing something. In sadness, you feel that something has been done to you. You have been at the passive end, at the receiving end. Something has been done to you and you were helpless and you could not retort, you could not retaliate, you could not react.

In anger, you feel a little good. After a big bout of anger, one feels a little relaxed – feels good. You are alive. You can also do things. Of course you cannot do them to the boss, but you can do them to the wife.

Then the wife waits for the children to come home because it is uneconomical to be angry with the husband. The whole of life seems to be economics. He is the boss, and the wife depends on him, and it is risky to be angry at him. She will wait for the children. They will come home from school, and then she can jump and she can beat them – for their own sake.

What will the children do? They will go in their rooms, they will throw their books, tear them, or beat their dolls, or beat their dogs, or torture their cats. They will have to do something. Everybody has to do something, otherwise one becomes sad.

The people you see on the streets who have become sad, so permanently that the face has taken a certain mold, are the people who are so helpless, so down the rung of the ladder, that they can't find anybody to be angry with. These are the sad people. Higher up on the rung you will find angry people. The higher you go, the angrier are the people you will find. The lower you come, the sadder are the people.

In India, go and see the untouchables, the lowest class. They are sad. Then go to the brahmins – they are angry. A brahmin is always angry; for any small thing he will go mad. He is a brahmin. An untouchable is simply sad because there is nobody else below him on whom he can throw his anger. Anger and sadness are both faces of the same energy; repressed.

Patience comes when you are neither angry nor sad. Patience is a great phenomenon. When you are neither angry against anybody nor sad against anybody – sadness and anger have both gone; your energies have settled, centered; you are at home. Patience means you have come back home. Now nothing distracts, nothing disturbs. You are so happy, so blissful inside, that everything else is irrelevant.

Somebody insults you, you need not get insulted. You are so happy. Have you watched? When you are happy and somebody insults, you don't get so angry. When you are unhappy, you get too angry. That simply shows the mathematics of it. When you are unhappy, you are ready to be angry, waiting to be angry. When you are happy, the same thing doesn't matter.

When one is deeply blissful, simply enjoying each moment of life as a gift from existence, who bothers? Nothing is worth it then. You have such a precious thing with you that everything else is simply irrelevant.

A religious person is not a repressed person, although the religious persons you have come across are all repressed persons. But a religious mind is not repressed. A religious mind is a happy mind, a blissful mind, a celebrating being.

I will tell you one anecdote:

Armstrong played a twosome on the golf course with the minister of his church one or two times a month. Reverend Brown was a good golfer and the competition between them was keen, but Armstrong had to admit that the matches offered a special strain on his internal workings.

Armstrong had, as so many of us do, a gift for rich invective, and on foozling a shot he had a habit of voicing his feelings by addressing the ball, the green, and the general surroundings with a wealth of purple passion. Yet in the presence of Reverend Brown, he found himself restrained from indulging himself, and by the end of the round he would be pale with repressed verbiage.

The minister, on the other hand, though he also foozled shots now and then would, on such occasion, observe a patient silence that irritated Armstrong even more.

Finally Armstrong said, "Reverend Brown, I must ask. Tell me, how is it that you manage to keep your temper when you slice the ball into the rough, or when you miss your putt because there's a twig on the green you didn't see?"

Reverend Brown replied, "My good friend, it is a matter of sublimation. I need not shout or use vile language. Surely that will not alter the situation and will, on the other hand, imperil my soul. Yet, since I must do something, I sublimate. I spit."

"You spit?"

"That's right." Here Reverend Brown's eyes darkened. "But let me tell you this! Where I spit, the grass never grows again!"

The people you have known as religious have been sublimating things. But sublimation is just a trick of the mind. There is nothing sublime in it. The word is a misnomer. Because of these sublimations, many things have happened to humanity which could have been avoided. After each ten years a great war is needed because of sublimation – because people go on repressing. Then the whole thing becomes too heavy; it has to be thrown off.

Have you seen? Whenever there is a war people look so happy, so vibrant with life; their dullness disappears. Something is happening. Now they can call the other country names that they have been avoiding up to now. The other country becomes the Devil; the other country becomes the enemy of truth; the other country becomes the very personification of evil. And the other country has to be destroyed, uprooted completely.

Now destruction is allowed – not only allowed, but praised. Violence is allowed – not only allowed, but praised. People are allowed whatsoever was not allowed before: anger, hatred, jealousy, violence, the murderous instincts; everything is allowed. People feel very good.

After each ten years a great world war is needed; less than that won't do because man has been taught to sublimate: repress sex, repress anger, repress cruelty, repress everything, and try to smile, try to wear a mask, have a false personality. Deep down you go on sitting on a volcano and on the face you go on smiling. The smile is false, painted. Nobody is deceived by it, but you go on thinking that you are sublimating. Nothing is sublimated.

Understanding transforms, it does not sublimate. If you understand anger, anger disappears and the same energy becomes compassion. Not that you sublimate: anger simply disappears, and the energy that was involved, invested in anger, is released and becomes compassion. When you understand hate, hate disappears and the same energy becomes love.

Love is not against hate – it is absence of hate. Religious people go on conditioning you, "Love your enemy." They go on saying to you, "Wherever you feel hatred, repress it and show love."

I cannot say that to you. I will say, "Wherever you feel hatred, become aware." No need to love your enemies. You have not even loved yourself, how can you love your enemies? You have not even loved your friends, how can you love your enemies? That is impossible. First love yourself, love the friends, then you can love the strangers and then you can love the enemies.

It is as if you throw a small pebble in the silent lake – small ripples arise and then they go on spreading to the farthest shore. First you have to love yourself, then your small circle of friends, then the great circle of strangers, and then the enemies. Not that you have to force love for your enemies. Otherwise you will take revenge in some other way. You will sublimate.

You may not swear, you will spit – and the grass will never grow wherever you spit. Then you will sublimate and you will create the idea of hell for your enemies. Here you cannot create a hell for them; then you will create a hell for them somewhere underground, where they will be put into fire, into burning oil, tortured in every way.

Just look at what type of a hell the Christians, the Hindus, the Mohammedans have created. If you read their stories about hell you cannot improve upon them. They have done the last thing; the sadist imagination has reached its peak.

If you repress, you will take your revenge somewhere or other. All your so-called saints go on hoping that somewhere in hell their enemies will be put into fire and tortured. That is their hope. And here they go on showing love. That love is bogus. That love is impotent.

I don't teach you to sublimate. I simply teach you one thing – understanding. Let understanding be the only law. Understand anger, watch anger, become aware of anger. Don't do anything, just let it be there in front of you. Look deeply into it and suddenly you will see that just by looking into it, a transformation starts happening. Just by observation anger starts changing into compassion.

There is the key. Nothing has to be done – just awareness does everything for you. And, of course, then you are patient. Not that you have controlled your anger. You are patient because you are so happy. You are patient because your anger is transformed into compassion. You are patient because your hatred has become love. You are patient because your greed has become a sharing. You are patient because now you are enjoying life at its peak. Who bothers what others say? One is not concerned at all.

A Zen master was going to his temple after his morning walk with his disciple. A man came, hit him hard on the back with a staff, and ran away. The master did not even look back; he continued his walk. The disciple could not believe it. He said, "What is the matter with you? Are you mad? The man has hit so hard and he has escaped and you have not even looked back."

The Zen master said, "That is his problem. How am I concerned with it? He must be mad, poor fellow. I feel much compassion for him. And I cannot look back, because he is already mad; my looking back may make him more mad. Already he will feel guilty back home; with my looking back he may feel that I have condemned him. No, that won't be human. He is already in trouble. Now there is no need to create more trouble for him. That is his problem."

When you are happy, then others' problems are no longer your problems. Let me say it in this way: when you have no problems, then nobody can throw his problem on you. Because you have problems, others can throw their problems on you and you become hooked.

Patience is a byproduct of inner bliss.

The fifth question:

Osho,
The ego feels so cunning that even moments of inner silence, moments of let-go, seem to be but subtle tricks of the control monster. It is like a skillful fisherman playing with the fish he has hooked, giving it room to run and get tired before pulling it in.

Yes, the ego is very subtle – the subtlest thing in the world. In fact it does not exist, hence its subtlety. In fact it is just a shadow, it has no existence. So wherever you go, the shadow follows you. And if you start running from the shadow, the shadow will run with you. The faster you run, the faster the shadow will follow you. And then you will feel that it is impossible for you to escape from this shadow.

No, it is not impossible. Just go under a tree, sit under the shade, and the shadow disappears. Don't run. That is not the way to go away from it. It is a shadow. You cannot go away from it. It has no existence, hence it is so subtle. Because it has no existence it is so powerful. Because it is not, ergo you cannot escape from it.

Try to understand. Move under the shadow of a big tree and sit there and look around – the shadow is no longer there. That big tree is what I call meditation. Come under the shelter of meditation and the ego disappears.

But people do many other things. They try to become humble; that is an escape. They feel the grip of the shadow, the grip of the ego. They try to become humble, they try to become simple, they renounce everything. Because they think the ego comes from riches, they renounce the riches – but then the ego comes through renunciation of the riches. They think the ego comes from prestige and from power – renounce power, renounce prestige – but then the ego comes from your humbleness.

Let me tell you an anecdote. I love it tremendously:

The beloved rabbi was on his deathbed, and life was slowly ebbing away. Around the bed was a group of sorrowing disciples who felt the coming loss keenly and who talked in whispers among themselves of the manifold virtues of the old man now leaving them. One said, "So pious, so pious! Which of the many commandments of the Law did he fail to keep? Where at any point did he deviate in the slightest form from the commandments of God?"

And another mourned, "And so learned. The vast commentaries of the rabbis of the past were, so to speak, imprinted on his brain. At any moment he could call to mind some saying which would illuminate any possible theological question."

Still a third said, "And so charitable, so generous. Where was the poor man whom he did not help? Who in town is ignorant of his kindness? Why, he kept for himself only enough to hold body and soul together."

But as this litany of praise continued, a faint tremor appeared on the rabbi's face. It became obvious that he was trying to say something. All the disciples leaned forward, with bated breath, to hear those last words.

Faintly from the rabbinical lips, there came the words, "Piety, learning, charity! And of my great modesty you say nothing?"

"Of my great modesty you say nothing." Then the ego will hide behind the modesty. Then the ego will hide behind humbleness. Then the ego will hide behind simplicity. The ways of the ego are subtle because it is your shadow – wherever you go, it follows you. Unless you find a place where you are in shade, then it disappears.

Through meditation, by and by you will come under the shade of a great tree. Sheltered, you will look all around and the ego will not be found. Except meditation, nothing can help. Your austerities won't help you. Your renunciations won't help you. Except meditation, nothing is of help.

What is meditation then? Meditation is a state of no-mind. The mind is like hot, burning sun. Under the mind you move – a shadow falls, a shadow is created. When the hot, burning sun is not there, suddenly silence.

Meditation is a state of no-mind. Meditation is the interval when there are no thoughts floating in you, when the clouds of thoughts have disappeared. You are without thoughts, but not asleep. You are without thoughts, yet alert. An alert thoughtlessness is meditation.

In the beginning there will be only rare moments; only for a split second will you feel the shade of the tree. But in that split second this ego will disappear completely. You will find you are not, because the feeling of "I am" is nothing but accumulated thoughts. It is the piling up of thoughts that gives you the feeling "I am." If thoughts disappear, the "I" disappears.

You can take a torch in your hand and you can move your hand fast: a circle of fire will be created. The circle does not exist, but it appears because the torch is moving fast. A circle of fire is seen. In fact there is no circle, only a torch, but you can see the fire-circle.

Buddha used to take this symbol often – a circle of fire. Stop movement, stop your hand, and there is only a torch and the circle disappears.

Stop your mind and the circle of thought disappears. Suddenly only your being is there and the circle is no longer there. That circle is the ego. All thoughts together make it appear as if you are. When thoughts disperse, you are, but you don't feel that you are. The "I" disappears, only "amness" remains.

In the West, one man, Rene Descartes, led the whole Western mind on a wrong track. His dictum is very famous; on that dictum the whole of Western philosophy stands. His dictum is: *cogito ergo sum*. I think, therefore I am.

This is absolute nonsense. I think, therefore I am? That means that when thinking stops, you will disappear, you will not be. In fact, when thinking disappears, for the first time you are. With the disappearance of the thinking, the ego disappears; not you, not your being.

His dictum – *cogito ergo sum*: I think, therefore I am – is illogical, because from "I think," you cannot derive "I am." From "I think," you can derive only "I think." The dictum can be: *cogito ergo cogito*. I think, therefore I think. That's okay. But, I think, therefore I am, has no relation with I think. I am, therefore I am. *Sum ergo sum*: I am, therefore I am.

But this amness can be felt only when the mind is completely unclouded, when all thoughts have disappeared.

These moments come to you also, even without meditation, but they are very, very atomic and you miss. Between two thoughts there is always an interval – very small. Between two words there is an interval – very small. In that interval you are and yet you cannot say "I am." Being is, but the ego is not.

Meditation is an experience of pure being, without thoughts. The ego can disappear only that way, otherwise not.

So don't try other ways, otherwise it will go on following you. It can become subtle. It can become very pious. There are very many pious egoists: religious people, monks, popes; very pious people, but very egoistic.

The only way that can lead you beyond the ego is the way of meditation. There is nothing else.

The last question:

Osho,
What will happen if the Eastern mind meets with the Western mind?

The greatest thing that can happen, the greatest synthesis that is possible.

The Western mind is the male mind. The Eastern mind is the female mind. The Western mind is the active mind: too restless, too active; almost aggressive, aggressively active. The Eastern mind is passive, relaxed – almost lazy.

You can see the difference. The East is lazy and the West is constantly running for nothing. The question is not where you are going; the only question in the West is how fast you are going. Don't ask where; that is not the point. Don't waste time. Go fast.

In the East, nothing seems to move; everything seems as if there is no movement, time has stopped. The Western mind lives with time, is very time-conscious. The Eastern mind is relaxed in eternity.

There are benefits to both and there are dangers, harmful effects to both. If you are too active you will become tense; you will get ulcers. Life will be just a constant running, reaching nowhere. You will produce many things, your markets will be full of things, your life will have a better standard. Economically, medically, scientifically, technologically, you will be far more developed. That's good.

But then there are the harmful effects. Inside, you will be very empty. The supermarket will be full, but inside will be totally empty.

The outside will become richer and richer and inside will become poorer and poorer. The standard of living will go higher, but by and by life will disappear from your hands. You won't be able to say why you are living.

You will live comfortably, conveniently. You will live comfortably, you will die comfortably, but you will not live at all – because the interior will be empty. And one has to live from the innermost core of his being. The real richness comes from the innermost core. Things are good, but not good enough. They are needed – but man cannot live by bread alone.

In the East, people are relaxed; so much so that they are almost lazy. It is not good to say "relaxed." They are lazy. Of course, in that laziness they can have glimpses of their inner being more clearly. They have nowhere to go, so they go on diving deep within their own beings. All their movement has become inward. Their inner core is richer, but their outward life is so poor and ugly; horrible, nauseating. They are beggars.

If the Eastern mind and the Western mind meet, that will be the greatest synthesis of the male and the female mind, of the passive and the active mind. And there will arise a balance, and for the first time humanity will be born – a global humanity, neither Eastern nor Western. It will be simply humanity – whole, total. A Western man is half, an Eastern man is also half.

I have heard about one man...

He was an Indian, but he lived almost his whole life in Germany. He died, and of course, as all Indians expect, he expected to go to heaven. But as it almost always happens, he went to hell.

He was very worried. He went to the officer in charge. He said, "There must have been some mistake. I am an Indian. I should go to heaven. I am not a German. I was just living in Germany."

The officer in charge took pity on him and he said, "I can understand your difficulty, but now only one thing can be done. That too is not regular, but for you I will make a concession. You can choose either the Indian hell or the German hell."

"But what is the difference?" the man asked.

"In the German hell," explained the officer in charge, "you spend half your time eating all the food you want, listening to music and disporting yourself with girls. In the other half of the time you are pinioned to the wall and beaten mercilessly. Your nails and teeth are pulled out and boiling oil is poured over you."

"And in the Indian hell?"

"In the Indian hell you spend half your time eating all the food you want, listening to music and disporting yourself with girls. In the other half of the time you are pinioned to the wall and beaten mercilessly. Your nails and teeth are pulled out and boiling oil is poured over you."

"But there is no difference."

"There is, in some of the details. In the German hell you have German food, German music and German girls, whereas in the Indian hell you have Indian food, Indian music and Indian girls. But both nationalities are first class in this respect. Certainly, as for the more painful part," said the officer in charge, "the tortures in the German hell are conducted in the usual German fashion, whereas..."

The man suddenly jumped and said, "I will take the Indian."

The Indians are so lazy that there cannot be much discipline in their hell. There will be chaos. They cannot do anything in a planned way. But, of course, in a German hell things are done in a German way.

The Eastern mind, because of the interior journey, has become by and by completely oblivious to the outside world. Much is lost that way. Much is gained, much is lost. One becomes more attuned to his inner being, but then poverty, illness, disease, chaos outside.

You can close your eyes and enjoy yourself, but open your eyes in India and everywhere it is horrible. It is impossible to tolerate it, to bear it. That's why Indians have learned the trick of closing their eyes and meditating. With open eyes you cannot meditate. It is so ugly all around that it will not be possible to meditate.

In the West, everything is beautiful on the outside – the world has attained much through technology – but that too is one-sided. And people have completely forgotten how to go in. They have forgotten how to close their eyes.

Both are incomplete. And to me, the only possibility for the new man is a great synthesis between the East and the West. And that's what I am trying here in Pune.

I am neither an Eastern man nor a Western man. I don't belong to any country, to any nation, to any religion, because if you belong to any country you cannot belong to all, and if you belong to any religion, all religions cannot be yours. I don't belong to any. I have no roots in any country, in any religion, in any partial humanity.

The whole effort here is to create a situation in which the division between the East and the West drops. And that is the same division between man and woman – on a different level, but the same division – between yin and yang: the same division between the active and the passive, the same division between the positive and the negative.

If it can be dropped – and it can be dropped – I have dropped it, you can drop it. Then suddenly you will see within you a new light arising which is neither of the East nor of the West. You will see within yourself the birth of a new man to whom the whole belongs and who belongs to the whole.

Enough for today.

CHAPTER 7

the infinite journey

The master Foso Hoyen said: They say that Buddha uttered five thousand and forty-eight separate truths during his lifetime. They include the truth of emptiness and the truth of being. They include the truth of sudden enlightenment and the truth of gradual enlightenment. Are not all these yea-sayings?

But on the other hand, Yoka, in the Song of Enlightenment says there are no beings and no Buddhas; sages are sea-bubbles; and great minds are only flickerings of lightning. Are not all these nay-sayings?

Oh my disciples, if you say yea, you deny Yoka; and if you say nay, you contradict Buddha. If Buddha were here with you, how would he solve this problem?

If we knew where we stand, we would question Buddha every morning, and greet him every night. But as we don't know where we stand, I will let you into a secret: when I say this is so, perhaps it is not a yea-saying. When I say this is not so, perhaps it is not a nay-saying. Turn to the East and see the holy Western Land; face South to see the Northern Star.

Nirvana, Tao or truth, is an existential experience. One has to be it to know it. One has to dissolve into it to be it. Even to call it an experience is not exactly right, because it is more like experiencing than like an experience.

The word *experience* gives the feeling that the thing is finished, completed. It is never completed, never finished. It is a process – a dynamic process – which goes on moving. The very movement is its life; it never comes to an end.

The goal is in the journey. Except for the journey there is no goal. The journey is the goal. That's why even to call it an experience is to call it wrongly. It is an experiencing. It is never finished. You enter into it but you never come out of it. By the time you can come out of it, you are no more. It is a point of no return.

Experience exists between the experiencer and the experienced. But in the experience of truth – or call it godliness, or whatsoever you like – the experiencer is dissolved, the experienced is dissolved. There remains only a dynamic process of experiencing. It is a river without banks. The duality is not there. There exists no division.

So how to express it? – because all expressions will be limitations, all limitations are falsifications. If you say "God is," you falsify. If you say "God is not," again you falsify from the other end. When you say "God is," you have uttered an untruth.

Let me explain it to you. We can say "The house is," we can say "The tree is," we can say "The man is," because one day the tree will not be, one day the tree was not; one day the house will not be, one day the house was not. Between two nothings, there is just a lightning of existence.

We can say about the house "It is," but we cannot say "God is." In the same sense, the word will become a falsification – because God has always been there, is there, will be there. So in the same sense as we say "The house is," we cannot say "God is." "God is" makes God also a thing – and it is not a thing. God is all things together – all things that have ever been, and all things that will ever be there. God is the totality of past, present and future.

So how to say "God is"? In fact, the sentence "God is" is a tautology, a repetition – as if you are saying "*Isness* is." *God* means isness – the isness of all that is.

The isness of the house is God, the isness of the tree is God, the isness of man is God.

You cannot say "God is" because then God will also be one of the million things; he will not be the totality. You cannot say "God is." It is a falsification.

You cannot say "God is not," because the totality is. How can you deny it? Even if you say it is an illusion, the illusion is. Even if you say it is a dream, the dream is, the dreamer is, the dreamed is. You cannot simply say "God is not." You are, and the person to whom you are saying "God is not," is – the *isness* cannot be denied.

So what to do? How to express God? How to express nirvana? How to express Tao or the truth? They cannot be expressed. They can be understood, they can be indicated, but they cannot be expressed.

Expression is very limited and the truth is infinite. The infinite cannot be put into words. You can force the infinite into words but then it is no longer infinite; that is the falsification. All that is beautiful, all that is lovely, all that is good and true, remains unexpressed.

Lao Tzu has said, "Truth cannot be expressed. The moment you express it, it is no longer truth." This is one of the most fundamental things to be understood. Truth can be shown, but cannot be said. You can show truth – a buddha is an arrow, showing the truth, but he is not saying it. And whatsoever he says is a falsification.

Zen monks say that Buddha uttered infinite lies – because whatsoever is uttered becomes a lie. It is not a question of what it is – the moment you utter it, it becomes a lie. The utterance is very finite, and the uttered is infinite.

Have you watched? If you have fallen in love with a man or a woman and you say "I love you," suddenly you feel the impotence of language. "I love you" does not carry much. It looks absurd to say; it looks as if you have betrayed your inner feeling. Real lovers never say "I love you." They may do many things to show their love, but they will never say "I love you," because to say it is to corrupt it. It is vaster than the word *love*.

Whenever you say to somebody "I love you," you will feel a little guilty. If you don't love them there is no problem; then you can go on saying it. Then these are clichés, then, they don't mean much. Then you can go on playing with words. But if you really love, then your heart will beat faster when you say "I love you," and you will feel a little embarrassed. It is something which cannot be said.

Yes, through your eyes you can show it, through your touch you can show it, through a thousand and one things you can indicate toward it, but how can you say it? Language is not capable of it.

If you cannot say love, how can you say prayer? Prayer is falling in love with the whole. It is the greatest love there is. How can you say prayer?

A really religious person sits silently in his prayerfulness. And those who go on talking to God, saying things to God, don't know what prayer is. They are repeating clichés. They are repeating words.

A real prayerfulness is bound to be silent. One remains mystified. One is overpowered by the infinite. One wonders, one is in a deep awe. But how can you say anything? Words falter, the mind stops, the thinking cannot move. Suddenly you are in a deep emptiness. You are there, but words are not there. You feel your own heart beating, you can feel your own breathing; when you become totally silent you can even feel your own blood circulating – but there is no mind.

Prayerfulness cannot be done. It is not an act; it is nothing like a doing. It is something that you can be in, but you cannot do. You can be prayerful, but you cannot pray. It is a state of mind, not an activity.

God, nirvana, Tao, truth: just meaningless sounds; indicative, pointing toward the infinite, toward the beyond – fingers pointing to the moon.

But fingers are not the moon. If I show you the moon with my finger, don't catch hold of my finger – it has nothing to do with the moon. Don't be attached to my finger, otherwise you will miss the moon. The finger has to be forgotten. You have to move away from the finger to see the moon.

So whatsoever a buddha has said has to be forgotten. Scriptures have to be dropped – they are fingers pointing to the moon. But you become a Christian, you become a Hindu, you become a Buddhist – there you miss. Suddenly you are caught by empty words, verbiage, rubbish, and the more you are caught in the verbiage, the further away you are from truth.

Truth is an experiencing, it is not an intellectual effort. It has nothing to do with intellect. Your intelligence burns bright. Yes, your intelligence has a clarity, but the mirror is completely clean of words.

Once Goethe was asked, "What is the meaning, the secret, of life?"

He replied, "That which the plant does unconsciously, do consciously – that is to say, grow."

The meaning of life is in growth. The meaning of nirvana is in your growth. The meaning of truth is in your growth; grow. There is no end to this growth. You go on growing, you go on growing. The journey is infinite. There never comes a goal. Many goals come and go, many peaks of experience come and go, but still the infinite waits and it goes on waiting. You cannot exhaust it.

That is the trouble with language: language is exhaustive. When I say to you "I love you," I have said everything, exhausted – but love goes on. Love is a growth, an alive process. "I love you" is dead language. Something has died in the words. Words are like corpses.

A buddha, one who is enlightened, helps you to grow. If he talks, he talks only to help you to drop all talking. If he uses words, he uses them only to help you to become wordless. If he talks, he talks only to indicate toward silence.

So always remember, when a buddha says anything, the container is not important at all, but the content. The word is the container and the meaning is the content. But that meaning can come to you only when you grow. Unless you taste something of buddhahood, you will not understand.

So it is not a question of knowledge; it is a question of understanding. Knowledge you can go on gathering; you need not grow. You can go on stuffing yourself with knowledge and deep down inside you remain the same – no growth happens, no transformation happens.

In fact, all the knowledge that you gather hinders growth. One becomes too burdened by what one knows. The more you know, the less the possibility of knowing. Then, your capacity to know is too burdened. Then, your capacity to know is too clouded.

Religion is not a process of learning. In fact, it is just the contrary – a process of unlearning. Whatsoever you know has to be dropped, unlearned again, so that you can become a child once more, so that you can be reborn. And this second birth is the real birth. The first birth is not the real birth; it is only an opportunity for the second birth, that's all. If the second birth happens, you used your first birth. If the second never happens, then the opportunity was lost.

The first birth is only the birth of the body and the mind. The second birth is the birth of your spirit, of your soul. And unless you know something of the innermost eternal core of your being, you have not known anything.

But humanity loves knowledge, information. It is very ego-satisfying. Whenever you can say that you know, whenever you can give some advice to somebody else, you feel very high. Not knowing who you are, not knowing where you are, you go on playing the role of a teacher.

Just look around, everybody is giving advice to everybody else. Of course nobody takes it – and it is good that nobody takes it otherwise the world would be in much more trouble. It is already in much trouble. It is good that nobody takes your advice, your advice is worthless – in trouble, in crisis, you will not listen to your own advice. It is just dead junk. It has nothing to do with your inner growth.

Real knowing is part of growth: grow. Each moment go on growing, expanding, exploding. Each moment should be a new birth.

Why is it not so? Because you go on carrying the past with you. If you want each moment to be a new birth, you also have to die each moment to the past. Die to the past so that you can be reborn herenow.

All knowledge is of the past. Mind is always of the past. Consciousness is always of the present. A buddha helps you to become more conscious; he does not help you to become more knowledgeable.

I have heard an anecdote:

A worried fellow entered the psychiatrist's office wearing love-beads, bell-bottom pants, shoulder-length hair, and smoking a joint.

The psychiatrist said, "You claim you are not a hippie. Then how do you explain the clothes, the hair and the pot?"

"Doctor," sighed the chap, "that's what I'm here to find out."

Nobody knows why you are the way you are. Nobody knows who you are. Nobody knows why you have landed in the state of mind in which you have landed. Completely unaware, you go on drifting. You go on imitating others because you don't know who you are. The only way to get an identity, an image, is to imitate others.

I was reading Alan Watts' autobiography. He relates one incident from his childhood. When he was a child, there was a boy named Peter living in the same street, and he appreciated that boy very much. That boy was a sort of hero to Alan Watts. Sometimes he would come home so impressed by his hero Peter, that he would start behaving like him and his mother would say, "Alan, remember, you are Alan, not Peter."

From the very childhood, everybody is trying to be somebody else, because you don't know who you are and it is very difficult to live without an identity. It is very difficult to live without knowing who you are. There are only two possibilities. Either you go in, which is a tremendous adventure and needs tremendous courage, or you imitate others – a bit from somebody and a bit from somebody else – and you become a patchwork.

Look at yourself and you can find you have become a patchwork. Whenever you say something, inside just watch where it is coming from: your mother, your father, your brother, the friend, the teacher, the priest – from where has this bit come? And go on discarding all that has come from others.

A deep cleansing is needed for growth, because you cannot imitate growth. Growth has to happen to you; you cannot go on imitating. Drop all imitation, and then by and by you will have a clarity, by and by you will have a ground to stand on. You will know who you are.

In the beginning it remains vague, confused, chaotic, but if you are courageous, by and by things settle and for the first time you become aware of your own being. And each being is unique. Never has there been anybody else like you, and there never will be again. Existence has staked much on you. It expects much from you. You are a novel experiment. Don't miss the opportunity.

But people go on imitating and people go on collecting knowledge, and people go on creating a false identity just to cling to so they don't feel alone, so they don't feel lost. If you really want to get home, first you will have to get lost. If you really want to know something, first you will have to drop all knowledge. If you really want to be yourself – and who does not want to be? – you will have to stop imitating.

Enough is enough. You have imitated enough and wasted much opportunity. But it is never too late. Drop it; cleanse your mirror of being.

In the beginning you will be afraid, because it will feel empty. But emptiness has a freshness about it. Emptiness has a beauty about it. Emptiness is virgin, and everything comes out of that virgin emptiness. That womb of emptiness creates everything.

Even if you start working on your inner growth you are always divided – in a certain way split, schizophrenic. A part of you goes on clinging to the outside image, which is cheap. One part goes on working inside, but this dual activity, which is contradictory, dissipates energy.

Take a decision. If you really want to grow, then unburden yourself of all that has come to you from others. They may have given it in deep love; that is not the point. They may have given it to you because they wanted to help you; that too is not the point. Feel grateful to them, but keep yourself unburdened from all the advice given to you, from all the knowledge thrown at you, from all the conditionings that the society has forced you to be in.

Unconditioning is needed. That's what I mean when I say unlearning. Once the mind is unconditioned, things again become pure; the stream of consciousness again flows; it is no longer blocked. You are no longer frozen. The complexes by and by melt. You become a wild energy.

Remember, existence is wild. Existence is not yet civilized, and never will be. Once existence is civilized, it will be dead. Existence is wild, raw energy, with tremendous potentiality and no limitations. If you want to move in step with existence, you will also have to be like it, a little bit at least – a little wild. A sheer delight in energy is needed. Not knowledge, not character, but a sheer delight in energy, a sheer delight of being. Just a celebration that "I am here," just the happiness that "I can breathe," that "I can see," that "I can hear," that "I can dance," that "I can love," just a sheer delight and a gratitude arises in you.

That gratitude is the quality of a religious man, and in that gratitude, by and by one starts tasting what nirvana is.

Nirvana is cessation of the ego – and when the ego ceases, godliness enters; when the host is no longer there, then the guest comes.

Be more poetic about life and less philosophical. Allow poetry to enter in you and stop philosophizing. All philosophy is borrowed. Poetry need not be borrowed. Every child is born as a poet. Every child is a poet. To be a poet is natural, it is a gift of nature.

I was reading a few lines of Rainer Maria Rilke:

> O tell us poet, what do you do?
> – I praise.
> But those dark, deadly, devastating ways,
> how do you bear them, suffer them?
> – I praise.
> And then the Nameless, beyond guess or gaze,
> how do you call it, conjure it?
> – I praise.

And whence your right, in every kind of maze,
in every mask, to remain true?
– I praise.
And that the mildest and the wildest ways
know you like star and storm?
– Because I praise.

This is what I mean when I say a sheer delight in energy. Then you simply start praising. Not that there is a God, but a praise arises in you, and because of that praise, everything becomes holy, sacred.

People come to me and they tell me that if I can convince them that there is a God then they will pray, and I tell them, "If you pray, you will be convinced that there is God." God is a by-product. God is not a primary experience, but a secondary experience. The basic thing is the capacity to be prayerful and praise and to celebrate. Forget all about God – just feel happy. A tremendous opportunity has been given to you for no reason at all. You are alive. You have not earned it. You have not done anything to get it. It has been showered on you.

Suddenly one day you are alive. Loving, moving, breathing, and all the beauties and the experiences of life are available to you. The sun rises in the morning, the moon comes in the night, and the whole expanse of sky fills with the stars.

Praise. Be prayerful. Feel grateful. The gift is so valuable that you cannot imagine how it can be earned. It is beyond valuation. Can you think, can you imagine something that you can do which will give you more life? How will you do it? What will you do? You cannot create even a single moment of life. It is a gift.

When one starts praising, things become more and more beautiful. Trees become greener, flowers bloom as they had never bloomed before, because you were blind and you could not see. And birds sing as they have never sung before. Not that they were not singing, but you were deaf. Suddenly, your sensations are open; suddenly, your senses have become sensitive, receptive – and the whole life becomes a celebration.

Be a poet, and then there is the possibility to know what is. Godliness is known by the poetic intelligence within you. Nirvana is attained by the poetic possibility, potentiality within you. It has nothing to do with philosophy. Philosophy always goes on denying. It always goes on saying "no." Logic is no-saying. Life is bridged by a deep yes-saying. You say "no"– the bridge is broken.

The Zen story:

The master Foso Hoyen said: They say that Buddha uttered five
thousand and forty-eight separate truths during his lifetime.

This is just a way of saying that he uttered millions of truths. The
truth is one, but a buddha goes on saying it in different ways because
it cannot be said. So he goes on devising new ways to say it again.
Again he fails, again he tries, again he fails. The failure is absolutely
certain, but the compassion of a buddha goes on. He would like to
tell it to you, he would like to share it with you. He has attained and
you are stumbling in the dark. He would like to call you to the path.

His compassion says, "Say. Go to the rooftops and shriek so that
all those who are stumbling in the dark can hear." And he tries, every
moment of his life he tries – again and again he fails, because truth
cannot be said.

That's why five thousand and forty-eight times, five thousand
and forty-eight truths he uttered. This number is a symbolic number,
it shows infinity. It shows that millions of times he uttered, but still the
truth remains unuttered. He devised many ways. He said it from one
side, felt that it had not been communicated, so he said it from the
opposite side – maybe it could be communicated that way – failed
from there, then he found another side.

Zen Buddhists say that after Buddha became enlightened he did
not utter a single word, and they also say that he has said five thousand and forty-eight truths. What do they mean? They mean that he
tried hard, but he could not say it. He spoke, but the truth cannot be
said and could not be said. He tried hard and missed, again and
again, because the very nature of truth is such that it is inexpressible.

The master Foso Hoyen said: They say that Buddha uttered five
thousand and forty-eight separate truths during his lifetime. One thing
will be of great value to understand: truth cannot be said, but at the
same time, you cannot hide it. You cannot say it, but you cannot hide it.
It tries to assert itself in millions of ways. The very experience is such
that it wants to be shared, and it is also such that it cannot be shared.

Just a few days ago, Anupama asked a question, saying that
when she goes deep in meditation something happens to her but she
cannot share it with her lover, so she feels a little guilty. Lovers want
to share everything, whatsoever they have. Love is an unconditional

sharing. So she wants to share it, but feels it is impossible to share. Guilt arises – one feels as if one is hiding something.

But the very nature of truth is such that if you try to express it, you cannot express. The glimpse comes to you when there are no words, when the mind stops functioning – then comes the glimpse. And by the time words have come back to the mind, the glimpse is gone. They never meet.

When the glimpse is there, words are not there; the mind is not there to recognize, to formulate. When the mind comes back, the glimpse is gone. From one door you enter; the truth leaves the house from another door. You never meet.

Truth leaves the moment the mind enters, but still the mind can feel the fragrance. Something has happened, something tremendously valuable has happened. Somebody has been in the house. You can feel, somebody has passed. The room has a different quality to it now. Your whole being is throbbing with some experience. Something has happened, a light in the darkness, but the mind cannot encapsulate what has happened. It can feel a little bit – something certainly has happened, the being is not the same, the house has changed. But still, what has happened remains incomprehensible to the mind.

The mind would like to share it with all those you love. With all those you feel for, you would like to share, but if you try, you will fail.

So these two things are part of the nature of the experience itself. First, you would like to share, you will have a tremendous urge to share, and then you will fail – sharing is not possible. And the second thing: still you cannot hide it. It will show from your eyes, from the way you walk, from the way you talk, from the way you remain silent. It will show. Have you watched it?

One day a man came to me and he said, "I am very stupid. Can silence help me?"

I told him, "Try. At least this is good, that you accept that you are stupid. This is the beginning of wisdom."

But if a man is stupid and he becomes silent, the silence will have something of the stupidity. A stupid man who is silent will still be a stupid man. The silence of one who is enlightened and the silence of one who is stupid are going to be totally different. The stupid man's silence will be stupid. His talk will be stupid, his silence will also be stupid. The silence of a buddha will have a light, a flavor, a fragrance. His talk will also have the same quality.

It is not a question of being silent or talking. It is a question of your being – the very quality.

When you have touched something of the no-mind, it will start expressing itself in many ways. Through the mind it will be difficult to express, but through your totality it will be expressed. You will see in a different way. If somebody looks into your eyes, your eyes will become silent pools of energy. If somebody touches your hand or your body, he will feel a certain coolness, tranquility. Something has happened inside. You are carrying something in your womb.

Have you seen a woman when she is walking with a child in her womb? She walks differently. She carries something within her being.

Whenever an experience of truth – even a glimpse, a satori – has happened, you walk differently. You are no longer the same. You cannot hide it. You cannot express it and you cannot hide it.

...five thousand and forty-eight separate truths. They include the truth of emptiness and the truth of being. They include the truth of sudden enlightenment and the truth of gradual enlightenment.

Very paradoxical. Sometimes Buddha says that your innermost being is totally empty, and sometimes he says your innermost being is a positive being, full of bliss, peace, tranquility. What is true?

You can have a glass full of water and then you can empty it, you can throw the water out. The glass is empty now in a way, but still full in another way. The water has been emptied out, but now air has entered into the glass. The glass is still not empty. You can say it is empty of water, but you cannot say it is empty. It is full of air.

You can empty your room of all furniture, and then you will say, "This room is empty." But have you watched? Now the room is full of room, space, full of emptiness. Of course, the furniture is removed. The furniture was a barrier against the room existing in its totality. Now the room is simply a room – *room* means space. Now it is a space full of space. You can move more easily, you can be more easily in it. Now nothing hinders the way.

Sometimes Buddha says that the innermost being is empty and sometimes he says that the innermost being is absolute being: empty of the mind and full of no-mind; empty of thoughts, full of no-thoughts, intervals, gaps – full of room.

If you can enter a man of meditation, you will find in him infinite space and no barriers. If you can enter in me, you will not find any barrier anywhere. You can go on and on and on. The furniture has been removed. I am totally empty in a way, in a sense, and totally full in another way. I am empty of myself, but full of godliness. *Godliness* means room. *Godliness* means space.

You can be emptied of intellect and then you are full of intelligence. You can be emptied of knowledge – then you are full of understanding. Both are true together.

They include the truth of sudden enlightenment and the truth of gradual enlightenment. Sometimes Buddha says you proceed gradually, by and by in steps, and sometimes he says that enlightenment is sudden – it cannot be divided into steps, it is more like a jump than like going on a staircase.

Both are true. Try to see. This is where the poetry of religion becomes something beyond logic. For logic this is difficult. The logic will say either–or, and poetry says both–and. The logic always gives you a choice – either this or that. Either say the innermost being is empty or say it is full of being. It gives you alternatives. But the poetry of being says and–both – it is empty of something *and* full of something.

You heat water; gradually it becomes hotter and hotter. Gradually it becomes hotter and hotter; of course, step by step: ninety degrees, ninety-one degrees, ninety-two degrees, ninety-nine degrees. Then it comes to the point of one hundred degrees – the evaporating point. Then suddenly a jump and the water disappears into vapor, it evaporates.

Now, both things are happening. If you ask me, "Is evaporation a sudden jump?" I will say, "Yes, it is a sudden jump," because exactly at one hundred degrees the water takes a jump. The form changes; it is transfigured. It is no longer water; it becomes vapor. And it happens in a sudden jump.

The process of being heated is gradual. Of course, the water is water at ninety degrees, at eighty degrees. Even at ninety-nine degrees it is still water – hot, getting closer and closer to one hundred degrees. You can stop it at ninety-nine degrees. It will never evaporate, it will cool down again. Turn the fire off. The water will remain water. The sudden jump never happened, but it was getting ready. But you cannot help water to suddenly jump from ninety degrees and become vapor. That's not possible.

Gradual and sudden are not contradictions. There is no question of choosing between them. Both are needed in their own ways. Because of such contradictions, a logical mind thinks that religious people are mad. A logical mind cannot make any sense out of these things. It goes on saying that either this is possible or that is possible; both are not possible.

For example, Zen masters say that Buddha never uttered a single word, and at the same time they go on saying that he uttered five thousand and forty-eight truths. Which is true? Both are true. He uttered millions of words and still he could not utter a single word of truth.

The Master Foso Hoyen said...Are not all these yea-sayings?
But on the other hand, Yoka...

another enlightened master

...in the Song of Enlightenment says there are no beings and no
Buddhas; sages are sea-bubbles; and great minds are only
flickerings of lightning. Are not all these nay-sayings?

Now, Yoka is a follower of Buddha, a disciple of Buddha, a lover of Buddha. Still he says that *...there are no beings and no Buddhas*; and *sages are sea-bubbles...*

This Yoka was worshipping every morning, every evening, bowing down at the stone Buddha of his temple. And at the same time singing in his *Song of Enlightenment* that *...sages are sea-bubbles...*

What does it mean? What does he mean? If sages are sea-bubbles then stop praising Buddha, praying to Buddha, touching his feet, bowing down – stop all this nonsense.

But if you ask Yoka, he will say, "I have learned this – that sages are sea-bubbles and Buddhas don't exist – from this man Gautam Buddha, so I have to pay my respects. This understanding has come to me through him. He indicated the path."

Once it happened...

A Zen master was celebrating his master's birthday. The master had died. Somebody asked him, "Why are you celebrating? – Because as far as I know, the master denied you. He never accepted you as his disciple. You tried long, that I know. You tried again and again, that I know, but every time you were refused. You were never initiated by him. So why are you celebrating his birthday? Traditionally it is to be celebrated only by the accepted disciples."

The master laughed and he said, "Precisely because he refused me, I celebrate. Now I can understand his compassion. If he had accepted me, I may have become just an imitator. Because he threw me into myself continuously, by and by I stood on my own feet. By and by I dropped the desperate search to cling to somebody else. He helped me. He was my master. In his rejection he accepted me."

This is illogical. But still, if you look through the eyes of a poet, through the eyes of a lover, you can understand it. Intellectually it will be difficult, but if you are intelligent it is a simple fact.

Sometimes, to deny is to give. Sometimes, to reject is to accept. Sometimes, not to help is the only way to help.

But on the other hand, Yoka, in the Song of Enlightenment says there are no beings and no Buddhas; sages are sea-bubbles; and great minds are only flickerings of lightning. Are not all these nay-sayings? The master is telling his audience that Buddha says something which looks like a yes-saying; and then his disciple Yoka, says something which looks absolutely negative, a nay-saying...

Oh my disciples, if you say yea, you deny Yoka; if you say nay, you contradict Buddha. If Buddha were here with you, how would he solve this problem?
If we knew where we stand, we would question Buddha every morning, and greet him every night.

Look at the contradiction: *...we would question Buddha every morning and greet him every night.* That is the quality of a real inquirer. He inquires with deep love, reverence. He does not inquire out of his knowledge, he inquires out of his living problems. The very crisis of life creates his inquiry. He is not bogus. He does not ask a question because he has read a book and the question has arisen. He asks because his life has created a problem.

When he asks he has nothing inside him – no prejudice, no concept. He asks with the purity of the heart, like an innocent child. He does not ask to be convinced about something, he is already convinced. He does not ask in order to argue, to debate, to discuss. He asks to know. He asks to understand.

If we knew where we stand... The whole point is, if you know where to stand, if you have come to an unwavering state of your mind, only then is right questioning possible. If you are trembling inside, if you are wavering inside, then you cannot ask the right question. The right question comes only to a mind which has come to a state of unwavering, a certain tranquility. Out of that silence, right questioning arises.

One day I was reading about a man who went to his doctor. The doctor examined his hands; they were trembling. The doctor said, "My God! You are drinking too much! Your whole blood system has been poisoned. Almost alcohol is running in your veins instead of blood. You are drinking too much."

The man said, "No, I can hardly drink, because almost the whole thing is spilt when I take hold of the glass – almost the whole thing is spilt. I can hardly drink."

If you are wavering inside, the whole intelligence is spilt. Intelligence becomes a reservoir if you are unwavering.

Always remember not to cooperate with the inner wavering, not to help it. Don't give it your energy. Remain indifferent to it – a little aloof, far away – and by and by you will see that the wavering becomes less and less and less. And if you remain indifferent and don't get involved and identified with it, a day comes when suddenly you are in a moment of total stillness. Then you stand on the right ground. Then you stand in your being. Then for the first time you become capable of standing.

If we knew where we stand, we would question Buddha every morning, and greet him every night. Morning and night are symbolic. The morning means the beginning of activity. When the mind is active, we will ask Buddha every morning. The night means inactivity, passivity, receptivity. And when the mind is passive, non-active, we will greet Buddha.

Active and passive... If your mind is active and you are standing unwavering, you can ask a right question which can be helpful. And if your mind is unwavering, soon you will see the inactive phase coming, where you will greet and praise Buddha, where you will bow down and respect the man who has helped you to come out of a crisis.

But as we don't know where we stand, I will let you into a secret: when I say this is so, perhaps it is not a yea-saying. When I say this is not so, perhaps it is not a nay-saying.

Remember, all yea-sayings are not yea-sayings. If your mind is negative, your yea-saying will also be negative. And all nay-sayings are not negative. If your mind is positive, your nay-saying will also eventually turn to be positive.

Jesus tells a story:

A father asked his elder son to go to the garden and work there. The son said, "Yes father, I will go," but he never went. His yes-saying was not exactly yes-saying. He was cunning. He was false, inauthentic.

The father asked his younger son. He said, "No, I don't have any time and I will not go," but then he thought over it and went. His no-saying was not a no-saying.

The real thing is what is inside you, not what you say. Buddha says "There is no God," but you cannot find more divine a person anywhere else. H. G. Wells has written that Gautam Buddha is the most godless and the most godlike man of human history. He says there is no God – but don't think this is a nay-saying.

Look at Buddha. He is so positively one with existence that to say "There is God" will be wrong. That will create a division. He says there is no God. Don't be bothered by his words. Look at him, watch him, and you will see God walking on earth. In your questioning whether there is God, you have already missed. You should have watched. Godliness was before you.

Buddha goes on saying, "There is no God," and he never means it. He simply shatters your mind, hammers your mind. He is simply saying no to your prejudice, not to godliness.

One day it happened, a man came in the morning and Buddha said, "There is no God." And another man came in the afternoon and Buddha said, "Yes there is." And then a third man came in the evening and Buddha kept silent and didn't answer this way or that.

His disciple, Ananda, became very puzzled because he was present the whole time. He said, "I will not be able to sleep tonight unless you explain it to me. What do you mean? To one person you say no, to another you say yes. They asked the same question. And to the third, who has also asked the same question, you kept silent, you didn't answer at all. What do you mean?"

Buddha said, "The first man, to whom I said no, was a theist. He has a concept of God, an ideology about it. I had to shatter that ideology so that he can be freed from his bondage and can become available to truth. I had to say no. To help him to know, I had to say no to his ideology that God exists – otherwise he would remain confined within words.

"The man to whom I said, 'Yes, there is God,' is an atheist. He has a belief that there is no God. I had to shatter him. Everybody has to be brought out of his belief system so that experience becomes possible.

"To the third person, who is neither, who is a true seeker with no prejudice, I kept quiet. I told him, 'Be silent. These questions are futile, meaningless. Just be silent and you will know.' And he understood, and he bowed down and went away with deep understanding."

So all yea-sayings are not yea-sayings. All nay-sayings are not nay-sayings.

Let me tell you an anecdote:

Over a glass of beer, Johnson said to Smith, "My psychiatrist keeps talking about something he calls ambivalence, and I'm darned if I can understand it."

"No problem," said Smith. "To be ambivalent is to feel contradictory emotions – to be both pleased and displeased with something, to both love and hate someone."

"That's what he says too," said Johnson, "but I just don't see how you can experience two contradictory emotions simultaneously."

"Here is an example then. Suppose you had just bought a brand-new Cadillac for ten thousand dollars, and suppose the very first day you owned it, its brakes failed and it went over a cliff a mile high. How would you feel?"

"I would feel terrible."

"But suppose your mother-in-law was the only one in the car at the time. Then?"

Your yes and your no do not mean much; they are ambivalent. Sometimes when you want to say no, you say yes just to hide the no.

Sometimes when you want to say yes, you don't say yes, you say no, just to show your ego, your strength, your power. No gives a certain power. Whenever you say no, you feel powerful. Whenever you say yes, you feel a little humiliated.

Watch; your yes may be hiding a no, your no may be hiding a yes. When you cry and weep, it is not necessary that you are not smiling within, because the reverse happens every day – you smile, and you are simply hiding your tears.

But if you watch people and don't get caught in their words, you will find immediately what is happening. The truth cannot be hidden. If somebody is smiling just to hide his tears, don't listen to his smile. Just watch him, and immediately you will see – behind the smile there are tears ready to come out. Whenever somebody says no, just watch the person. Watch the whole person. There must be indications which will show that deep down he is saying yes.

Always listen to the depth and don't be worried what people say. The world can become very, very beautiful, and life can become really a celebration if you stop listening to people's words and you start listening to people's hearts. Then you will not be deceived.

It happened...

A woman had died, and the funeral cortège was being set up for the wife of the dour Sandy MacTavish, who was dressed somberly in the appropriate black.

The funeral director said to him in a respectful whisper, "And you will be sitting in the lead car with your mother-in-law."

Sandy frowned, "With my mother-in-law?"

"Yes, of course."

"Is that necessary?"

"It is essential. The bereaved husband and the bereaved mother – the two closest survivors together."

Sandy turned to look at the large and sobbing figure of his mother-in-law and said, "Well, all right then, but I tell you right now that this is going to spoil the pleasure of the occasion."

...dressed in somber black appropriate for the occasion – but deep down happy that the wife has died.

Just watch people, and you will be able to see that their yes does not mean yes and their no does not mean no. People are contradictory.

The same also happens to a buddha, for different reasons. You are ambiguous; that's why your statements do not mean what they tend to show. A buddha is contradictory because he is trying to bring a truth into language which comprehends both the extremes in it.

You are contradictory because your inner being is split. A buddha is contradictory not because his inner being is split – his inner being has become one – but because he is trying to bring a truth which is beyond duality into language. He has to contradict.

In the Upanishads they say: "God is near, nearer than the nearest, and farther than the farthest," because it is both – the near and the far. It has to be both because it is all. It is both; life and death. It has to be both. It is both; Devil and God. It has to be both.

The English word *devil* is very beautiful. It comes from a root, a Sanskrit root, *deva*. From the same root *deva*, comes *divine*. And from the same root comes *devil*. *Devil* and *divine* come from the same root, from the single word *dev*. The Devil is also divine, and the divine must have something of the Devil in it.

Christianity has cut the duality in two separate, clear-cut parts. The Devil is fighting God and God is fighting the Devil. But in the East we have never split reality because reality cannot be split. The Devil is God and God is the Devil. It is the same energy expressing through opposite polarities.

When a buddha talks, he has to use contradictions.

...when I say this is so, perhaps it is not a yea-saying. When I say this is not so, perhaps it is not a nay-saying. Turn to the East and see the holy Western Land; face South to see the Northern Star.

Paradoxes, but truth can only be expressed through paradoxes. Your inner fullness can only be expressed by emptiness, and your real life is possible only through death. Resurrection happens only after crucifixion. If you really want to be alive, be as if you are dead. If you really want to be intelligent, live as if you are an idiot.

Lao Tzu has said, "The whole world is wise except me. I am an idiot." The word *idiot* is beautiful. It comes from the same root as the word *idiom*. An idiom is a personal style. An idiom means a personal style and an idiot means one who lives his own way; an idiot means one who is doing his own thing and is not worried about the world. One who is not an imitator is an idiot. It has nothing to do with stupidity.

Saint Francis used to call himself an idiot, and Jesus was also known in his country as an idiot. Feodor Dostoevsky has written a book, *The Idiot*. It is worth reading. The book is about a very simple man, very humble, unique. But because he is humble and unique and simple, the crowd thinks he is an idiot.

If you try to live your life in your own way, you will look like an idiot. The crowd will not respect you. It respects only masks, false personalities, not authentic people. If you really want to be intelligent, be like an idiot. And if you want to be an idiot, collect knowledge. Be a pundit and then you will be an idiot.

Try to go deep into these paradoxes. The whole of religion is expressed in the idiom of paradox.

Turn to the East and see the holy Western Land... Because if you want to *...see the holy Western Land...* ordinarily you will turn to the west. Why turn to the east? But this is how it happens in real life. Turn to the opposite polarity.

Have you watched an old clock? The pendulum goes on moving – from right to left, from left to right. When it is going to the left, what is really happening inside the clock? When it is going to the left, it is gathering momentum to go to the right. When it is going to the right, it is already getting ready to go to the left. To go to the right it goes to the left. To go to the left it goes to the right.

In the day you work hard, then in the night you have a deep sleep. Work hard if you want deep sleep. Contradictions. The ordinary logic will say to practice relaxation the whole day if you want a good sleep. Rehearse it. Lie down on the bed, remain on the bed the whole day, because if you practice it the whole day, of course it is going to be better in the night. It is ordinary logic.

That is what is happening in Western countries. Insomnia has become common. And the reason? The reason has nothing to do with sleep, it has something to do with labor. If you don't work hard, you cannot move into sleep. If you don't sleep deeply, the next morning you will not be able to work hard.

Life exists in contradictions. If somebody comes to me and says that he has trouble with sleep, I say to forget about sleep. Run four miles in the morning and four miles in the evening. Sleep is not the problem. You must be relaxing too much; then sleep is not needed.

Always remember that deeper down all contradictions meet and are part of one whole. People come to me and they want to become silent, they want to move into a state of thoughtlessness. I tell them to do hard work, cathartic meditations – Dynamic, Kundalini. Jump, move, shake.

They say, "But we want to be silent. Can't we just sit and be silent just like Buddha?" You can sit, but you will not be silent; inside all turmoil will go fast. Rather, do the opposite – jump, run, jog, dance. Exert yourself, exhaust yourself, and after that the pendulum starts moving to the opposite end. Silence is possible only if you are exhausted; then sit silently, then relaxation happens easily.

Always remember this basic law. Otherwise, if you look at and follow ordinary logic, Aristotelian logic, then you will miss life. Just move to the opposite.

If you want to be really sane, be capable of being insane, be capable of going into craziness. That is what I teach. Be crazy if you really want to be sane. If you try too much to be sane, you are going to be crazy. All too-sane people become crazy. They have to become crazy. They try hard to remain sane – that very effort helps the pendulum to move to the opposite side.

Don't try to be sane and you will be sane. Whenever there is an opportunity to be crazy, relax and go crazy. Don't miss any opportunity. If people are dancing, dance, go crazy. Wherever you can find an opportunity to be crazy, be crazy – and I can guarantee you will never become crazy; you will remain sane. You will have a sanity which cannot be disturbed by anybody, which cannot be disturbed by any circumstance.

Yes, Foso Hoyen is right:

Turn to the East and see the holy Western Land; face South to see the Northern Star.

Enough for today.

CHAPTER 8

collecting seashells

The first question:

Osho,
How can I feel life fresh day by day? Please explain.

Life is fresh but you are stale, and you become stale because you go on carrying the yesterdays. The past functions as a barrier between you and life. Die every moment to the past and then life can be felt and lived as fresh as it is.

Life is never old; each moment it renews itself, rejuvenates itself, reorients itself. It is eternally fresh. But the mind cannot be fresh. The very mechanism of the mind does not allow it to be fresh. It has to be old, it has to be dead.

The moment you know something, it is already past. Knowledge is already dead. A bird sings in the tree. The moment your mind says "beautiful," it is already old. It is no longer in the present, it has already passed. The moment you say to someone "I love you," it is already past. The moment the mind catches anything, it immediately dies.

To be fresh means to be without mind. Listen to the birds without the mind interfering. See the trees without the mind interfering. You will have to learn how to remain without verbalization. This is the root of all disease.

You see a rose and immediately the mind starts spinning: "A beautiful rose, I have never seen such a beautiful rose before." You are no longer seeing this rose now. You have moved into the past. You are comparing with other roses. And when you are comparing with other roses, you have completely forgotten this rose.

Those other roses are just in the memory – past impressions. And the most amazing thing is that when those other roses were alive, you must have been comparing them with some other roses which were dead. Again this amazing thing will happen. Some other day, seeing another rose, you may compare with this rose which you are not seeing at all.

Look at life and don't allow words to interfere. Look without words. Look without thinking – and suddenly everything is fresh, suddenly everything is as new as it can be.

This has to be learned. Every child knows it. It is a capacity which comes with your birth, it is something inborn. But then the society takes over and starts teaching, forces the child to learn. What the society is trying is nothing but creating a pattern of verbalization inside. And by and by, layer upon layer will gather there and the child will miss life.

Psychologists say that up to the age of four the child remains absolutely fresh and absolutely intelligent. Every child is intelligent up to the age of four. There is no stupid child; it doesn't happen. Every healthy child is intelligent, and up to the age of four, a child learns the most. Fifty percent of his whole life's learning is finished by the age of four.

By the age of eight, the child is no longer a child. He has become part of society, he has learned tricks, gimmicks. Now he is no longer a person, he is a mechanism. And by the age of eight, learning stops. Then accumulation continues – he goes on accumulating knowledge – but learning stops, freshness disappears.

Watch small children below the age of four, and you will find them bubbling with fresh energy. Just watch them, look at their response to things, and you will always find them original, open, fresh, unique. Each child is a genius, but the society cannot allow so many geniuses, and the society cannot allow so many open people. They will create chaos.

An original man is a danger. Only rarely does somebody escape from the imprisonment of the society. A little quota of original people the society can tolerate. Somewhere here and there a Buddha, an Einstein, can be tolerated. But a very small quantity of genuine intelligence, and sometimes even that becomes too much. Then a Jesus has to be crucified, a Socrates has to be poisoned.

These people remain children. They remain fresh, they remain young. They remain original. They remain unique and open.

Look! Don't call adults people, they are not. They are machines. Only small children are people. Adults are already dead. Adults have utility. As I have been watching, if some adult comes to me, either he is a doctor or a professor or an engineer, but not a man or a woman. He has some utility, some function in the society. He is not a person anymore.

When small children come, they are simply people. Nobody is a doctor, nobody is an engineer, nobody is a scientist; they are simply people – open-ended, fresh, with no accumulation.

Look into the eyes of children; such infinite silence and yet not dead – vibrant with life. Look at children; so resilient, so flexible, so responsive. As they grow, they start taking a mode, a fixed mode, a fixed structure. Then they function only through that structure.

When somebody comes and says, "I am a doctor," I immediately understand that I cannot meet the person, I can only meet the doctor. The doctor will be in between. When somebody comes and says that he is a professor, then I know well that I can shake hands, but I will not find the hands; they are hidden under the gloves – the gloves of a professor, the gloves of a doctor. The man is not available, he is hiding behind a utility.

What does being a doctor mean? – that he is functioning in a certain way in the society. He is of a certain utility to the society. To become a utility is to become a commodity. To become a utility is to become a thing.

Children cannot be used, they are purposeless hence they are people. If you shake hands with a child, you shake hands with him. There are no gloves, they are nude and naked. But by the age of eight, almost always something closes in. The doors and windows close. And then for your whole life you will go on missing life, and whatsoever you do will be a duty, a drudgery, a drag. One has to do it somehow. It will not be a celebration.

I have heard…

Two friends met on a street. They had not seen each other for a long time. One asked the other, "Who are you working for nowadays?"

"The same company," said the other, "the wife and the six kids."

Even for your wife, for your children, you are not functioning out of love – a duty, a responsibility, a burden. They too are a company you are working for.

You would like to escape, but sanity does not allow you. You would like to escape, but you know, where would you go? You would like to escape, but you have lost the energy to escape. You would like to escape, but now you have become too habituated to the pattern. It would be difficult for you to live without this company. But life is slipping from your hands.

Once it happened...

Two seedy individuals stopped on the street to watch a funeral procession pass. It was done in elaborate style, from the long, gleaming hearse, through the cars packed with flowers, to the impressive line of automobiles following.

One of the individuals said, "It's a rich guy. I've watched funerals like that before. There's a solid mahogany casket, polished so you can see your face in it, with a satin lining and gold carved handles. They put it in a big mausoleum, with stone doors, statues, flowers, praying and singing."

"Wow," said the other, eyes shining, "now that's what I call living."

By and by your life becomes so deathlike that even death looks like living – if it is luxurious, comfortable, costly. Then even death can create a jealousy in you.

Your life is almost insignificant. You have not lived at all. You have learned a few tricks and you go on doing those tricks. And you know you are missing your life, but still you go on clinging with those tricks because those tricks have become your securities; you are afraid to lose them. You are afraid to lose the comfort that comes through dead habits.

You ask me how to live life fresh. Just become a child again – unlearn whatsoever you have learned. Drop verbalization. Listen to these birds with no word arising in you. Suddenly a wave of freshness passes through you; an energy arises in you which is not old.

This bird has never been there before and this bird is completely unaware of the past. He has never sung like that before. Today is absolutely fresh. He is absolutely and totally herenow. If you can listen without words, suddenly, as if a knife penetrates your being, the freshness of life will penetrate your accumulated dust – as if a ray of light penetrates darkness.

All around you, except for human beings, everything is fresh. Touch the tree, have a little talk with the river, look at the sky, watch the stars, lie down on the earth, relax. Go to the sea, watch the waves infinitely coming and coming and coming – without any business, without any utility, for no purpose, simply a delight in energy. And by and by you will become aware that the dust is disappearing; your mind, mirror is getting cleaned.

Language and addiction with language is the root cause. Words and words and words – and your being is hiding behind. The more words gather, the farther away you are from yourself, and the more difficult it becomes to come back home – because there is a forest, a wild forest of words. It is almost like a maze, a chaos.

Life is fresh. Mind can never be fresh. If you understand this, then look at life without the mind. Put the mind aside. I am not saying throw away the mind completely. It is useful. Use it. It is a bio-computer; use it – but don't be used by it. When it is needed, use it.

There are many, many situations where it is needed. You have to calculate; it will be needed. You have to remember the way to go to the station; you will need it. You have to remember many things and you will need it. So whenever it is needed, use it. Whenever it is not needed, put it aside, let it rest.

If the mind is allowed to rest, two things will happen to you: life will become fresh and the mind will become very, very powerful. Your mind is simply tired. Twenty-four hours in use – even a mechanism needs to relax. Even a car needs to be put to rest. Even a machine gets tired. Ask scientists. The latest research says that even a machine gets tired, even metal gets tired. It needs rest.

And your mind goes on working and working, day and night. Awake or asleep, the mind goes on working. It gets tired, so it cannot function well. It is a constant grinding machine, it goes on grinding. If there is nothing to grind, then too it goes on grinding. It goes on chewing old stuff again and again and again.

Learn how to give rest to the mind. You will have a more powerful mind. You will have a more powerful memory. You will have a more powerful logic and reason. And if you can put it aside, you will always be available to fresh life and the fresh life will be available to you.

When you come home, put the mind away. It is needed in the office; it is not needed with your children. Play with them. No need to be an adult. Become a person. No need to be a doctor with your wife. With a patient it is perfectly okay, but she is your wife; you need not be a doctor. With a friend you need not be an engineer, you need not be a businessman. You need not be anybody. You can simply be yourself – again a child playing on the shore, collecting seashells for no purpose at all.

These purposeless moments will allow you to be fresh.

The second question:

Osho,
What am I for?

For nothing. For no purpose at all.

Do you want to become a thing? Things are for something. If you ask me what this chair is for, the question is relevant and the answer is simple – to sit upon. If you ask me what this mike is for – to speak through. If there is nobody to sit upon the chair, it will be completely useless, it will have to be thrown away. If there is nobody to speak through the mike, there is no need for it. It will be simply useless, it will not have any purpose for existing.

But what are you for? – for nothing. You are not a chair, you are not a mike. You are not a house to live in. You are purposeless. And that is the beauty and that is the glory of life. It is a purposeless phenomenon. It exists for nothing. Or, it exists for itself. Both are the same.

Things exist for something else; they are means. Persons exist for themselves; they are ends.

You love somebody. For what? – for love itself. If you say you love for the money the person has, then you don't love. If you say you love for the prestige that comes from loving this person, then you don't love, then you are doing something else. Some other activity is going on, but not love – business, politics, maybe something else, but not love at all.

Love is an end in itself. You simply love for love's sake.

For what are these birds singing? For what? – just the sheer delight of singing. They are not singing there to get any award. They are not singing there for any competition. They are not even singing for you to listen to them. They are simply singing. They are full of energy and the energy overflows. The energy is too much – what to do with it? They share with existence. They are spendthrifts, not misers.

If you sing, first you look for what. Are the people going to appreciate it? Are you going to be awarded in some way, gross or subtle? Then you are not a singer you are a businessman. If you dance for some audience to see and you are looking for their appreciation, their applause, then you are not a dancer.

A dancer simply dances. If people see and appreciate and enjoy, that is another thing. That is not the goal. A dancer can dance alone, with nobody there to see. A singer can sing alone. The activity in itself is paying so much that there is no need to have any other goal, any other purpose.

You exist for yourself. The very question shows that you are looking at life through the head. The head is purposive. The heart is non-purposive. The very question shows that you would like to become a thing, a commodity to be sold in the market.

A prostitute loves, but that is not love; it is a commodity in the market. You love, but then it is not a commodity; it is an overflowing energy. You share your happiness, your bliss, with someone. You feel good with someone, you feel a certain harmony. With someone you feel in accord. The very activity in itself is valuable, the value is intrinsic. There is nothing outside it as a goal. It is not leading anywhere. It is leading to itself.

This has to be understood. All that is beautiful in life is intrinsic; it has intrinsic value. And all that is ordinary is purposive.

People go on asking why God created the world. "Why did he create it?" They think of God as if he is a manufacturer. Why? Why did he create the world? There is no "why" to it, and all answers that have been given to this "why" are patent nonsense. He created because he enjoyed. Creation in itself is enjoyment. He loved to create. He felt happy to create.

The Christian story says that God created the world and then he looked at creation and said, "Good, good." To whom was he saying this? There was nobody. He was saying "Good" to himself. He enjoyed it; a tremendous joy came to him. He created the world and loved it, just like a painter paints, and then goes far away from the painting and looks at it from this angle and that, and feels happy, tremendously happy. Not that the painting is going to give him much money – it may not give any at all.

One of the greatest painters, Vincent van Gogh, lived as a beggar because he could not sell a single painting. Not only could he not sell, he was condemned from everywhere that he was mad. Who would purchase those paintings? – they were worthless.

Now each of his paintings is worth millions of dollars, but in his own time nobody was ready to purchase them. He would go and give his paintings to his friends and even they were afraid to hang them in their drawing rooms, because people would think them mad. Not even a single painting was sold in his whole life.

His own brother, Theo van Gogh, was very worried. He was a businessman, and he could not think how a man could go on painting when nothing was selling. So he persuaded a friend and gave him money, and told him to go to van Gogh and at least purchase one painting. He would feel good.

The man went. Of course, he was not interested in paintings at all; he was just obliging the brother. The brother had given him the money and he was just to purchase any painting whatsoever. Van Gogh immediately suspected something, because the man was not even looking at the paintings. He said, "Okay, this will do. Take this money."

Van Gogh threw the money out of the house and threw the man out also, and he said, "Never come here again! I suspect this money is not yours and you are not in any way interested in paintings. My brother must be behind the whole thing. Get away from here. I am not going to sell it."

He killed himself when he was very young – thirty-six, thirty-seven – because he felt that whatsoever he could create he had created, and now just to drag on in a miserable life, with not even enough to eat... He was eating only three days per week, because his brother was giving him enough money to eat, but he had to purchase colors and canvas and brushes. So for four days he would save the money for colors and paintings, and for three days he would eat.

But he was a tremendously happy person. There was nobody to appreciate his work, so he would look at his own paintings. He must have said, just like God said, "Good. Good, I have done it again."

Never ask what you are for; you are for yourself. And unless you realize this, you will miss much. Deep down, your innermost being is always waiting for someone who will love you for yourself; for nothing else, just for yourself; somebody who will say, "I love you for love's sake. I love you the way you are. I love you because you are. I love you, your being, and there is no end to it, no purpose behind it."

Unless somebody comes and loves you meaninglessly, you will not have the glory of life. Remember, in that meaninglessness is hidden the whole significance of life. When somebody loves you meaningfully, he has already reduced you to an object. You are a thing and he is a purchaser.

When somebody loves you just for you, for no other reason at all, then suddenly your inner flower blooms. You are accepted as you are.

Love always accepts you as you are, and through that acceptance, much transformation happens. You can bloom. Now, there is no fear. Now, nothing is expected from you; you can relax. Now there is no goal beyond you; you are the goal. You can dance and celebrate.

It happened...

In the fourth century B.C. the great Athenian philosopher Plato established a school, The Academy, at which mathematics was a key portion of the curriculum.

Plato loved mathematics tremendously. He was a poet of mathematics, a lover. On his academy door it was written: "If you don't know mathematics, please don't enter." One had to learn mathematics before one could enter The Academy. It was taught with the utmost rigor of which the times were capable, and it dealt with idealized shapes on which idealized operations were performed.

One student, who was put to stern mental exercises over the Platonic conception of mathematics, kept searching in vain for some application to the various forms of artisanship for which he knew mathematical concepts were useful.

Finally he said to Plato, "But, master, to what particular use can these theorems be put? I don't see any practical use. The theorems are beautiful, they are pure mathematics, but what is the utility? To what use can these theorems be put? What can be gained from them?"

The old philosopher glared at the inquiring student, turned to a slave and said, "Give this young man a penny that he might feel he has gained something from my teachings and then expel him."

It is difficult to understand, because for Plato mathematics was his love, his beloved. Profit was not the question, achieving anything was not the question. Just to contemplate those forms – pure forms of mathematics – was enough. That very contemplation leads one into the unknown.

It is not a question of any gain. Life itself is enough unto itself. And if you are trying to fulfill some goal, you will miss life.

That's what has been taught to you from the very beginning. Every parent is trying to force you into some utility. They are worried that you may become a vagabond, you may become a wanderer. They are worried that you may become useless. They are worried that you may not prove yourself of any use in the world. Then who will appreciate you?

Their egos are worried because through you they are planning some fulfillment of their own unfulfilled egos. Their parents did the same with them, now they are doing the same with you. And you will go on doing the same with your children.

Dead people go on haunting you. Your father may be dead, but he will go on haunting you. Whenever you relax, you will hear the voice of your father, "What are you doing? – getting lazy! Do something!" and you will jump out of your laziness and run around and do something because you are getting useless.

Because everybody has been conditioned to be of some utility, the question arises "For what?" And if you cannot find the answer, you feel very puzzled and confused. Drop all that nonsense. You are enough as you are.

I'm not saying become lazy. I'm not saying become a parasite. I am saying to live your life as an intrinsic value. Do whatsoever you want to do, but don't do it to prove that you are useful. Do it because you love it. Do it because you feel happy doing it. Do it because it is your love. And suddenly everything has a different color and everything becomes luminous.

My own parents wanted me to become a scientist – if not a pure scientist then at least a doctor, an engineer. I betrayed them. Now they have completely forgotten and they are happy. They are very good and simple people. But at the time when I betrayed them, they felt very hurt. They were hoping for much.

All parents hope, and through their hope they destroy their children. You have to get free of your parents – just as a child has to get out of the womb of the mother one day, otherwise the womb will become death. After nine months the child has to come out of the womb. He has to leave the mother howsoever painful, and howsoever the mother may feel empty – but the child has to come out.

Then another day in life, the child has to come out of the expectations of the parents. Only then, for the first time he becomes a being in his own right, on his own. Then he stands on his own feet. Then he becomes really free.

If parents become alert, more understanding, they will help the children to become as free as possible and as soon as possible. They will not condition the children to be of use; they will help the children to be lovers.

A totally different world is waiting to be born, where people will be working. The carpenter will be working because he loves the wood. The teacher will be teaching in the school because he loves teaching. The shoemaker will go on making shoes because he loves making shoes.

Right now something very confusing is happening. The shoemaker has become a surgeon, the surgeon has become a shoemaker. Both are angry. The carpenter has become the politician, the politician has become the carpenter. Both are angry.

The whole of life seems to be deep in anger. Look at people – everybody seems to be angry. Everybody seems to be somewhere where he was not meant to be. Everybody seems to be a misfit. Everybody seems to be unfulfilled because of this concept of utility; it goes on haunting.

I have heard one very beautiful story:

Mrs. Ginsberg, having arrived in heaven, addressed the recording angel bashfully. "Tell me," she said, "would it be possible to have an interview with someone who is here in heaven?"

The recording angel said, "Certainly, assuming the person you have in mind is here in heaven."

"Oh, she is. I'm sure of that," said Mrs. Ginsberg. "Actually, I want to see the Virgin Mary."

The recording angel cleared his throat. "Ah, yes. As it happens, she is in a different section, but if you insist I will forward the request. She is a gracious lady and she may wish to visit the old neighborhood."

The request was duly forwarded, and the Virgin was gracious indeed. It was not long at all before Mrs. Ginsberg was favored with the Virgin's presence.

Mrs. Ginsberg looked long at the radiant figure before her and finally said, "Please forgive my curiosity, but I have always wanted to ask you. Tell me, how does it feel to have a son who is so wonderful that ever since his time hundreds of millions of people have worshipped him as a God?"

And the Virgin replied, "Frankly, Mrs. Ginsberg, we were hoping he would be a doctor."

Parents are always hoping – and their hope becomes poisonous. Let me tell you: love your children, but never hope through them.

Love your children as much as you can and give them a feeling that they are loved for themselves, and not for any use that they can be. Love your children tremendously and give them a feeling that they are accepted as they are; they are not to fulfill any demands. Whether they do this or that, it will not make any difference to the love that has been given to them. The love is unconditional.

Then a totally new world can be created. Then people will move naturally to things that they like. People will move naturally to directions that instinctively they feel like flowing in.

But what to say of ordinary parents?

I will tell you another story:

Rabbi Joshua, having lived an exemplary life that had been admired by all, died in the fullness of time and went to heaven. There he was greeted with hosannas of delight. Inexplicably, he shrank back, covered his face with his trembling old hands, and refused to participate in the festivities held in his honor.

All persuasion having failed, he was ushered respectfully before the high judgment seat of God himself.

The tender presence of God bathed the noble rabbi, and the divine voice filled his ears. "My child," said God, "it is on record that you have lived entirely in accord with my wishes, and yet you refuse the honors that have, most fittingly, been prepared for you. Why is this?"

Rabbi Joshua, head bent low and voice meek, said, "Oh, Holy

One, I am not deserving. Somehow my life must have taken a wrong turning, for my son, heedless of my example and my precepts, turned Christian."

"Alas," came the still voice, sweet with infinite sympathy, "I understand entirely and forgive. After all, my son did the same."

Expectations, expectations!

People go on hoping through others. People go on being ambitious through others. Drop that trip of your parents. Remember, that is the only way you will be able to forgive them. And remember also, that is the only way that one day you will be able to respect them.

Unless you are fulfilled, unless you have found something that is not just a profession to do but something like a vocation, a calling, you will never be able to feel happy about your parents, because they are the cause of bringing you into this miserable world. You cannot feel grateful, there is nothing to be grateful about. Once you are fulfilled, then you will feel tremendously grateful.

Your fulfillment is possible only if you don't become a thing. Your destiny is to become a person. Your destiny is to become an intrinsic value. Your destiny is to become an end in yourself.

The third question:

Osho,
You said yesterday that everything is perfect herenow, nothing has to be changed, everything is as it should be. Then, Osho, what are we doing here in the meditation camps? Please explain.

If you understand what I have said, then there is no need to do anything. If you don't understand, then much will have to be done.

You are doing meditations because understanding is missing. If understanding comes to you, there is no need for any meditation. If you understand, then your whole life becomes a meditation. Then whatsoever you do, you do meditatively.

You eat meditatively, you sleep meditatively, you walk meditatively. Then meditation is not something set apart – it is like breathing or the beating of the heart. It becomes a quality of your being. Not that you do meditation, you become meditative. Whatsoever you do, meditation follows you like a shadow.

If you understand, then meditation is not something to be done, it is a consequence of understanding. But if you don't understand, then meditation has to be done, because only through meditation, by and by you will be cleansed and understanding will become possible.

They are interrelated. Either you understand – then meditation follows; or you don't understand – then you have to meditate and understanding follows. They are interdependent.

Don't ask which is first – the egg or the hen. Neither is first; they are interdependent. The hen cannot be there if the egg has not been before, and the egg cannot be there if the hen has not been before.

But one has to start from somewhere. Don't get confused. Go to the market – either purchase a hen or bring an egg, but do something. Just don't sit and contemplate philosophically that first you must decide which is which and which is first. Then you will never be able to decide. Nobody has ever been able to decide which comes first.

In fact, they appear as two; they are not two. The egg is nothing but unmanifested hen, and the hen is nothing but manifested egg. The hen is nothing but the egg's way of producing more eggs. They are interconnected.

So either understanding or meditation. If you understand, then there is no need. But don't deceive yourself, because deception is very easy. You can think, "Yes, I understand." You can think that you understand, because it is very ego-enhancing to think that you understand – and then what is the need to meditate?

But if understanding really happens, then all problems disappear immediately. If problems still linger on, then you must have deceived. If anger continues to be there, if hatred continues to be there, if jealousy continues to be there, if fear continues to be there, then you have deceived yourself. Then please, start meditating. Then much cleansing has to be done.

Meditation is nothing but catharsis. Meditation is throwing out all junk from inside. If the mirror is clear, it reflects perfectly. That is what understanding is – a clear mirror of consciousness. But if the mirror is covered with dust, then first you have to wash the dust, clean the mirror. That is what meditation is.

Meditation is just cleaning the mirror. Understanding is the clean mirror, the cleaned mirror.

So if you feel that you are not yet able to understand what is being said to you here, then continue meditating. Someday you will be able to see it. If you have understood, then there is no point. But understanding means that now there are no problems.

Just a few days ago, a man came and he said that he had been meditating for years, and I asked him, "How are you feeling?"

He said, "Beautiful, perfect. Meditation has helped me tremendously. I have become completely silent and I see visions and light and things like that."

I said, "Then it is perfectly okay. Why have you come to me?"

He said, "But this anger and sex and greed continue."

Then I said, "You must have deceived yourself. You must have seen a dream of light, of visions, of silence. You must have persuaded yourself that you have become silent, because it is impossible to become silent, to be full with light, and then continue to be angry, greedy – it is impossible. Either you have deceived yourself or you are trying to deceive me."

If you understand, then there is no need to do anything. Then simply everything disappears. You are awake. The sleep is gone and all the dreams have disappeared.

A Zen master awoke one morning. He called a disciple who was passing by and said, "Listen. I had a dream. Would you like to interpret it?"

The disciple said, "Wait." And he went out and brought a bucket of water and told the old man to wash his face. The old man did, and laughed and blessed the disciple and said, "Right. This is the right interpretation of the dream."

Then another disciple who was passing was called and the master said, "Look, I had a dream and I asked this disciple to interpret it and he brought a bucket of water. Now, would you like to interpret it?"

The disciple said, "Wait." He went out and came back with a cup of tea. He said, "Please drink a cup of tea. Finished! The dream is finished, so why bother about it?"

When you are awake, you are awake. When you have understood that it is a dream, it needs no interpretation. Finished! A dream means it is not. What is the need to interpret something which is not?

Of course, Freud would not like the story at all. He has created a great business. He was a Jew. He turned psychoanalysis into a great business. Now it is one of the greatest firms in the world. Even General Electric and Ford are nothing; psychoanalysis is going to remain.

The Eastern attitude says that once you realize a dream is a dream – finished! A full point has come.

If you understand what I am saying, that very understanding is enough. If you don't understand, then you have to meditate. Then, don't deceive. Intellectual understanding won't help. Of course, whatsoever I am saying you can understand intellectually. Intellectual understanding is not understanding. Whatsoever I say – you hear, you listen, you know the language, and everything is clear – but that is not understanding.

Understanding is a total phenomenon. Just listening, and just by listening something happens within you – a turning, what Buddha used to call a *paravritti*, a conversion. Buddha used to say that there is only one miracle. He called it the turning about in the deepest seed of consciousness – *paravritti*.

Listening to me, something happens in your consciousness – a turn about. You are no longer the same. Not that you have accumulated some intellectual knowledge from me, and you have become more informed. No, suddenly you are no longer the same. Somebody had come to listen to me, somebody else goes back. A gap, a discontinuity, a death has happened; a crucifixion and a resurrection. It rarely happens.

Understanding is very rare. It needs tremendous courage to die and be reborn in a single moment. But it happens. If it has not happened, then go on continuing meditations. One day meditations will prepare you. The mirror will become more and more clear. One day the reflection will be perfect and understanding will come to you.

Understanding means a total transformation of your being.

Don't be too concerned with words, rather, be concerned with me. Don't be too concerned with what I say to you, rather, be concerned with what I am herenow. Then there is more possibility for transformation and understanding. If you just go on listening to me, you can find ways to avoid, escape.

Words are just words, no word is real. They are just artificial devices – useful, but very limited. Language comes into existence by coincidences. It has no ultimacy about it. That's why there are so many languages. For the same reason, there are thousands of words in the world. There are almost thousands of languages. It is artificial.

Whether you call a rose a rose or you call it "*gulab*" makes no difference to the rose. The rose is blissfully unaware of what you call it. Otherwise the rose would get confused. There are one thousand words for the rose. It will be impossible for the rose to bloom anymore if it becomes too linguistic, if it becomes too intellectual. The rose does not bother about what you call it. And whether you call it a rose or you call it *gulab* – what difference does it make? A rose remains a rose. Language is artificial, coincidental.

I have heard a very beautiful story, almost unbelievably true...

A very ancient story tells of Joseph and Mary on their way to Bethlehem to be taxed. Mary, being great with child, was on the donkey of course. Joseph walked patiently at her side.

It happened that Joseph turned his ankle on an unexpected stone in the road and nearly fell. Caught by surprise, he muttered under his breath, "Jesus!"

Mary turned to him, eyes sparkling, and said, "Just the name for the child."

That's how all language comes up – just coincidences.

Don't be very concerned with what I say, be concerned with what I am. And then a different type of understanding, not intellectual at all but total – that goes deep down in your guts, that starts circulating in your blood, that starts beating in your heart, that you start breathing in and out, that becomes a part of your very being – arises. Then there is no need of meditation.

But before that, please don't deceive yourself. Because I know, many of you will be thinking, "Very good. So now there is no need to meditate."

No, meditation cannot be dropped unless you have come to understanding. Continue.

I know everything is right now as it should be; everything is perfect. I can see you as perfect beings, buddhas, luminous beings full of light, but you are not aware. Just by my saying it, it cannot happen to you. You will have to cleanse your eyes, your perception.

Meditation is just medicinal. It helps to clean the eyes. It helps to clean the perception. It gives you clarity to see.

The last question; listen to it carefully, because this is how the mind tries to be clever, tries to be cunning, and can deceive you. Of course, nobody else is deceived, but you can deceive yourself. And when you deceive yourself, there is no possibility of getting out of it, because there is nobody else to get out of it. You are alone there. The deception can become permanent.

Listen first to the question – a beautiful question in a way:

Osho,
The other day you said, "Don't follow me!" Later, you advised us to become sannyasins. It seems to me a contradiction. I don't follow you. Please explain.

Whatsoever I am saying is all contradictory. Now drop worrying about contradictions. I totally accept my contradictoriness, so you need not worry, that is finished forever. Now think about something else.

It is so easy to see a contradiction, even a child can do that. It is not of any worth. It does not show a great intelligence. In fact intelligence is not needed to see a contradiction. Even a stupid mind can see the contradiction. But if you can see something in the contradiction which is not contradictory, you rise in intelligence, you rise higher.

It is easy to see the contradiction between life and death. They are contradictory. No need to prove it, no logic is needed. It is a simple fact, apparently so – but go a little deeper. Life and death are not contradictory; they are two poles of the same energy, of the same wheel.

Death is not against life; death is the very culmination of life, the very crescendo. Death does not end life, in fact, death allows life to be. If there is no death, there will be no life. Death creates the very possibility for life to be. How can they be contradictory? They are complementary.

If you have intelligence – not just a logical, trained mind, but intelligence which can see deep, beyond the surfaces, can move to the very center – then you will see that all great religions and all great religious teachers have always been contradictory and yet consistent.

Now let me tell you how it happens: "The other day you said, 'Don't follow me.'" You have seen the contradiction. Now let me create another contradiction. "The other day you said, "'Don't follow me.'" Now, if you don't follow me, you will be following me. Get it? If I say don't follow me and you don't follow me, of course, you are following me. The only way then, not to follow me is to follow me. Become a sannyasin.

You can see my contradiction; you cannot see your own? You say, "I don't follow you." Exactly, precisely that is what all of my followers are expected to do.

Let me tell you one anecdote:

A stranger came into a bar in which there were only the bartender, a dog and a cat.

As the stranger ordered his drink, the dog rose, yawned, and said, "Well, so long, Joe," then walked out.

The stranger's jaw dropped. He said to the bartender, "Did you hear that! The dog talked."

"Don't be a jackass," said the bartender. "A dog can't talk."

"But I heard him."

"You just think you heard him. I tell you dogs can't talk. It's just that wise-guy cat over there. He's a ventriloquist."

It is easier to see others' contradictions – very easy. One really relishes it. But a real intelligence tries to see the contradictions in oneself.

Yes, I say don't follow me. But for that, great preparation is needed. Because if you don't follow me, you will follow somebody else. That will not make much of a difference.

When I say don't follow me, I mean don't follow. If you don't follow me and you follow Jesus, if you don't follow me and you follow Buddha, what difference does it make? If you don't follow me and you follow Karl Marx or Mao Zedong, what difference does it make? Or – let me come to the exact point – if you don't follow me and you follow yourself, what difference does it make?

When I say don't follow me, I mean don't follow.

But a great preparation will be needed so that all the tendencies within you which help you to follow can be dropped. That is the meaning of sannyas. Sannyas is nothing but a situation in which all the inner tendencies to follow, to imitate, to believe, by and by drop.

Sannyas is not following me. Sannyas is just being with me. Let the difference be absolutely clear to you. Sannyas is not following me. Sannyas is just being with me, in my presence. Sannyas is not imitating me. Sannyas is just to be with me to follow your own destiny. I am here to help you to be yourself.

Sannyas is just a trust, it is not a belief. I don't promise you anything. I don't give you any system of thought. Hence I am contradictory, because if I am not contradictory, you will create a system of thought around me.

I am continuously contradictory, each moment I go on contradicting. And the reason is that when you look at all of my assertions you will not be able to create any system. If you follow me, people will laugh at you. They will say, "You are contradictory."

Only through intense contradiction can the logic, the system-making mind be destroyed and shattered. There is no other way.

I am contradictory so that if you really love me and if you are really close to me, by and by you will be able to drop the mind which says it is contradictory, it is illogical.

It is – because it is beyond logic. It is – because it is higher than logic. There is logic in it which is higher than all logic. It is a little crazy – but the craziness is a little higher than what you call sanity.

R. D. Laing has said somewhere that each breakdown is a breakthrough also. I don't totally agree. Each breakdown, he says, is a breakthrough also. I don't agree. I know each breakthrough is preceded by a breakdown, but each breakdown is not followed by a breakthrough. A breakdown is simply a situation in which your so-called logical mind cannot function. It comes to a barrier beyond which there is no go for it – it simply breaks down. That's when we say a man has become mad.

I also help you to become mad. Of course, my madness is with a method. First you have to break down so that a new breakthrough can be possible. First you have to be dismantled, destroyed, so that you can be recreated.

I am not in favor of renovation of old buildings, no. Laxmi is in favor of it, but I am not. She has her difficulties. I am completely in favor of dismantling and then making a new start from the very *abc*.

By becoming a sannyasin, you allow me to destroy you. A great trust is needed – it is not a following, following is very cheap – it is moving into danger, it is taking a tremendous risk. And moving with such a man who is so contradictory that you are going to get crazy sooner or later.

Whatsoever I am saying today, tomorrow I will contradict. Only one thing is certain: that I will remain contradictory. Only with one thing am I consistent, and that is my inconsistency.

But if you allow me – sannyas is simply a gesture that you allow me – then I can dismantle you. And then, out of that dismantling, a totally new being can arise; Whatsoever society has done, I can undo, that's all.

Sannyas is not a following. It is a friendship. You are not going to become my shadows and follow me. You are going to come along with me, hand in hand, shoulder to shoulder. It is a love affair, a friendship.

But remember, if you don't follow me, you will be following me. So better take sannyas.

Enough for today.

CHAPTER 9

a conscious death

The master Fugai was a fine painter, and he was considered to be wise and generous. But he was also most severe, both to himself and to his disciples.
It is told that Fugai met his end in an extraordinary manner.
Feeling that his last day had come, he quickly had a hole dug, then climbed in and ordered the digger to cover him with earth. The astonished man ran off.
On his return to the spot he found the master standing in the hole with great dignity – dead.

Life is an opportunity. You can use it, you can misuse it, or you can simply waste it. It depends totally on you. Except you, nobody is going to be responsible. Responsibility is of the individual. Once you realize this then you start becoming alert, aware. Then you start living in a totally different way. Then, in fact, for the first time you become alive. Otherwise, people live in a sort of dream – half-asleep, half-awake – just somewhere in between consciousness and unconsciousness. That life is not really a life. You exist – but you don't live.

Existence is given to you. Existence is a gift. Life has to be earned. When existence turns upon itself, it becomes life. Existence has been given by the whole, you have not done anything for it. It is simply there, a given fact. When existence becomes life... The moment you start existing in a conscious way, immediately existence becomes life.

Existence lived consciously is life.

Life is a great challenge, an adventure into the unknown, an adventure into oneself, an adventure into that which is. If you live an unconscious life, if you simply exist, you will always remain afraid of death. Death will always be just somewhere near the corner, hanging around you. Only life goes beyond death.

Existence comes, disappears. It is given to you, taken away. It is a wave in the ocean – arises, falls back, disappears.

But life is eternal. Once you have it, you have it forever. Life knows no death. Life is not afraid of death. Once you know what life is, death disappears. If you are still afraid of death, know well you have not known life yet.

Death exists only in ignorance – in the ignorance of what life is. One goes on living. One goes on moving from one moment to another, from one action to another, completely unaware what one is doing, why one is doing, why one is drifting from this point to that point.

If you become a little meditative, many times in a day you will catch hold of yourself completely drifting, unconscious.

The whole effort of religion is to make you aware of your existence.

Existence plus awareness is life eternal – what Jesus calls life in abundance, what Jesus calls the kingdom of God. That kingdom of God is within you. You already have the seed within you. You just have to allow it to sprout. You have to allow it to come in the sunlit world of the sky, to become free, to move in freedom, to move higher and higher, to touch the very infinity. It is possible to soar high – but the basic thing is awareness.

Shortly before Carl Jung died, he said in an interview, "We need more understanding of human nature, because the only real danger that exists is man himself. He is the great danger and we are pitifully unaware of it. We know nothing of man."

One fallacy continues and that fallacy is that because you are, you think you know who you are. You feel that you are, but you don't know who you are. Just a confused feeling, a mixed feeling, a shadowy feeling that you are, is not enough. It should become crystal clear. It should become an unwavering light within you. Only then one knows what man is.

In Sanskrit, for man we have the word *purusha*. That word is tremendously beautiful. It is difficult to translate it because it has three meanings. It can be pronounced with three different emphases. The word is *purusha*. It can be pronounced as *pur-u-sha*. Then it means "the dawn in the city, he who is filled with light." It can be pronounced as *puru-sha*. Then it means "filled with wisdom and eternal happiness, a citizen of heaven." It can be pronounced as *pu-rusha*. Then it means "whose passions are purified and who has become deathless."

There are many possibilities within you, layer upon layer. The first layer is of the body. If you get identified with the body, you are getting identified with the temporal, the momentary. Then there is bound to be fear of death.

The body is a flux, like a river – continuously changing, moving. It has nothing of the eternal in it. Each moment the body is changing. In fact, the body is dying every moment. It is not that after seventy years suddenly one day you die. The body dies every day. Death continues for seventy years, it is a process. Death is not an event, it is a long process. By and by, by and by, the body comes to a point where it cannot hold itself. It disintegrates.

If you are identified with the body, of course the fear will be constantly there that death is approaching. You can live, but you can live only in fear. And what type of life is possible when one's foundations are constantly shaking, and one is sitting on a volcano and death is possible any moment? Only one thing is certain – that death is coming – and everything else is uncertain. How can one live? How can one celebrate? How can one dance and sing and be? Impossible. Death won't allow it. Death is too much and too close.

Then there is a second layer within you: that of the mind – which is even more temporal and more fleeting than the body. Mind is also continuously disintegrating.

Mind is the inner part of the body and the body is the outer part of the mind. These are not two things. Mind and body is not a right expression. The right expression is mind-body. You are psychosomatic. Not that the body exists and the mind exists. The body is the gross mind, and the mind is the subtle body – aspects of the same coin – one outer, the second inner.

So there are people who are identified with the body. These are the materialists. They cannot live. Desperately they try, of course, but they cannot live. A materialist only pretends that he is living, he cannot live.

His life cannot be very deep; it can only be superficial, shallow – because he is trying to live through the body which is continuously dying. He is living in a house which is on fire. He is trying to rest in a house which is on fire. How can you rest? How can you love?

The materialist can only have sex, cannot love, because sex is temporal; love is something of the eternal. He can make hit-and-run contacts with people but he cannot relate. He is constantly running, because he is identified with the body. The body is never at rest, it is a continuous movement.

At the most he can have sex – a temporal, a momentary thing; nothing deeper, nothing of the soul, nothing of the innermost core. Beings remain far away, bodies meet and mingle and separate again. The materialist is the most idiotic person, because he is trying to live through death. That is the stupidity.

Then another type of person is the idealist – one who is identified with the mind, with ideas, ideologies, ideals. He lives in a very ephemeral world – not in any way better than the materialist. Of course, more ego-fulfilling, because he can condemn the materialist.

He talks about God, he talks about the soul, he talks about religion and great things. He talks about the other world – but that is all mere talk. He lives in the mind: continuously thinking, brooding, playing with ideas and words. He creates utopias of the mind, great beautiful dreams, but he is also wasting the opportunity, because the opportunity is here and now, and he always thinks of somewhere else.

The word *utopia* is beautiful. It means "that which never comes." He thinks of something which never comes, which cannot come. He lives somewhere else. He exists here and lives somewhere else. He lives in a dichotomy, in a dualism. With great tension he exists. The politicians, the revolutionaries, the so-called theologians, the priests, all live a life identified with the mind.

Real life is beyond both body and mind. You are in the body, you are in the mind, but you are neither. The body is your outer shell, the mind is your inner shell, but you are beyond both.

This insight is the beginning of real life. How to start this insight? That's what meditation is all about. Start witnessing. Walking on the street, become a witness. Watch the body walking and you, from the innermost core, are just watching, witnessing, observing. Suddenly you will have a sense of freedom. Suddenly you will see that the body is walking, you are not walking.

Sometimes the body is healthy, sometimes the body is ill. Watch, just watch, and suddenly you will have a sense of a totally different quality of being. You are not the body. The body is ill, of course, but you are not ill. The body is healthy, but it has nothing to do with you.

You are a witness, a watcher on the hills, far beyond – of course, tethered to the body, but not identified with the body; rooted in the body, but always beyond and transcending.

The first meditation is to separate yourself from the body. And by and by, when you become more acute in your observation of the body, start observing the thoughts that continuously go on within your mind. But first watch the body, because it is gross, can be observed more easily, will not need much awareness. Once you become attuned, then start watching the mind.

Whatsoever can be watched becomes separate from you. Whatsoever you can witness, you are not it. You are the witnessing consciousness. The witnessed is the object; you are the subjectivity.

The body and the mind remain far away when you become a witness. Suddenly you are there, with no body and with no mind – a pure consciousness, just simple sheer purity, an innocence, a mirror.

In this innocence, for the first time you know who you are. In this purity, for the first time existence becomes life. For the first time you are. Before it, you were simply asleep, dreaming. Now you are.

And when you are, then there is no death. Then you know that you will be witnessing your death also. One who has become capable of witnessing life has become capable of witnessing death, because death is not the end of life, it is the very culmination of it, it is the very pinnacle of it. Life comes to its peak in death. Because you are afraid, you miss. Otherwise death is the greatest orgasm there is.

You have known the small orgasm of sex. In sex also, a small, a little death happens. Some life-energy is released from your body – you feel orgasmic, unburdened, relaxed, Just think of death. The whole energy that you have is released. Death is the greatest orgasm.

In sexual orgasm just a small, minute part of your energy is relaxed. Then too you feel so beautiful. Then too you feel so relaxed and you fall in deep sleep, all tensions dissolved. You become a harmony. Think of death as the whole life released. From every pore of your body, the whole life released back to the whole. It is the greatest orgasm there is.

Yes, death is the greatest orgasm, but people go on missing it because of fear. The same happens with sexual orgasm. Many people go on missing it. They cannot have any orgasm because of the fear. They cannot move totally in it. Remember this, people who are afraid of death will be afraid of sex also.

You can watch this happening in this country. This country has remained afraid of sex, and this country is very much afraid of death also. You cannot find more cowards anywhere, you cannot find more cowardly people anywhere. What has happened? Those people who are afraid of death will become afraid of sex also, because a small death happens in sex. Those people who become afraid of sex, cling too much to life. They become miserly. Misers miss sexual orgasms and then they miss the great orgasm, the fulfillment of the whole life.

Once you know what death is, you will receive it with great cele-bration. You will welcome it. It is the fulfillment of your whole life's effort. It is the fruition of your whole life's effort. The journey ends. One comes back home.

But in death you don't die. Just the energy that was given to you through the body and through the mind is released, goes back to the world. You return back home.

If you don't die rightly, you will be born again. Now let me explain it to you. If you don't die rightly, if you don't achieve the total orgasm that death is, you will be born again, because you missed and you have to be given another opportunity.

Existence is very patient with you. It goes on giving you more opportunities. It has compassion. If you have missed this life, it will give you another. If you have failed this time, for another session you will be sent back to the world. Unless you fulfill the goal, you will be sent back again and again. That is the meaning of the theory of rebirth.

The Christian God is a little miserly. He gives only one life. That creates much tension. Just one life? – no time even to err, no time to go astray. That creates very deep inner tension. In the East we have created the concept of a more compassionate God who goes on giving: "You have missed this one? Take another."

In a way it is very sensible. There is no God as personified, who gives life to you. It is in fact you. Have you watched sometimes? In the night you go to sleep. Just watch. When you fall asleep, when you are falling asleep, just watch the last thought, the last desire, the last fragment in your mind. And then when in the morning you feel awake, don't open the eyes; just again watch. The last fragment will be the first fragment again.

If you were thinking of money when you were falling asleep, exactly the same thought will be the first thought in the morning. You will be thinking of money again – because that thought remained in your mind, waited for you to come back to it. If you were thinking of sex, in the morning you will be thinking of sex. Whatsoever – if you were thinking of God and you prayed and that was your last thing in the night, first thing in the morning you will find a prayerfulness arising in you.

The last thought in the night is the first thought in the morning. The last thought of this life will be the first thought of another life. The last thought when you are dying this time will become the first seed of your next life.

But when a Buddha dies, a man who has attained, he simply dies with no thought. He enjoys the orgasm. It is so fulfilling, it is so totally fulfilling that there is no need to come back. He disappears into the cosmos. There is no need to be embodied again.

In the East we have been watching the death experience of people. How you die reflects your whole life, how you lived. If I can see just your death, I can write your whole biography – because in that one moment your whole life becomes condensed. In that one moment, like a lightning, you show everything.

A miserly person will die with clenched fists – still holding and clinging, still trying not to die, still trying not to relax. A loving person will die with open fists, sharing – even sharing his death as he shared his life. You can see everything written on the face – whether this man has lived his life fully alert, aware. Then on his face there will be a light shining; around his body there will be an aura. You come close to him and you will feel silent – not sad, but silent. It even happens that if a person has died blissfully in a total orgasm you will feel suddenly happy near him.

It happened in my childhood:

A very saintly person in my village died. I had a certain attachment toward him. He was a priest in a small temple, a very poor man. And whenever I would pass – and I used to pass at least twice a day; when going to the school near the temple, I would pass – he would call me and he would always give me some fruit, some sweet.

When he died, I was the only child who went to see him. The

whole town gathered. Suddenly I could not believe what happened – I started laughing. My father was there, he tried to stop me because he felt embarrassed. A death is not a time to laugh. He tried to shut me up. He told me again and again, "Keep quiet!"

I have never felt that urge again. Since then I have never felt it; never before had I ever felt it – to laugh so loudly, as if something beautiful has happened.

I could not hold myself. I laughed loudly, everybody was angry, I was sent back, and my father told me, "Never again are you to be allowed in any serious situation! Because of you, even I was feeling very embarrassed. Why were you laughing? What was happening there? What is there in death to laugh about? Everybody was crying and weeping and you were laughing."

I told him, "Something happened. That old man released something and it was tremendously beautiful. He died an orgasmic death." Not exactly those words, but I told him that I felt he was very happy dying, very blissful dying, and I wanted to participate in his laughter. He was laughing, his energy was laughing.

I was thought mad. How can a man die laughing? Since then I have been watching many deaths, but I have not seen that type of death again.

When you die, you release your energy and with that energy your whole life's experience. Whatsoever you have been – sad, happy, loving, angry, passionate, compassionate – whatsoever you have been, that energy carries the vibrations of your whole life. Whenever a saint is dying, just being near him is a great gift, just to be showered with his energy is a great inspiration. You will be put in a totally different dimension. You will be drugged by his energy, you will feel drunk.

Death can be a total fulfillment, but that is possible only if life has been lived.

An absentminded scientist suddenly decided one day that he was being neglectful of his family, so that evening he went home, kissed his wife and children, shaved, showered and changed before dinner and exerted himself to tell several amusing stories during the meal.

When it was over, he whistled as he cleared the table and insisted on washing and drying all the dishes by himself. When he had tidied everything up, he went into the living room to find his wife in tears.

"Everything has gone wrong today," she sobbed. "The hoover broke down, Georgie threw a baseball through our bedroom window, Polly fell and tore her best dress, and now you come home so drunk you don't know what you are doing."

Nobody knows what he is doing. No intoxicant is needed. You are simply absent-minded. You are simply unconscious – as if you go on creating your own unconsciousness within yourself. As if you continuously create some alcoholic beverage in your blood, in your bloodstream. You go on creating some drugs within you. And it is exactly so.

Unless you try hard to become aware, to clench yourself away from the drunkenness that you find yourself in, you will not be able to see exactly what is happening.

Ordinarily, whatsoever you do, you do like an automaton. You drive a car: no need to be aware of it, you simply drive the car like a mechanism. You have learned the trick. You go on singing or smoking and talking and thinking a thousand and one thoughts and the body goes on driving the car.

You eat: you eat like an automaton. You walk: you walk like an automaton. The body has learned the trick, it goes on performing. Your attention is not needed.

Your attention is needed only when there is some accident. If something goes wrong, then your attention is needed. Otherwise you can go on playing with your thoughts and you can go on moving anywhere you like. You need not be there in your action; to be present is not needed.

For example, if some new sound starts in the engine, then suddenly you become aware. Otherwise, if the car goes on humming as usual, you go on driving. You go on typing if everything is going okay. The mind is almost like a computer: once trained, fed rightly, informed, it goes on functioning on its own. The more efficient you become in your life, the more unconscious you become.

Children are more conscious. They have to be, because they don't know anything. Remember when you started writing for the first time? Then each word was so slow, and you had to write it with such attention. Look at a small child writing. His whole body is engaged, his whole mind is engaged. He becomes just his eyes. And it may be nothing; he may be writing just a small word.

A few children write me letters. They write *luv*, but I know how much effort they must have put in it. They must have thought and brooded, and they are writing just a small letter – *luv*. Of course, *l-u-v* – but they have put their whole attention in it. It carries much more meaning than when you write *love*, because you simply write as a habit. You may not even be aware of what you are writing.

I know one man who is a very cultured man, very mannerly. I was sitting in his room once when he became angry, and he became so angry with his servant that he said, "Go to hell, please!"
Then I asked him, "What do you mean by 'please'?"
He said, "Just old habit."

You may be writing *love*; that may be just old habit. You may not be at all aware of what you are saying. Do you mean it exactly? Because to utter the word *love* is to utter something sacred, something tremendously significant. But the way you write it or you use it...
I know people who say, "I love my car. I love my house," or, "I love ice cream." Now, those people are profaning a sacred word. When they say to a woman, "I love you," it doesn't mean much. They say the same thing to ice cream also. It has nothing of their heart, their awareness, their being in it.
A child is more aware. Watch a child – full of energy, fresh, aware, open, alert. But we teach him something else. The society does not want awareness. Awareness is dangerous for this so-called society, because the society is ill and this society has investments in unconsciousness.
If people are aware, then what will happen to the industry which goes on producing cigarettes? What will happen to the industry which goes on producing alcohol? What will happen to the industry which goes on exploiting people's sexuality and their sexual desire? What will happen to the politicians? What will happen to the priests? They all exist because you are unconscious. They all can exploit you because you are unconscious.
If a society becomes more alert, that society will live a rebellion; it will live in revolution. Not that it will make a revolution, because the whole thing of making a revolution is nonsense. Revolution is not a thing that you can do and be finished with. Revolution is a way of life; it is a process. You cannot do it and be finished with it. You live with so much awareness that you live in rebellion.

Awareness is not good for this society. This society exists on unawareness.

I have heard a story:

A small germ cell, a germ cell of cancer, met another germ cell of cancer in the bloodstream of a body where both were swimming. The first one asked the other, "You don't look good. Are you ill or something?"

He said, "It seems I have caught penicillin."

You never catch penicillin. You catch flu, you catch other diseases. But think of the germ cells – they catch penicillin.

This society is ill. Awareness will kill it. This society cannot exist with many people alert and aware. They will be dangerous to it. Immediately it catches hold of children and closes their minds, makes them unaware, drugs them – and that drugging this society calls schooling, education.

Go to a school for small children, a kindergarten school. Watch through the window. Children are very alive. Nothing is excluded from their consciousness, everything is included. A bird starts singing; of course, they look out of the window. The teacher becomes angry. He says, "Be attentive! Pay attention to me!"

Now, how is a child supposed to pay attention? What will he do? He pretends. He looks at the teacher, strains his head, strains his eyes and pretends that he is paying attention. And the teacher is happy. His ego feels enhanced. All the children are paying attention to him. From everywhere all eyes are looking at him. Small children are being corrupted because of this man's ego.

Again and again their focus will become wider. Again and again the bird will call, a dog will bark, somebody will talk on the street, a car will pass. A thousand and one things are happening, the world is vast, and a child is alive. But the teacher wants him to be attentive.

The teacher is happy when all the children are paying attention to him. He may be simply talking nonsense. He may be teaching history – which is simply stupidity, better to be dropped forever. What is the need of knowing that some time a madman like Alexander existed? Or Adolf Hitler? Better to forget. Nightmares – but pay attention to these nightmares!

I was reading a story:

Jones stopped his large and expensive car on the country road and gazed about in confusion. He noticed a young farmhand leaning on a fence nearby and called out, "Hey, you! How far to New York?"

The farmhand thought about it and said, "Don't know."

"Well then, what is the best way to get there?"

Again the farmhand thought and said, "Don't know."

"Well look, where is the nearest gas station where I can pick up a map?"

The farmhand thought a little longer, but said again, "Don't know."

The man in the car said with contempt, "You don't know much, do you?"

The farmhand said, "I'm not lost."

The children are not lost, and we go on teaching them. All our teaching is going to become a barrier to life, because life needs a wide mind, open from all sides. And teaching asks for a narrow mind – concentration, attention, not awareness.

Awareness is a mind flowing in all directions simultaneously. You listen to me. You listen to this truck passing by in the street also. You listen to the birds. Nothing is excluded and nothing is a distraction. All things exist together. I go on speaking; the birds are not disturbed. The birds go on singing – why should I be disturbed? And if you can listen, just aware, they both become part of one harmony.

The whole of teaching depends on concentration. Concentration means poisoning the child. Concentration means narrowing his being. Just a small slit will be open and everything else will be closed. Just a small hole, which you call concentration, will be open, and this vast sky will be closed, all doors and windows closed. Just sit near the keyhole and go on looking through the keyhole – that's what concentration is.

But the teacher feels beautiful, the teacher feels wonderful. All are looking at him, everybody is paying attention to him. And the children pretend – because how to pay attention to something which is not naturally attractive?

When a dog barks outside, the dog doesn't say, "Pay attention to me." It simply barks and the child wants to go and see what is happening. It is more attractive than the teacher. When a bird starts singing, its single note repeating, it is more attractive than the teacher.

It doesn't say, it doesn't advertise, it doesn't force anybody. You are free to pay attention or not to pay. But the child wants to pay attention. Life is tremendously beautiful – and this teacher is standing there.

By and by the teacher will force the child, because we are playing such ugly games. We are playing such ugly games, we will use all kinds of coercion. Just think. A small child is sitting for six hours; forced to sit on a bench, a hard bench, not allowed to fidget. Ask the psychologists what they say. They say a child who fidgets more is more intelligent. And a child who sits there as if dumb, deaf, is almost stupid.

Energy fidgets, energy is alive. A really alive child cannot sit silently for long. He is alive, he is not dead. He would like to jump and run and do millions of things. He is overflowing. And we force him to sit.

What happens? He is almost paralyzed by the time he comes out of the university. For twenty years continuously forced to concentrate – and to that concentration the whole society gives so much significance. Then there are examinations. If he fails, he is condemned. If he succeeds, he is appreciated. Now we are playing the ego game. We are teaching him how to be egoistic. We are teaching him an ugly competition – to be inimical with everybody else. And we are teaching him that the only value in this society is to be more efficient, not to be aware.

Now comes the point to be understood. If you want to be more efficient, less awareness is good, because a mechanism is more efficient than a man. A mechanism simply repeats. It never errs, it never goes wrong. So the mind should become like a machine: you push the button and here comes the answer. You just push the button and here flows efficiency.

The whole effort of the society is to reduce you to efficient mechanisms. And vast amounts of money are wasted to cripple you, to destroy you, to paralyze you. Then suddenly one day you find you are missing everything. You haven't tasted life yet.

You have lived and yet you cannot say that you have lived. You have loved and yet you cannot say that love has happened to you. You have been alive and yet you cannot say what the taste of being alive is, what the fragrance of being alive is.

Whatsoever has been called education up to now, is the greatest calamity that has happened to humanity. And the day this whole structure of education is dropped and a totally new education, based not on efficiency – because what does it matter if people are a little less efficient? What does it matter, if they are more alive and a little less efficient? It doesn't matter at all.

Once we base education on awareness then people may not be so efficient in killing, in war; may not be so efficient as clerks, may not be so efficient as government officers – but it is good. Because if people are inefficient in killing, perfectly good! Fewer people will be killed. If the man who dropped the atom bomb on Hiroshima had been less efficient and had dropped it somewhere in a forest, what would have been wrong? It would have been perfectly good. It would have been fortunate.

If German people were less efficient, then Hitler would not have been such a great calamity to mankind. If they had been a little lazy, less disciplined, less skilled, less robot-like, Hitler would have failed. But he had chosen a right country to be born in. These people are always very, very clever. They always choose the right countries to be born in. And then he managed to make the whole country a war camp.

Less efficiency is not a problem. More awareness is needed. And when I say less efficient, I don't mean that necessarily it is going to be so. If you try anything, for example, walking. If you walk alert and aware, you will feel that you cannot walk as efficiently as before. If you drive a car with awareness, you will feel that you cannot drive the car as efficiently as before. But this will be just in the beginning. After a few days you will see – efficiency is coming back, and not at the cost of awareness. When efficiency comes with awareness, it is perfectly good, it is to be welcomed. Otherwise you will live a life almost dead.

It happened once...

A man had been seeing a headshrinker for some months because he thought he was a poodle. One day a friend asked him how the treatment was progressing.

"Well," said the patient, "I can't say that I am cured yet. But I have made some progress. My psychiatrist has stopped me from chasing cars."

At the most, if you continue unconscious and robot-like, this type of change is possible. You will remain a poodle; at the most you may stop chasing cars.

The whole mechanism of the society tries to make you remain as unconscious as ever. The society just becomes worried once your unconsciousness disturbs its working. Then it tries to help you. If you don't chase cars – because that will create trouble in the traffic – if you don't chase cars and inside your mind you continue to dream about yourself as a poodle, perfectly okay; the society is not worried.

The society is not worried about you and your mind. The society is worried only if you create some trouble for it. Otherwise it is perfectly okay, an innocent thing, if you think you are a poodle. It is not a sin – just don't chase cars. Once you act out your fantasies then it becomes a crime. If you remain in your fantasies and don't act them out it is perfectly okay; the society is not worried.

This is the difference between sin and crime. Sin is if you think yourself a poodle and you are not a poodle. It is a sin – because you will miss being a man. If you chase cars it becomes a crime, because you create disturbance in the traffic and the policeman becomes disturbed. Now you have to be treated.

People are almost crazy, but the society is not worried about them unless a crazy person creates some trouble. Between the crazy people who are in the mad asylums and you, the difference is not of quality; it is only of quantity, degrees. They may be a hundred and one degrees, you may be ninety-nine degrees. You may be this side, they are that side, but the difference is not vast – just one or two steps and you can become crazy. But the society tolerates you. Your madness is perfectly accepted if it is private. Once you make it public then the disturbance arises.

Unless you become conscious you remain mad. You may not think you are mad, nobody will be telling you that you are mad, but you remain mad. Only a buddha is not mad. Only enlightened consciousness is not mad. Unless that is attained, everything is being lost – and the opportunity is disappearing every moment.

People decide many times to change themselves. But that decision is also part of their unconscious state, it doesn't help much; hence the importance of a master, the importance of trusting a master. You are fast asleep, you cannot wake yourself. At the most you can dream that you are awake already. You will need to trust an alarm clock.

But an alarm clock is an alarm clock. It may create some situation to disturb your sleep, but you can be very cunning with it. You can think, you can create a dream that you are sitting in a temple and the temple bells are ringing. Now, the alarm clock is useless; it cannot help.

You need an alive alarm clock – that is what a master is – who you cannot deceive, who will go on shaking you; who will shake you out of your sleep. Your decisions are not of much value because they are your decisions. You cannot rely on them.

A man was saying to his friend...

"I have made up my mind; it is time I changed. I am never going to look at another woman. Tonight I am going to confess to my wife and ask her forgiveness."

The friend said, "I am glad to hear it. It is high time you did."

That night his wife was most hurt by his confession and demanded to know who it was who had stolen his affections. "Was it that blonde in the post office?"

"I'm sorry," he replied gallantly, "I won't say."

His wife continued, "I bet it was that model in the next avenue."

He kept his silence.

"I know who it was – that brunette at the Green Dragon."

"Sorry, I can't tell you."

"All right," said his wife angrily. "If you won't tell me who it was I won't forgive you."

The following day, going to work, he saw his friend. "Well," said the friend expectantly, "did she forgive you?"

"No," came the reply, "but she gave me three good contacts."

That's how things go on in an unconscious mind. You cannot rely on it.

Now the Zen story, one of the most beautiful.

The master Fugai was a fine painter, and he was considered to be wise and generous. But he was also most severe, both to himself and to his disciples.

Before we enter into the story, a few things have to be understood. Zen is the only religion in the world which has been creative. All other religions helped people to become uncreative and that is not good. In fact, an uncreative person can be silent, but cannot be happy. An uncreative person may become very peaceful, but can never be blissful.

All bliss arises out of creativity. Unless you create something, you cannot feel blissful. Impossible! Only existence can be blissful. And in creating something, you become a little godly.

When you create something, you participate with existence. When you create something, you allow existence to flow through you. In fact, whenever something is created, it is always created by existence; you become the instrument, the medium. You are possessed by it.

Whenever a great painting arises, the painter is just instrumental. Existence paints it. Whenever great poetry is made, the poet is not the creator; the poetry flows through him. The poet simply allows it. The poet remains in a let-go. The poet allows himself to be possessed by something greater than him, bigger than him, deeper than him, higher than him.

Zen is the only religion in the world which is creative. And that is something tremendously important.

I would like you also to be creative. Because if you become uncreative, of course, you can become more easily silent, because an uncreative person becomes unrelated to the world. An uncreative person is an escapist. He escapes to the Himalayas. He hides in a cave, sits, watches his navel, forgets the whole world.

In a way, good, because he will not do any harm – but that is the only good. He will not be mischievous, he will not become a politician, he will not become a general, he will not exploit people. He will be out of the way. Good. But the good is very negative, not enough. More is needed. He will not do bad, but he will not be able to do good.

When you don't do bad, you feel peaceful, because whenever you do something bad, you become disturbed. He will be silent, but his silence will have the quality of sadness – isolated, alone. His silence will not be alive; it will be something dead – the silence of the cemetery, the silence of a corpse – not the silence of a flower, not the silence of the stars. He will miss something. He will miss the blissfulness of life. One needs to be creative also.

Attain to your inner being. Attain to that which is not body, not mind, then start flowing. Whatsoever way your inner being finds easy starts flowing. Any small thing will do. You can become a gardener or a painter or a poet or a shoemaker, or whatsoever it is – because it is not a question of utility; it is a question of creativity. Create something so your innermost being is expressed, manifested.

Zen masters were either poets or painters or gardeners, and

whatsoever they did, they did with a difference. A Zen garden is totally different from any other garden in the world. It has to be, because all other gardens are made by unconscious people. A Zen garden is made by conscious people. It has a different aura around it.

One Zen master was a great gardener. Even the emperor used to learn from him. And the master said, "Prepare the garden in the palace. After three years I will come to see it. If I approve, then you have passed the examination. If I disapprove, then again for three years you will have to make it, again you will have to learn."

Of course, it was the emperor's palace; thousands of gardeners were working there. The emperor simply ordered them and whatsoever he learned was immediately used in the garden. It became a tremendously beautiful garden.

After three years the master came. He looked around. The emperor became afraid, the emperor started perspiring, because the master was looking very hard. He wouldn't smile. And then he said: "You failed. Because I don't see even a single dead leaf in the garden. How can life exist without death? And how can so many trees exist without dead leaves? Because there are no dead leaves, the garden is dead."

The king had cleaned the whole garden just that morning; not even a single dead leaf was left. And he failed.

The master went out. Outside, there was a heap of dead leaves which had been removed from the garden. He brought all the dead leaves back, threw them on the paths. Winds started playing with the leaves, the garden became alive. The sound of the dead leaves running hither and thither – the garden became alive. And the master said: "Now, now everything is okay. Life cannot exist without death. You failed. Now three years more discipline will be needed."

Zen masters created gardens. That type of garden doesn't exist anywhere else, cannot exist anywhere else.

The master said to the emperor, "Your garden is beautiful, but it shows so much of the human mind. The divine is absent. You have planned it too much.

Whenever anything is planned too much, it loses naturalness. Plan it in such a way," he said, "that nobody can see the planning. The art is greatest when the art cannot be detected. If you can detect it, then the human signature is there. If you cannot detect it, if a garden looks wild, then something of the divine exists there."

There have been painters, there have been poets – small poems, haikus; tremendously beautiful, very indicative. In so few words, only seventeen syllables, a haiku can say as much as a book will find difficult to say.

One haiku of Basho:

> *An old pond*
> *a frog jumps in*
> *plop.*

Finished.

"An old pond..." Let the picture arise in your mind. An old pond, an ancient pond, everything silent, awaiting...

> *An old pond*
> *a frog jumps in*
> *plop.*

Finished, the poetry is finished – but it has said many things. It has almost painted the whole thing. You can hear the plop. You can see the frog. You can see the old pond. You can almost touch it. You can feel it.

Whatsoever Zen masters have been doing, small or big, has the quality – the quality that comes by the touch of an enlightened person.

The master Fugai was a fine painter, and he was considered to be wise and generous. But he was also most severe... Yes, they are very compassionate and hence very severe. Because of their compassion they are severe. Unless they are severe they will not be of much help to you.

Just the other night a girl came to see me. She said that she would think about sannyas because she is not yet ready for it. I could see in her that she is ready. Just the head is not ready; the heart is ready – but the head was trying to boss over the heart.

So I said, "Okay, you think – but remember one thing: next time you come and ask for sannyas I will have to think also. And I may reject. This moment I can give you sannyas – if you take it without thinking. If you think, then I will also have to think. Next time you ask, I may reject."

It was hard on the poor girl. I could see her face. She said, "Okay," but she felt hurt. Then I talked to other sannyasins – their problems, their meditations – and then Govinddas was there to play on his instrument and then I told everybody to dance. The girl also danced. That dance helped – she relaxed from the head to the heart.

And after the dance I asked, "Are you ready now?" She said, "Yes. Now I feel very open and close to you."

Now she is a sannyasin. I had to be a little severe. If I had not said that... It was unkind to say that I would reject her – I never reject anybody. You can reject me, you can accept me – I accept you always. I was not going to reject, but I had to say it. That helped. She needed to be hit on the head.

Remember, compassion can be severe. In fact, only compassion can be severe. Otherwise, what is the need? Who is worried? Who bothers? People come to me and they ask, "Why do you insist on sannyas?" Because I love you and I would like to share something that can be shared only when you have come close to me.

...he was also most severe, both to himself and to his disciples.
It is told that Fugai met his end in an extraordinary manner.
Feeling that his last day had come...

If you can be a witness to your body and mind, you will be able to see before you die – almost six months before – that now you are going to die. Six months before, the body starts disintegrating inside. You and the body start loosening, separating, falling apart. It takes almost six months to bring the process to a completion. But exactly three days before, one can say the hour, the minute, the second. Exactly three days before, something clicks inside and one is ready to die.

If you have lived rightly, fully aware, you will be able to know when your death is coming. Right now you are not even aware of life, that it has come. Then you will even be aware of death, the footsteps of death. You will be able to hear the subtle sound coming closer and closer and closer.

Right now you cannot even live, and then you will be able even to die. And it will be a conscious thing. It is not that death will happen to you; you will die consciously. You will surrender to death consciously. You will welcome death consciously. This is the meaning of this story.

It is told that Fugai met his end in an extraordinary manner.
Feeling that his last day had come, he quickly had a hole dug...

This is the way. One should go a little way, a few steps, to meet death. When you know death is coming, go and meet it at the gate. Let death be welcomed.

...he quickly had a hole dug, then climbed in and ordered the digger to cover him with earth.

He must have been a very rare man. He wanted to savor death in its completeness. He would not even like to be buried in the earth in unconsciousness, when he was gone. He would like even that to happen while he is there and watching and witnessing. Standing there being buried with earth.

...and ordered the digger to cover him with earth. The astonished man ran off.

He couldn't believe what was happening. And he would be caught later on and accused, that he murdered the master. He simply ran off.

On his return to the spot he found the master standing in the hole with great dignity – dead.

A man of understanding has dignity even in his death. A man who lives an unconscious life, even in his life has no dignity. An unconscious life is the life of a beggar – with no dignity and a thousand and one humiliations. A conscious death – even a death, when conscious, has dignity, tremendous dignity and beauty and grace.

I was reading:

Charles de Talleyrand-Perigord was a French politician, remarkably capable but utterly unprincipled – as politicians are – who survived innumerable changes in the government by adroitly betraying his associates in time. A republican during the French Revolution, he served as Napoleon's foreign minister, intrigued with Napoleon's enemies in time to survive the emperor's fall, and then managed to survive the falls of the restored kings as well.

Finally in 1838, having reached the age of eighty-four, it was time for him to die, and King Louis Philippe was at his bedside.

"Oh," muttered Talleyrand, who was in great pain, "I suffer the tortures of hell."

And Louis Philippe, unmoved, said politely, "Already?"

A man who has lived an unconscious life suffers hell while he is alive, suffers hell when he dies – because the hell is created of your unconsciousness, by your unconsciousness, with your unconsciousness. The hell is nothing but the horror that is created by your unconsciousness.

A man who has kindled his lamp of inner being, lives in heaven, dies in heaven, because consciousness is paradise.

Enough for today.

living in nirvana

The first question:

Osho,
During one of your lectures we learned that if we try to leave our
ego just by trying to be humble for example, then the ego comes
through humility. We also learned that the only way to get rid of
the ego is meditation. But doesn't the ego come through that also?
I ask this because I've seen live examples in this place.

Let me answer you through an anecdote:
A psychologist was giving a young man some personality
tests. He drew a vertical line and asked, "What does this
make you think of?"

"Sex," said the young man.

Next the psychologist drew a circle. "And what does this make
you think of?"

"Sex," said the young man again.

The psychologist drew a star. "And this?" he asked.

"Why, sex of course," the young man said.

The psychologist put down his pencil. "In my opinion," he said, "you have an obsession about sex."

"I have an obsession!" protested the young man. "For goodness' sake, who's been drawing all those off-color pictures?"

If you are obsessed with the ego, wherever you go you will find live examples of it, and you will think others are being egoistic – it is your projection. Once you become humble, the whole world becomes humble. Suddenly, the ego not only disappears from you, it disappears simultaneously from the whole world.

To a non-egoistic person, the ego never comes across. Not that others become egoless because he has become egoless, but because he is egoless, he cannot see the egos of others. It simply disappears for him. It is your attitude.

So the first thing to remember is: whatsoever you come across, first try to find the causes within you. Don't be worried why others are egoistic. Let them be if they are. They will have enough punishments for their egos; their own egos will be punishing them enough. You need not be worried.

Whenever you see that somebody is egoistic, immediately turn within, close your eyes, and try to find out the cause in you. That is going to help. If you find a cause within yourself, it can be dropped, it can be transformed. And if you become egoless, suddenly you become tremendously blissful.

Why be worried about others? Just think of you. Be a little more selfish. You are trying to be too unselfish, too altruistic. Be a little more selfish. Think of your own being and of your own wastage of life.

Whatsoever you come across, the more the possibility is that somewhere, hidden deep, that is your problem.

Watch it in this way. Whenever you become angry, it is not because the others have created anger in you. It was already there, it may have been in a dormant state. The others can only provoke that which is already there. Their insults cannot create anger in you. If it is not there, insults cannot create it. Insults can only bring it out if it is there already. Anger is not created by anybody else, it is there or it is not there. And if nobody is going to create the anger, then you will start trying to find some excuse.

I have seen people angry with their shoes, throwing them in anger. I have seen people angry with the doors, slamming them in anger. What has the door done to you? What can the shoe do to you? But you cannot find human objects. Nobody has insulted you, nobody has become an excuse for you, and you are bubbling with anger. You are already on the verge of explosion – anything will do.

Everything that you come across in others is more or less a projection of your own mind. This is the basic religious attitude. If you think it is coming from the other, that is the political attitude. That's why a politician goes on changing others: a revolution is needed – in the society, not in himself. The world has to be changed, only then can he live peacefully.

The politician can never live peacefully, it is impossible. The world is not going to be changed. It is not that easy. Your life is short, and the world has remained almost the same and it is going to remain almost the same. Only you can change, because only you can become conscious.

Consciousness is revolution. Consciousness is transformation. So become conscious within yourself.

If you find somebody else egoistic, thank him immediately. He has helped you to become aware of your own ego. Be grateful to him and forget all about him. Now go within. Now try to find out where the cause lies – why you felt that this man is egoistic. Somewhere your own ego has been hurt.

The second question:

Osho,
Every time I think I want to do something, the complete opposite happens and I feel as if I am going crazy. It feels as if I have no more power over what is happening to me.

Nobody has – because nobody is. The power is possible if you are there. You are not there. The whole is. These individual egos are not there. These are false entities, just illusion. An illusion cannot have power. How can that which is not, that which does not exist, be powerful? Naturally, it is impotent.

So the first thing to be understood: the ego is impotent.

The whole is omnipotent, the part is impotent. But the part is impotent only if it tries to be separate from the whole. Once it dissolves itself into the whole, it becomes the whole. Then it is no longer impotent, then that part also becomes omnipotent.

If you are trying to do something, you will feel helpless. Life happens, it has nothing to do with doing. In the very effort you are creating trouble for yourself. Don't try to swim upstream. Then you will feel as if the river is fighting you. It is not the river.

The river is completely unaware of you. The river is completely unconcerned with you. The river is not doing anything to you, the river is not being nasty to you. Only you are trying to swim upstream, hence you feel the river is going against you.

If you start floating with the river, all enmity disappears from the river. Not that it was coming from the river, it was coming from you. If you are trying to do something, the opposite will happen. That is the misery of human ego, that is the hell.

I have heard a very beautiful story:

An ascetic, a great ascetic, who lived his whole life as a celibate, who remained virgin, who was very much against sex and whose whole life was just an effort to fight against sex, against love, died. His chief disciple could not survive the shock, after just a few hours he also died.

When the chief disciple reached the other world he could not believe his eyes, he was shocked. The master was sitting there – the great ascetic – and Marilyn Monroe was sitting in his lap, almost naked, kissing and hugging the man! He was very shocked, but then, even in his dense head, understanding arose. He thought, "Of course, God is just, and my great master has been well rewarded for all his austerities."

So he went and touched the feet of his master and said, "Master, now I can believe that God is just. In heaven you have been well rewarded for all your austerities, *tapascharya*, that you did in your life."

The master looked very angry, and with deep condemnation he said, "You blockhead! We are not in heaven and I am not being rewarded – she is being punished."

The opposite is bound to happen. The ascetic is going to meet Marilyn Monroe; it is going to happen. The ascetic has created the whole thing himself.

In India there are many stories of great *rishis*, great seers. I don't see why they have been called great seers, because they seem almost blind. The stories are that whenever those great seers were deep in their austerities, in their fasts, in their *sadhana*, beautiful women from the other world will come; *apsaras*, heavenly damsels will come and try to seduce them.

It seems almost impossible. Why should it happen? Why is the other world so interested in seducing poor seers? And who is managing this whole nonsense? They are doing austerities to get out of the world, to stop the wheel of samsara; they are passing through the nightmare of nirvana, they are trying to become desireless – why are they being punished? Why do beautiful women come to them and try to seduce them?

But still, the stories are logical. Nobody is sending those beautiful women. There is nobody to send them. There are no beautiful women to be sent. They are fighting upstream. The more you fight with sex, the more your fantasy becomes real. The more you avoid sex, the more you fight with it, the more you go against it – the more your own dreaming creates damsels of the other world around you. It is your own upstream effort.

I'm not saying that transcendence of sex is not possible. Almost always it is possible – but it is possible only if you flow with the stream, never against the stream. If you are not fighting with the stream, things will happen that you always wanted to happen, but because you wanted, they were not happening.

There is a proverb that "Man proposes and God disposes." But why should God be so against man? Why should he be so cruel? There is no God to dispose anything, and if there is, he cannot be so cruel as to dispose your poor desires. You don't ask much. You ask almost nothing, trivia. Why should he dispose? He can't be so miserly.

The real thing is: the moment you propose, in your very proposal you have created the disposal. You are fighting against the stream. Now you are moving upstream, and you will feel as if the river is moving against you.

Start floating with the river, and suddenly you will see the river is taking you to the ocean. And it is not against you; it is very friendly, it is very lovely. No need even to swim, no need to make any effort – effortlessly, just float and the river takes you. Don't waste your energy.

The question is: "Every time I think I want to do something, the complete opposite happens..." It will happen. It is your doing. Please stop proposing. Rather, allow happenings to happen. Move with things.

Don't bring your will and your ego. The whole is vast and you are a tiny part. Accept this. Dissolve in the whole, merge yourself in the whole. Don't try to create an illusion that you are separate. You are not. Once this illusion is dropped...

That is what I mean when I say drop the ego. Ego is nothing but the illusion of separation from the whole. Humbleness is nothing but a reunion with the whole, a remarriage with the whole. The ego is a divorce; humbleness is a remarriage, a reunion, *unio mystica* – when you are again united with the original source.

Then all that you always wanted to happen starts happening, but it never happens till you stop wanting.

This is the dilemma. If you go on wanting, your very want will create a situation in which it is not going to happen. And of course, the mind will say, "Make more effort." The mind will say, "This time you lost; next time bring more willpower."

Willpower is a dirty word. The idea of willpower is the greatest stupidity there is. The will belongs to the whole, it doesn't belong to the part. My leg cannot have its own will. If it tries to have its own will, it will be paralyzed. My hand cannot have its own will. The whole, my whole body, me, can have a will.

We are just the hands and legs of the whole. We cannot have wills – only the whole. The whole wills, and everything happens to us.

Once you accept this, then all effort, all struggle is gone. One moves effortlessly. All weight, all heaviness from the head disappears, all headache disappears. In fact, the head itself disappears. Then life is an ecstasy, a continuous bliss, an eternal celebration, a benediction.

But you go on trying to do something. It is exactly there, precisely there, where you miss. And the more you miss, the more you desire – a vicious circle is created.

Over a friendly game of chess, Father Shaughnessy said to Rabbi Ginsberg, "Tell me Rabbi, have you ever tasted ham? Be truthful now."

"Once," said the rabbi, reddening slightly, "when I was in college. I must admit curiosity overcame me and I had a ham sandwich. But tell me Father, be truthful now. Did you ever, perhaps with a girl...?"

It was Father Shaughnessy's turn to blush. He said, "I must confess that once in college, before I was ordained, I did have a little."

Silence fell, and the Father said with a sad smile, "It is better than ham, isn't it?"

The moment you fight with anything, you give it tremendous power. The moment you fight with anything, you give it tremendous attraction. The moment you fight with anything, it becomes infinitely inviting.

Sex is not as beautiful as people who have denied themselves think. In fact, if sex is completely allowed, totally free, sooner or later one gets fed up with it. Already it is happening in the West. People are fed up with sex; hence the attraction to drugs. And because the governments go on denying drugs– the same as they were doing with sex before – the drugs have a tremendous attraction. Once drugs are allowed they will lose all attraction.

Whatsoever is denied becomes tremendously powerful over you, because the mind goes on constantly fabricating fantasies around it. Try anything, try to fight with anything – small things. If I tell you that to touch your nose is a sin, it is absolutely nonsense. Such an innocent thing – touching your nose – but try it. For three weeks think that touching your nose is a sin – you will go crazy! You will find places where nobody can see and you will touch your nose. And you will enjoy it, I tell you. Then you will feel guilty that you have missed one more opportunity of getting to heaven.

The more you avoid it and the more you control yourself, the more you will ask, "What has happened?" The nose was never attractive, you never even bothered about it. You were not even aware that it existed. Suddenly it has become the very center of your mind. You will think of noses, beautiful noses – not one, rows of noses, longer and longer and longer rows. And in your dreams you will touch thousands of noses, and in the morning you will feel guilty and you will have to go to a priest to confess that again you have done the same sin. This is what has happened.

In my childhood, in my family, tomatoes were not allowed – because I was born in a Jaina family, and tomatoes look like meat. Just look – they are very innocent. You cannot find more innocent people than tomatoes! But they were not allowed. They had a tremendous attraction for me.

Once, staying with a friend, curiosity overtook me: he offered tomatoes and I ate. They were so beautiful; they have never been as beautiful since then. But in the night I vomited. I felt so guilty. And then, when I vomited, I understood that these tomatoes are really very dangerous things. I had never vomited before that. My whole being was upside down, I couldn't sleep the whole night, and the next day I fasted, just to repent. Now it all looks stupid, but then it was relevant.

Anything – whether it is sex, whether it is food, or whatsoever – once it is denied, once an authority says, "No, it is wrong," suddenly your innermost unconscious mind starts thinking about it, imagining how to get it. You go on projecting and you go on coloring it, making it more and more beautiful.

Drop all this nonsense. Float with life. Trust in life. And that's what I call trust in existence. Forget all gods; they are man-made, manufactured by the human mind. Trust life, and wherever life leads you, go with it. Don't try to swim upstream, and all that you would like will happen – but not because you would like it.

In fact, a deep desire for it exists in you because already life has planned to fulfill it for you. The deep desire simply indicates that life has planned it to be fulfilled for you. Just allow life, float with life, and it will lead you to the promised land. That's why a deep desire goes on asking.

People go on creating a paradise somewhere beyond the clouds. The paradise is herenow. You create a paradise because you deny yourself many things and you desire many things and you go on fighting and the whole life becomes miserable.

In this misery, you create hope, because otherwise the misery will be too much. Everybody would commit suicide if there was no paradise. Because of paradise you go on – it is only a few days' trouble and then everything will be okay; you will be with God in paradise.

You are never going to be with God in paradise unless you are with God herenow. Be with God today.

And what is the way of being with it today? Don't fight – surrender. Surrender to life. You are not surrendering to anybody: it is your life. So the moment I say surrender to life, don't create a duality in the mind. You are not surrendering to anybody else; it is your life, it is you, infinitely you, expanded you.

The third question:

Osho,
Several sannyasins have told me that you do not approve of macrobiotics. Is this so? I wonder whether your criticisms were

directed at obsessive attitudes toward diet rather than at the principles of macrobiotics. Macrobiotics is pure Taoism. There are no rules and no prohibitions. Its emphasis is on awareness, freedom, sensitivity and flexibility. It has nothing at all to do with food fads, rigid diets or obsessive attitudes. Brown rice is mistakenly regarded by some as the basis of macrobiotics, but it is only one element and can be used or discarded, recognized or ignored. Could you please comment?

The first thing: I am against all fads. Irrespective of what the fad is, I am against all fads, because fads attract obsessive people. Fads become hiding places for insane people. People who are abnormal hide themselves behind fads, and they create systems, theories, dogmas to rationalize.

I used to live with a woman. She was a very lovely woman, but almost crazy about cleanliness. The whole day she was cleaning the house, the whole day she was decorating – for no purpose, because she never allowed anybody in the house. If guests would come she would meet them on the lawn.

I asked her, "You continuously go on decorating and cleaning your house, but I see that nobody is ever allowed in."

She said, "Those people may make everything dirty."

"Then what is the purpose of it?"

She said, "Cleanliness is next to godliness."

Now, this woman is mad. Cleanliness has become just a hiding-place. It has become a ritual. Now, cleaning the whole day, she remains occupied. Cleaning the whole day has become her whole life – it is a sheer waste. But you cannot say that cleanliness is bad: cleanliness is good. So she has a reason. She is mad with a perfect rationality.

Even her husband was not allowed to come into the drawing room. And she never allowed herself to have any children, because children are dirty and they would create trouble and they would make things messy. Her whole life was sacrificed at the altar of cleanliness.

I said, "Of course, you have proved that cleanliness is second to godliness. You have made it an altar and you are sacrificing your whole life to it."

But she would say, "Am I wrong?"

You cannot say she is wrong. Cleanliness is good, hygienic – but there is a limit to it. The faddist always goes beyond the limit. He is deep down very troubled. I told the woman, "Do one thing: for three days don't clean the house. If you can remain sane for three days without cleaning the house, I will also join you and I will also clean your house the whole day."

She said, "Three days without cleaning? That is impossible. I will go mad."

She is already mad.

Whenever there is someone who is hiding behind a fad, whatsoever the fad is – it may be macrobiotics or something else – I am against it. I am against the attitude of obsessiveness.

Let me tell you an anecdote:

A man came home from the match. His wife looked up from the paper and said, "Look here, Fred, there's a report in the paper about a man who's just given his wife to a friend in return for a football season ticket. You're a keen fan but you wouldn't do a thing like that, would you?"

Fred said, "Of course I wouldn't. It is ridiculous and criminal – the season is half over!"

This is the mind of a fan, of a faddist. But these people can go on hiding behind beautiful reasons.

Mahatma Gandhi was continuously concerned about his bowel movements. He was almost obsessive about it. Sometimes when your stomach is disturbed, one can think about it, but continuously pondering and meditating and brooding over it is nonsense. But he was continuously brooding – as if that was the greatest subject in the world to think about.

He would do his prayer, or he was going to see the viceroy, or he was going to take part in the round-table conference, which was going to decide the fate of India and its freedom – but first he would take an enema. You would be surprised: in his diary, enema is as much referred to as God. The enema seems to be a second god.

But if you argued with him, he would look perfectly clear about it: the stomach has to be completely clean, because without a clean stomach the whole body gets toxins, this and that, and only with a clean stomach can the mind be clean. How can the mind be healthy without a healthy body? Then he would go on and on, arguing about it, thinking about it. But in fact, it is a fad and a sort of illness. And it doesn't show a healthy mind; it shows an unhealthy mind.

I am against this type of attitude. I have said so to many sannyasins because they come to me with their fads. One young man came and he said he had come to me to learn how to live only on water! I told him, "You will make me a criminal. If I tell you how to live on water, you will die!"

He was lean and thin, almost on the verge of collapse, but he had a fad that purity is possible only through water. Only water is pure and everything else is impure. His eyes were getting yellow, ill. He was not eating well, his body was starved, and by and by his brain would start being feverish. And the more feverish he would become, the more he would make efforts to purify himself. I have to tell such people that they are moving in a very, very dangerous direction.

Macrobiotic addicts also come to me. Now, this question is from Dharmananda. He has exactly caught the point. I am not against anything in particular, because I am not in favor of anything in particular. I am just in favor of life – life in its tremendous richness.

So if it is as Dharmananda says, I don't think macrobiotic people will agree with him. Now let me read the whole question again. I don't think macrobiotic people will agree with him, because he has destroyed the whole thing.

He says, "Macrobiotics is pure Taoism." No principle, no theory, can be pure Taoism. Even Taoism is not pure Taoism. Lao Tzu resisted for his whole life. He denied his disciples, he rejected all appeals to him to make a theory about his whole principle, because he said, "Once Tao is said, it is no longer Tao. Truth cannot be said, cannot be theorized." Only in the end he wrote something – and that too under pressure.

Lao Tzu was leaving China. It seems he was coming to India. Everybody has to come finally to India. India is not a geographical point; it is the very source of all human consciousness. Everyone who wants to be reoriented has to come to the orient. *Orient* simply means orientation.

Of course, Chinese scholars never say that he was going to India; that offends their ego. They say he was going to the south, but India is the south. They say he moved toward the south, but India is the south for China. And of course, it seems meaningful – Lao Tzu coming back to India. That seems absolutely relevant. Everybody has to come. India is everybody's home.

He was caught on the boundaries of China by the government officials and they said, "We will not allow you to go out of the country with your treasure. You have to leave the treasure."

He asked, "What do you mean?"

They said, "You have to write a book before you leave our country. You know something; you have to write it down and hand it over to the government. Then you can leave."

So he was forced on the boundary by these officials. In three days he went and quickly wrote the whole *Tao Te Ching*. But in the first line he says, "Tao cannot be uttered, and the Tao that is uttered is no longer Tao."

So even Taoism is not pure Tao – the "ism" makes it impure. So forget about macrobiotics – that it can be pure Taoism. It is a theory, a hypothesis.

"There are no rules and no prohibitions." If there are no rules and no prohibitions, then why be unnecessarily worried about macrobiotics? Then what is the point of calling yourself a follower of macrobiotics if there are no rules and no regulations? There are.

I would like for Dharmananda to be right. I would like it perfectly; that is what my whole standpoint is. But Dharmananda cannot be approved of by macrobiotic people. They have rules and regulations. In fact, Dharmananda is smuggling me into macrobiotics. He is my follower, so of course, it can be understood.

"Its emphasis is on awareness, freedom, sensitivity and flexibility. It has nothing at all to do with food fads, rigid diets or obsessive attitudes." No, they will not agree with you, Dharmananda. They will not.

"Macrobiotics has nothing to do with brown rice." They are mad about brown rice. They think brown rice is God, and unless you live on brown rice you will miss. But he says, "Brown rice is mistakenly regarded by some as the basis of macrobiotics but it is only one element and can be used or discarded, recognized or ignored." But then what remains? If even brown rice is discarded, ignored, and there are no principles and no regulations and it is pure Taoism, then what remains? Nothing remains. Then I can happily say, "Yes, be a macrobiotic follower, no problem."

I am against fads. I am against a disciplined life. I am not against discipline, I am against disciplined life. Discipline should come moment to moment from your inner being. It should be an inner light, not imposed from the outside. One should move in deep response to life. One should not follow any doctrine, because if you follow a doctrine then already you have accepted a conclusion. You live through that conclusion. You live from a center which is already fixed. Then you are not free. You cannot be flexible. Your principle, your idea, your center, your conclusion, will not allow you to be flexible. You will react according to your conclusion.

But if you are free and each moment decides its own conclusion, it is not carried over from the past, then it is perfectly okay. Then you have a discipline – real discipline – but you don't have a disciplined life.

Any man who is really alive has no character, cannot have a character. Character is always dead – a dead structure around you, carried over from the past, past experience. If you act out of your character, you don't act at all; you simply react. You don't respond.

Response is immediate. Life creates a situation, a challenge, and you respond. You respond out of your being, with no center, with no conclusion – not through the past. Herenow comes the response – pure, virgin.

That discipline I appreciate, that discipline I love. But any other discipline that you force yourself in, that you practice, is dangerous. That is going to kill you. That's how many people are already dead. Their discipline has killed them.

The fourth question:

Osho,
What is the difference between going within and going nowhere?

There is no difference. Going nowhere is going within. Going within is going nowhere. The difference is only that of terminology. If you ask the Upanishads, they say "Go within." If you ask Buddha, he says, "Go nowhere." And if you ask me, both mean the same; but still "nowhere" is better than "within."

Why? Because the moment you say "within" you have created a dichotomy of without and within – as if truth is only within and not without. It is without also. It is within also. It is the same life that is

within me and without, within you and without. It is the same phenomenon, so why create a dichotomy?

When Buddha says, "Go nowhere," that is what nirvana is – going
nowhere.

If you understand, going nowhere simply means not going.
Going nowhere does not mean going nowhere. It simply means
not going – just being, not going at all – because all going is motivated, all going is because of desire.

When there is no desire, everything stops. When there is no
desire, there is no movement. Time stops. Future drops, past disappears – only this moment, only this moment.

Just the other day I quoted Basho's haiku:

> The ancient pond
> a frog jumps in
> plop.

Time has stopped.

In Japanese it is even more beautiful; that cannot be translated.
If I try an exact translation then it will be like this:

> Ancient pond
> frog jumps in
> plop.

A process. When we say "a frog jumped in," it is as if something
has ended, finished, completed. In Japanese it is not "a frog jumped
in," it is "frog jumps in." Just the process – plop! – the sound, and
everything has stopped.

Basho has also made a picture of that frog and the pond. If you
look deep into the frog's eyes you will find Bodhidharma sitting there.
The eyes of the frog are almost like Bodhidharma, plopping out.

A moment when time stops. And why is the frog jumping in?
There is no "why?" A jump-in; for no motivation, for no desire. It just
happened. It just happened that the frog found himself jumping in. A
stirring, the pond stirred; the sound, the air stirred – and then nothing.
Nothing was before, nothing is after – just in between, a happening.

It is neither coming in, nor is it going out. It is going nowhere. It is
not going at all. A moment when everything stops, an unmotivated
moment. It does not mean that you will not be walking. You may
jump in the ancient pond – that is not the point – but there is no motivation. For nothing.

You move for the sheer joy of movement. You breathe for the

sheer joy of breathing. You don't desire anything out of it. You don't desire even the next moment. Plop. This moment is enough.

Buddha's saying "going nowhere," is a better expression. But don't be caught in words. All buddhas mean the same – Jesus, Mahavira, Zarathustra, Lao Tzu or Gautam Buddha. Whatsoever their expressions, they all mean the same. Don't try to be scholarly, and don't be a word chopper. It is all the same.

You can call it coming in, or you can even call it going out. Christianity, Islam, Judaism all say, "God is there, 'thou'" – somewhere outside you. You have to fall in love with that and disappear in that love. Hinduism, Buddhism, Jainism say, "God is in, somewhere within you." You have to disappear there. But these are all ways of talking, because it is out and it is in, because all outs and all ins are within it.

Don't be a word chopper, otherwise you can go on and on playing with words.

Let me tell you an anecdote:

"The last time I gave you money," said the old lady, "you promised you would not walk straight into the pub and spend it."

"That's right," said the tramp.

"Well, you did!"

"Lady, don't you know the difference between a walk and a sprint?"

Don't be a word chopper. Whether you run into the pub or you walk in, it is all the same. The tramp must have been a very clever man. He is saying, "Lady, don't you know the difference between a walk and a sprint? I had promised not to walk. I never promised not to run."

Remember, words can be a dangerous game. The whole point is, be unmotivated. Then whether you go out or you go in, or go somewhere or go nowhere, is irrelevant. Be unmotivated.

People come to me and they say, "We would like to be happy." Their whole life is motivated – they would like to be happy – and I feel very sad for them, because happiness is not a motivation. You can either be happy this moment or you will never be happy. So you cannot say, "I would like to be happy tomorrow." That is foolish.

Happiness needs no pre-requirements, no prerequisites. Just see the point of it. You can be happy right now, as you are. If you really want to be happy, then don't try to be happy – just be happy. Who is blocking the way? Who is hindering you? Who is forcing you to be unhappy?

But you say, "Right now I have to be unhappy, but tomorrow I would like to be happy." The tomorrow is going to be the same. It will come as a today. This today was also tomorrow yesterday. And yesterday you told me, "I'm going to be happy tomorrow."

If this is the way, if this is your logic, happiness is never going to happen. It is already happening. Just be happy. Give it a try. Just for twenty-four hours remain happy. Whenever you catch yourself getting unhappy again, give a good jerk and be happy. Shake the whole body and be happy again. It is just a knack. It has nothing to do with the tomorrow or the future. It is just a knack, an art.

I have never seen any situation in which a man cannot be happy. And I have also not seen any situation in which a man cannot be unhappy. It depends on you. It is your decision.

Happiness comes when you remain in an unmotivated moment, a sheer delight in being.

The last question:

Osho,
How to be creative while doing jobs which seem not to leave any space for creativity, like cleaning?

It is from Krishna Radha. She cleans. But I also do the same thing: every morning, every evening, twenty-four hours a day – cleaning your mind, cleansing. But I never feel that there is any need for any other creativity.

Cleaning a floor can be a tremendously creative act. Remember, creativity has nothing to do with any particular work. Creativity has something to do with the quality of your consciousness. Whatsoever you do can become creative. Whatsoever you do can become creative if you know what creativity means.

Creativity means enjoying any work as meditation; doing any work with deep love. If you love me and you clean this auditorium, it is creative. If you don't love me then of course it is a chore, it is a duty to be done somehow, it is a burden. Then you would like some other time to be creative. What will you do in that other time? Can you find a better thing to do? Are you thinking that if you paint, you will feel creative?

But painting is just as ordinary as cleaning the floor. You will be throwing colors on a canvas. Here you go on washing the floor, cleaning the floor. What is the difference? Talking to somebody, a friend, and you feel time is being wasted; you would like to write a great book – then you will be creative. But a friend has come: a little gossiping is perfectly beautiful. Be creative.

All the great scriptures are nothing but gossips of people who were creative. What do I go on doing here? – gossiping. They will become gospels someday, but originally they are gossips. But I enjoy doing them. I can go on and on for eternity. You may get tired some day, I am not going to get tired. It is sheer delight. It is possible that one day you may get so tired that you disappear and there is nobody – and I will be talking. If you really love something, it is creative.

But this happens to everybody. Many people come to me. When they come for the first time they will say, "Any work, Osho. Any work – even cleaning!" Exactly they say, "Even cleaning! – but your work, and we will be happy." And then after a few days they come to me and they say, "Cleaning! We would like to have some great creative work."

Let me tell you an anecdote:

Worried about their lackluster sex life, the young wife finally persuaded her husband to undergo hypnotic treatment. After a few sessions his sexual interest was kindled again, but during their lovemaking he would occasionally dash out of the bedroom, go to the bathroom and come back again.

Overcome by curiosity, the wife followed him one day to the bathroom. Tiptoeing to the doorway she saw him standing before the mirror staring fixedly at himself and muttering, "She is not my wife. She is not my wife."

When you fall in love with a woman, of course she is not your wife. You make love, you enjoy, but then things settle; then she is your wife. Then things become old. Then you know the face, you know the body, you know the topography, and then you get bored. The hypnotist did well. He simply suggested, "While making love to your wife, you go on thinking, 'She is not my wife. She is not my wife.'"

So, Krishna Radha, while cleaning, go on thinking you are painting. This is not cleaning. This is great creativity. And it will be. It is just your mind playing tricks. If you understand, then you bring your creativity to every act that you do.

A man of understanding is continuously creative. Not that he is trying to be creative. The way he sits is a creative act. Watch him sitting. You will find in his movement a certain quality of dance, a certain dignity. Just the other day we were reading the story of the Zen master who stood in the hole with great dignity – dead. Even his death was a creative act. He did it perfectly well, you cannot improve upon it. Even dead he was standing with dignity, with grace.

When you understand, whatsoever you do – cooking, cleaning… Life consists of small things, just your ego goes on saying these are small things. You would like some great thing to do – a great poetry. You would like to become Shakespeare or Kalidas or Milton. It is your ego that is creating the trouble. Drop the ego and everything is creative.

I have heard…

A housewife was so pleased with the promptness shown by the grocer's boy that she asked him his name. "Shakespeare," replied the boy.

"Well, that is quite a famous name."

"It should be. I have been delivering in this neighborhood for almost three years now."

I like it. Why bother about being Shakespeare? Three years delivering in a neighborhood – it's almost as beautiful as writing a book, a novel, a play.

Life consists of small things. They become great if you love. Then everything is tremendously great. If you don't love, then your ego goes on saying, "This is not worthy of you. Cleaning? Krishna Radha, this is not worthy of you. Do something great – become Joan of Arc." All nonsense. All Joan of Arcs are nonsense.

Cleaning is great. Don't go on an ego trip. Whenever the ego comes and persuades you toward some great things, immediately become aware and drop the ego, and then by and by you will find the trivia is sacred. Nothing is profane, everything is sacred and holy.

Unless everything becomes holy to you, your life cannot be religious.

A holy man is not what you call a saint. A saint may be just on an ego trip. And also he will look a saint to you because you think he has done great deeds. A holy man is an ordinary man who loves ordinary life. Chopping wood, carrying water from the well, cooking, cleaning – whatsoever he touches becomes holy. Not that he is doing great things, but whatsoever he does, he does it greatly.

The greatness is not in the thing done. The greatness is in the consciousness that you bring while you do it. Try. Touch a pebble with great love; it becomes a Kohinoor, a great diamond. Smile, and suddenly you are a king or a queen. Laugh, delight. Each moment of your life has to be transformed by your meditative love.

When I say be creative, I don't mean that you should all go and become great painters and great poets. I simply mean let your life be a painting, let your life be a poetry.

Always remember it, otherwise the ego is going to land you in some trouble. Go to the criminals and ask why they have become criminals – because they could not find any great thing to do. They could not become a president of a country of course, not all persons can become presidents of a country – so they killed a president; that is easier. They became as famous as the president. They were in all the newspapers with their pictures on the front page.

A man, just a few months ago, killed seven people, and he was asked why – because those seven persons were totally unrelated to him. He wanted to become great, he said, and no newspaper was ready to publish his poems, his articles; they were refused from everywhere. Nobody was ready to publish his picture, and life was fleeting, so he killed seven people. They were not related to him, he was not angry with them; he just wanted to become famous.

Your politicians and your criminals are not a different type of people. All criminals are political and all politicians are criminal – not only Richard Nixon. Poor Richard Nixon was caught red-handed, that's all. Others seem to be more clever and more cunning.

Mrs. Moskowitz was bursting with pride, "Did you hear about my son Louie?" she asked her neighbor.

"No. What is with your son Louie?"

"He is going to a psychiatrist. Twice each week he is going to a psychiatrist."

"Is that good?"

"Of course it is good. Forty dollars an hour he pays. Forty dollars! And all he talks about is me," said the mother.

The mother is feeling very happy.

Never allow yourself this tendency for being great, famous, someone bigger than life-size – never. Life-size is perfect. To be exactly life-size, to be just ordinary, is perfectly as it should be. But live that ordinariness in an extraordinary way. That is what a nirvanic consciousness is all about.

Now let me tell you the last thing. If nirvana becomes a great goal for you to achieve, then you will be in a nightmare. Then nirvana can become the last and the greatest nightmare. But if nirvana is in small things – the way you live them, the way you transform every small activity into a holy act, into a prayerfulness – your house becomes a temple, your body becomes the abode of godliness. And wherever you look and whatsoever you touch is tremendously beautiful, sacred. Then nirvana is freedom.

Nirvana is to live the ordinary life so alert, so full of consciousness, so full of light, that everything becomes luminous.

It is possible. I say so because I have lived it so, I am living it so. When I say it, I say with authority. When I say it, I am not quoting Buddha or Jesus. When I say it, I am quoting only myself. It has become possible for me; it can become possible for you. Just don't hanker for the ego. Just love life, trust life, and life will give you all that you need. Life will become a blessing for you, a benediction.

Enough for today.

about Osho

Osho's unique contribution to the understanding of who we are defies categorization. Mystic and scientist, a rebellious spirit whose sole interest is to alert humanity to the urgent need to discover a new way of living. To continue as before is to invite threats to our very survival on this unique and beautiful planet.

His essential point is that only by changing ourselves, one individual at a time, can the outcome of all our "selves" – our societies, our cultures, our beliefs, our world – also change. The doorway to that change is meditation.

Osho the scientist has experimented and scrutinized all the approaches of the past and examined their effects on the modern human being and responded to their shortcomings by creating a new starting point for the hyperactive 21st Century mind: OSHO Active Meditations.

Once the agitation of a modern lifetime has started to settle, "activity" can melt into "passivity," a key starting point of real meditation. To support this next step, Osho has transformed the ancient "art of listening" into a subtle contemporary methodology: the OSHO Talks. Here words become music, the listener discovers who is listening, and the awareness moves from what is being heard to the individual doing the listening. Magically, as silence arises, what needs to be heard is understood directly, free from the distraction of a mind that can only interrupt and interfere with this delicate process.

These thousands of talks cover everything from the individual quest for meaning to the most urgent social and political issues facing society today. Osho's books are not written but are transcribed from audio and video recordings of these extemporaneous talks to international audiences. As he puts it, "So remember: whatever I am saying is not just for you...I am talking also for the future generations."

Osho has been described by *The Sunday Times* in London as one of the "1000 Makers of the 20th Century" and by American author Tom Robbins as "the most dangerous man since Jesus

Christ." *Sunday Mid-Day* (India) has selected Osho as one of ten people – along with Gandhi, Nehru and Buddha – who have changed the destiny of India.

About his own work Osho has said that he is helping to create the conditions for the birth of a new kind of human being. He often characterizes this new human being as "Zorba the Buddha" – capable both of enjoying the earthy pleasures of a Zorba the Greek and the silent serenity of a Gautama the Buddha.

Running like a thread through all aspects of Osho's talks and meditations is a vision that encompasses both the timeless wisdom of all ages past and the highest potential of today's (and tomorrow's) science and technology.

Osho is known for his revolutionary contribution to the science of inner transformation, with an approach to meditation that acknowledges the accelerated pace of contemporary life. His unique OSHO Active Meditations™ are designed to first release the accumulated stresses of body and mind, so that it is then easier to take an experience of stillness and thought-free relaxation into daily life.

Two autobiographical works by the author are available:
Autobiography of a Spiritually Incorrect Mystic,
St Martins Press, New York (book and eBook)
Glimpses of a Golden Childhood,
OSHO Media International, Pune, India

OSHO international meditation resort

Each year the Meditation Resort welcomes thousands of people from more than 100 countries. The unique campus provides an opportunity for a direct personal experience of a new way of living – with more awareness, relaxation, celebration and creativity. A great variety of around-the-clock and around-the-year program options are available. Doing nothing and just relaxing is one of them!

All of the programs are based on Osho's vision of "Zorba the Buddha" – a qualitatively new kind of human being who is able *both* to participate creatively in everyday life *and* to relax into silence and meditation.

Location
Located 100 miles southeast of Mumbai in the thriving modern city of Pune, India, the OSHO International Meditation Resort is a holiday destination with a difference. The Meditation Resort is spread over 28 acres of spectacular gardens in a beautiful tree-lined residential area.

OSHO Meditations
A full daily schedule of meditations for every type of person includes both traditional and revolutionary methods, and particularly the OSHO Active Meditations™. The daily meditation program takes place in what must be the world's largest meditation hall, the OSHO Auditorium.

OSHO Multiversity
Individual sessions, courses and workshops cover everything from creative arts to holistic health, personal transformation, relationship and life transition, transforming meditation into a lifestyle for life and work, esoteric sciences, and the "Zen" approach to sports and recreation. The secret of the OSHO Multiversity's success lies in the fact that all its programs are combined with meditation, supporting the

understanding that as human beings we are far more than the sum of our parts.

OSHO Basho Spa
The luxurious Basho Spa provides for leisurely open-air swimming surrounded by trees and tropical green. The uniquely styled, spacious Jacuzzi, the saunas, gym, tennis courts...all these are enhanced by their stunningly beautiful setting.

Cuisine
A variety of different eating areas serve delicious Western, Asian and Indian vegetarian food – most of it organically grown especially for the Meditation Resort. Breads and cakes are baked in the resort's own bakery.

Night life
There are many evening events to choose from – dancing being at the top of the list! Other activities include full-moon meditations beneath the stars, variety shows, music performances and meditations for daily life.

Facilities
You can buy all of your basic necessities and toiletries in the Galleria. The Multimedia Gallery sells a large range of OSHO media products. There is also a bank, a travel agency and a Cyber Café on-campus. For those who enjoy shopping, Pune provides all the options, ranging from traditional and ethnic Indian products to all of the global brand-name stores.

Accommodation
You can choose to stay in the elegant rooms of the OSHO Guesthouse, or for longer stays on campus you can select one of the OSHO Living-In programs. Additionally there is a plentiful variety of nearby hotels and serviced apartments.

www.osho.com/meditationresort
www.osho.com/guesthouse
www.osho.com/livingin

for more information

www.**OSHO**.com

a comprehensive multi-language website including a magazine, OSHO Books, OSHO Talks in audio and video formats, the OSHO Library text archive in English and Hindi and extensive information about OSHO Meditations. You will also find the program schedule of the OSHO Multiversity and information about the OSHO International Meditation Resort.

http://OSHO.com/AllAboutOSHO
http://OSHO.com/Resort
http://OSHO.com/Shop
http://www.youtube.com/OSHO
http://www.Twitter.com/OSHO
http://www.facebook.com/pages/OSHO.International

To contact OSHO International Foundation:
www.osho.com/oshointernational,
oshointernational@oshointernational.com